D0897597

Forty Days
Michaela M. Özelsel

Michaela Mihribân Özelsel, born in Germany in 1949, was raised mostly in Turkey. She received her B.A. and M.A. in clinical psychology from the University of North Carolina and a Ph.D. from the Goethe University in Frankfurt, Germany.

In various European and Asian countries—as well as in the United States—she has received recognition for her work in training professionals in clinical hypnosis, behavior modification, and systematic family therapy and in linking these modalites to ancient Sufi healing techniques. Dr. Özelsel receives invitations to present at conferences around the world. She is a lecturer in psychology for the University of Maryland, European Division, and is in private practice in Germany.

Because of her multi-cultural background and her Western scientific training, her Sufi master has designated and then prepared her to be a "bridge" or "translator"—i.e., to provide the service of conveying some of the traditional wisdom of Sufism to the West.

Forty Days

The Diary of a Traditional Solitary Sufi Retreat
With an Accompanying Interdisciplinary Scientific Commentary

Michaela M. Özelsel

Introduction by Annemarie Schimmel
Translated by Andy Gaus

THRESHOLD BOOKS

BRATTLEBORO, VERMONT

Dedicated to my Teacher

*Threshold Books is committed to publishing books
of spiritual significance and high literary quality.
All Threshold Books are printed on acid-free paper.
We will be happy to send you a catalog.*

Threshold Books, 139 Main Street, Brattleboro, Vermont 05301
802-254-8300

Cover illustration: Leslie Schiff
Cover & Book design: Threshold Design

ISBN 0-939660-52-0

1 2 3 4 5 6 7 8 9 10

Özelsel, Michaela, 1949-
Forty days:
the diary of a traditional solitary sufi retreat, with an accompanying
interdisciplinary scientific commentary/ Dr. Michaela Özelsel
240. p. 8.25"
Includes bibliographical references and appendix.
ISBN 0-939660-52-0 (printed case. :alk. paper)
1. Sufism. 2. Psychology. 3. Spirituality

Library of Congress Catalog Number: 96-060033

Contents

vii   INTRODUCTION by Annemarie Schimmel
xii   FORWARD

1   Diary

109   Commentary:

113   BLOOD SACRIFICE
117   OBSERVATIONS ON THE THESIS OF "MORPHIC
        RESONANCE"
126   THE PERSON OF THE TEACHER
131   ACCOMPANYING PSYCHOLOGICAL PHENOMENA
        Scientific Approaches
        The Physiology of Hallucinations
141   METHODS OF SUFI SCHOOLING
        Ritual Prayer
        Zhikr
149   THE PHYSIOLOGICAL DIMENSION
        Neurophysiological Effects of Bodily
           Movements
        The Electro-Physiological Dimension
        Conclusion
156   METHODS OF SUFI SCHOOLING:
        DO THEY MAKE YOU WELL OR MAKE YOU SICK?
162   THE FUNCTIONALITY OF MOURNING AND LOSS
163   THE CALL TO THE PATH AND ITS CONSEQUENCES
167   SPIRITUALITY AND SEXUALITY
171   THE AUTHENTICITY OF MYSTICAL EXPERIENCES

179   THE *HALVET* IN TRANSCULTURAL COMPARISON
                         Structure and Methodology
                         Altered States of Consciousness and
                         Emotional Occurrences
                         Sensory and Extra-Sensory Perception
                         Near-Death Experiences
                         Purpose and Goal
                         Conclusion

199   THE LAND OF TRUTH
200   APPENDIX: *Halvet* QUESTIONAIRE
209   GLOSSARY OF ISLAMIC PERSONAGES
214   GLOSSARY OF MEDICAL AND PSYCHOLOGICAL TERMS
217   BIBLIOGRAPHY
221   RECOMMENDED READING ON SUFISM

INTRODUCTION

Anne Marie Schimmel

Anyone who engages in scholarly research on Sufism finds, over and over, accounts of the *arbaīn* or *chilla*, the forty-day confinement, which in Turkish is called the *halvet* (from the Arabic *khalva*) "the solitude," cloistering or confinement. A Sufi in his beginning stages, at the point where his master deems it proper and necessary, is supposed to complete this severe exercise of forty days and nights alone in a narrow room with the least possible light, with only minimal food, occupied solely with reading the Quran, meditating, and reciting certain litanies or names of God. His master would usually stop by in the evening to check his progress and to interpret his dreams or, should he prove too weak, to perform the necessary exercises to bring him back out into the world again.

Many Sufi masters have repeated this exercise in the course of their lives, and it is said of particularly pious men that at the time of their death they had completed forty *chillas*.

But what happens in these forty days? The great Persian poet Farīdaddīn ʿAṭṭār (d. 1221) described the quest of the disciple in his narrow cell in poetic terms: every day he asks creation where to find God, and all of the created things—sun and moon, stars and planets, wind and animals—answer that they are looking for God too, till the seeker, on the advice of the Prophet of Islam (Peace be upon him), finds the long-sought God in the "ocean of his soul," for the soul, the heart, is the actual dwelling-place of the Beloved. ʿAṭṭār's epic is an exquisite expression of the infinite yearning, the "pining and sighing of creation" that streams through the whole universe.

Travelers to the Orient will be familiar with the tiny cells often attached to a mosque, the hollowed-out spaces under mighty trees, and the mountain crevices to which the seeker may retire; and under modern conditions a tiny apartment in a big noisy city can also be transformed to serve for a *halvet.*

But for the uninitiated person who knows this experience only from outside, it is hard to put oneself in the place of a person who undertakes this confinement. What does he or she experience? What changes occur to that person's heart and body? To be sure, authentic accounts are known of the psychic and physical effect of the *zhikr,* the repetition many thousands of times of a formula, a name of God, supplied by the master. Perhaps the clearest and most penetrating description accessible to the Western reader is that of Qushairī (d. 1074), whose *Risāla* has been for centuries a standard text of moderate Sufism. He has set his experiences down in a small work called *"Tartīb as-sulūk,"* "Prescriptions for Advancement," and in this piece, translated and edited by Fritz Meier with his accustomed precision and deep understanding, the reader learns step by step how the *zhikr* acquires independence, takes on a life of its own and sets a person aglow.

Other circumstances on this path include the appearance of lights of various colors, as described particularly in the writings of Najmaddīn Kubrā (d. ca. 1221) and his students (here again Fritz Meier has done pioneering work). Another good introduction is Henry Corbin's well-known work *L'Homme de lumière dans le Soufisme Iranien* (The Man of Light in Iranian Sufism), which introduces the reader to the various light phenomena.

But the disciple is not allowed to walk the path alone. Sufism, and this can't be stressed often enough in contrast to many of the religious movements of today, does not mean floating ecstatically in a pale blue ocean of love. Not at all: one can only call oneself a Sufi when one has been initiated by a genuine master, thus taking one's place in the spiritual chain that extends back across the leaders of the brotherhood in every age and the early medieval masters right back to the Prophet Muhammad (Peace be upon him), who is considered the source of mystic wisdom. In this manner, just as in the case of apostolic succession, the sanctifying power is handed down. Only at the hand of the master in whom absolute trust has been placed may one approach the decidedly severe conditions of the *halvet*, because only the spiritual director, on the basis of his inner insight, knows which *zhikr* formulas are appropriate for the seeker at any given moment. The wrong *zhikr* as often happens would have bad results not just for the soul, but also for the body. Medieval Arabic works like Ibn ʿAṭāʾ Allāh's *Miftāḥ al-falāḥ* (The Key to Salvation and the Illuminator of Souls), indicate precisely which divine name should be used by whom.

Religious historians, particularly those interested in the phenomenology of comparative religion, will find much in these "revelations" of Dr. Michaela M. Özelsel that fits into the general framework of mystical experience and religious experience in general. The blood sacrifice at the beginning is part of that, since "sacrifice" is in fact what the *halvet* experience really means: a sacrifice in order to reach a higher goal.

The interpretation of the "Morphic Resonance" strikes me as very important. In Ibn ʿArabi's work you find the idea that each person can only experience the true or the deepest religious experience in the world of his or her own images. There is a world tailored to each person, which the person hooks into, and which then provides him or her with the right possibilities of expression that explains the Christian mystic's vision of Christ and Mary and the Muslim's dream of Muhammad; and when Ibn ʿArabi has a vision of the divine in the shape of a letter of the alphabet—namely the final h of *Allāh*—that is because in Islamic teaching God is "embooked" in the world through the Quran, becoming visible in the book, in the letters of the words, whereas in Christian teaching God is "incarnated" and "made flesh" in Jesus.

The "morphic field" described by the author, formed in the course of countless generations, also shows up, so far as I understand, in the way that many places seem "loaded" with holiness, that it is like the Hasidic story about a room filled to the brim with prayers which are somehow "reflected back" upon the people praying. The "tuning in" to the master's spiritual power is part of the same thing. The connection, the *tavajju*, only works when there is perfect harmony between master and disciple—thus the necessity of finding the right master, and thus the tendency in certain orders such as the Naqshbandiyya to concentrate on the soul of some great holy person of early times. The force field is needed to find the right experience; a simple Sufi of our day has quite rightly compared relations between master and disciple with the process of fine-tuning a television.

A small clarification of terms seems necessary here. The philosophical expression *vaḥdat al-vudjūd* is generally translated as "unity of being," suggesting a kind of pantheism or mystic monism. But one forgets all too quickly that in the theosophy of Ibn ʿArabi, who never uses the expression in any of his works, the "unity of being" is contrasted with the *kathrat al-ʿilm*, the "multiplicity of knowing" (a point that William Chittick has brought out very clearly on several occasions). God's being, His essence, is absolutely one and indivisible. He is the Hidden God (*deus absconditus*), unreachable even by the highest thinking or the highest love, because the Absolute One eludes all definition, indeed all expressible experience. But the One Essence was, as the extra-Quranic word of God puts it, "a hidden treasure," and in one act of breaking-out the divine names sprang forth from the One Reality, and non-being was thereby blessed with the abundance of manifestations that now constitute for us the visible and palpable world which however would still vanish in an instant if the names were not keeping it here. Goethe's lines:

> . . . *then a groan of pain resounded*
> *as the mighty stroke of All*
> *broke into reality*. . . .

describe this act of creation, which poets have often compared to pouring light on invisible shards of glass which become visible only by reflecting the light.

So one must handle the much-abused notion of the *waḥdat al wujūd* with care, even if the "looser" form of this teaching that has developed in later centuries, predominantly in the eastern part of the Islamic world (*hama üst*, "Everything is Him") has opened the door to the modern interpretation.

Usually a master does not want a disciple's experiences during a *halvet* made public, knowing that the highest or deepest experience that the seeker can be blessed with is beyond words. Descriptions could only give a false impression to those on the outside, and anyone who has ever read the mystic literature of any of the most various religions of the earth knows that only paradoxes or seeming nonsense can suggest what happens to a person during such an interval. Islamic mysticism is full of such paradoxes, which are difficult for the cleverest (*especially* for the cleverest) readers to solve. So it is with this report of what a person experiences in the course of a *halvet*. The reader must do what Seyyed Hossein Nasr called "reading between the letters" and must not focus on the visible word alone.

The present book is, to my knowledge, the first attempt on the part of a European who is not only a Muslim—but one who holds a Ph.D in clinical psychology and is also a psychotherapist—to describe the *halvet* experience. In that light her critical observation of events is fascinating. Still, her self-analysis leaves no room for doubt that we are dealing here with what is finally a religious experience, an expression of grace: every step on the path, even momentary backslidings or weaknesses, becomes a sign of divine guidance. And when scholarly writings about the experiences of meditation, constant prayer, and solitude have largely emphasized and still emphasize the purely psychological components, that makes this account, precisely because of the deeply religious stance of the author, extraordinarily important, in fact unique as far as I know.

Perhaps this book will open the door to a new understanding of Sufism and the inner dimensions of Islam, whose image often appears in such distorted form. To the author who had the courage to undergo the rigors of the *halvet*, and to her master, who directed her to publish her journal entries, we are extraordinarily grateful, and we wish this unusual book many readers.

[*Ya Hazrati Mevlâna*]

Foreword

Talking cannot bring about understanding; talking can only bring you to the point where the listener gets the disturbing feeling that outside this world perceived by our senses lies another world that we must try to find.

Hazrati Mevlâna[1] (known as "Rumi" to the West)

This is a first-person account of a spiritual instruction in the framework of the Sufi tradition. In the forefront lies, first of all, an account of a forty-day *halvet*, a period of absolute isolation accompanied by stringent fasting. Experiences of this kind cannot be passed along by speeches or books alone. It might be asked why I embark on such an undertaking at all. Hz. Mevlâna says: "Don't give wisdom to those who are unworthy of it, so as not to do it injustice; and don't withhold it from those who are worthy, so as not to do them injustice" (FmF, p. 256).[2]

---

[1] *Hazrati*: "venerable" or "holy"

[2] The principal sources used in this book (which were also my reading-matter during the *halvet*) are cited using the following abbreviations: Hz. Mevlâna,

It isn't wisdom that I could give. Yet the experiences that I was permitted to undergo, surpass in depth and breadth everything I know as a transculturally active psychologist about our Western methods of growth. That is not surprising, since Sufism is so much older and therefore more fully matured than Western psychology with its relative youth.

So what happens to a Western-educated, ethnologically interested social scientist who gets involved on the plane of direct experience with an ancient spiritual tradition? This book is designed to offer insight into these processes. It is therefore a very personal book.

Hz. Mevlâna says: "Now I want to give my friends some advice. When the brides of spiritual truth unveil their faces deep inside you and secrets are revealed, be careful, oh be careful, not to tell strangers about them or describe them to other people! And these words that you are hearing from me now are not to be told to everyone" (FmF, p. 140). That brings up the question, pertaining to all esoteric traditions, of what may be transmitted to whom, and by whom, and under what conditions. So I am transmitting what I have been authorized to transmit.

Among Sufis it is said, "The secret protects itself." What that means is that experiences really can only be transmitted to those who are ready for them. Similar processes are observed when someone tries to explain a drug experience to someone who has never had any such experiences. Hz. Mevlâna points out the futility of such an effort:

It is better not to ask the fakir... because when one who is [still] tied down to his body asks him questions, he must respond according to the other's capacity and understanding, namely by manufacturing a lie... and even though everything the fakir says is true and cannot be a lie, it is still a lie compared to the right answer and assurance and truth; yet in relation to the hearer it seems right, indeed more than right. (FmF, p. 208)

Fihi ma Fihi: FmF; Hz. Mevlâna , *Open Secret*: OS; Ibn 'Arabi, *Fūsūs al Ḥikam*: FaH. Translations from FmF and FaH are from the German editions.

My way of dealing with this inherent difficulty is a multi-layered and partly indirect mode of transmitting knowledge, which is consistent with the principles of Sufism. For the account of the *halvet* I have retained the diary format of my notes to allow the reader the most direct possible access to the transformative processes. But these unfold in the presence of the whole context of my life in general and the whole context of training on the pathway in particular. This part is an extremely personal matter.

The diary section is followed by a section of commentary in which, on the basis of my direct experience, various aspects of the *halvet* are examined from ethnopsychological, psychotherapeutic and cultural-anthropological perspectives. I myself found these "bridges" helpful in my gradual penetration into other ways of seeing and my ultimate success in being at home there.

The predominant theme is the question of the possibility of an actual consciousness expansion and the physiological processes that go along with it. In that connection, recent scientific and medical research results are reported and reference is made to what I regard as particularly significant scientific positions from the realm of consciousness research. When these isolated investigations are seen in relation to one another, they bring up new considerations and lead to theories that make further interdisciplinary research look well worthwhile. The commentaries are supplemented by sayings that come from Sufism itself. For this purpose I cite authors from various centuries. My choice is necessarily subjective, as is my understanding of what they have to say to us across the distance of space and time.

The method of verbally transmitting information from different points of view—from reproducing direct experience to presenting objectively measurable scientific facts—builds the outward framework in which, *insh'Allah*,[3] further levels of understanding may ultimately open up. Hz. Mevlâna says, "Words are useful insofar as they make you look for the object of your desire and goad you on—not that the goal of the quest could ever be reached through

---

[3] God willing.

words. If it could, you wouldn't need so much effort and self-denial" (FmF, p. 311).

Esoteric paths, then as now, are for the few who are ready to pay the price: "No one who ever trod this path has ever complained, unless it was someone who set foot on it in a frivolous and lascivious spirit" (Hz. Mevlâna, FmF, p. 245). And so this book, in its openness, is in the last analysis also a warning against "frivolity."

"I say," explains Hz. Mevlâna, "whatever comes from the hidden place. If God wills, He will make these few words useful and allow them to take root in your breast, and it will bring you powerful advantages. If God does not so will, a hundred thousand words could be spoken and none would take root in your heart; they would all pass by and be forgotten" (FmF, p. 121).

This book also comes from a "hidden place," from the hidden place of my innermost experience. May it rouse in some seekers on the path something of that "disturbing feeling" described by Hz. Mevlâna.

Istanbul, September 1991
Michaela Mihribân Özelsel

Publisher's Preface

The following journal entries by Mrs. Özelsel are reproduced as they were written down on the spot in early 1991 in Istanbul. That means above all that stylistic corrections have been avoided and repetitions have been consciously accepted as part of the bargain, in order to transmit to the readers as well as possible the authenticity of the experience and of the author's personal development. It was also of decisive importance for Mrs. Özelsel in the diary sections to leave the Turkish form "Hz. Mevlâna" (Mevlâna Celaleddin Rumi) as the name of the famous mystic and poet who is known in the West as "Rumi" (Mevlâna Jalaluddin Rumi) and is so identified in other books from Threshold Books.

All translations from the English, French, Spanish, and Turkish are by the author herself when not otherwise marked.

A Leaf calligraphy from the 17th/18th Century, which relates the well known
saying of the Prophet Muhammad (peace be upon him):
"Paradise lies at the feet of mothers."

DIARY

*. . . take refuge in the cave: God will spread His grace over you,
and will endow you—whatever your outward condition—with
all that your soul may need!*

Quran 18:16

"*A*sya'ya hoş geldiniz, Mihribân Hanïm,*"*[1] says the shaikh[2] with
a smile, "Welcome to Asia." "*Hoş bulduk,*" I answer and tear myself
away from the sight of the great mosques behind us, looming high
against the slowly darkening evening sky of Istanbul.

The shaikh himself is sitting at the steering-wheel of the small
white car that gave us some trouble on this cold, rainy January day,
but finally started after all. We leave behind us the large modern
bridge connecting Europe with Asia. In no time we are in the thick
of the narrow streets of Üsküdar, the Asiatic part of this city on two
continents. We make two brief stops: "They have good olives
here. . . an apple now and then is also useful." Oh yes, and a pair of
plastic bathing sandals.

The drive proceeds, passing the walls of ancient cemeteries that
seem to stretch out to infinity. The headlights capture the silhou-
ettes of still, tall cypresses and narrow Islamic gravestones, standing there united in silence as the rain slowly turns into snow.

Last night I arrived in Istanbul. An unreal, spooky flight. The
huge Turkish Airlines jet almost empty except for a few business
people, with me the only woman and the only foreigner on board.

---

[1] In Turkish the formal mode of address consists of the first name followed by
Hanïm (Mrs.) or *Bey* (Mr.).

[2] *Shaikh, Pir.* and *Murshid* are designations for the spiritual leaders of Sufi orders.

1

In two days an ultimatum to Saddam Hussein would be expiring. "Who would be flying east today?" says the flight attendant. Then a brief meeting with Mehmet, my husband. "I've finished filing for our divorce. You just need to sign a general power of attorney for your lawyer, and the rest won't take long."

"Here we are," announces Murat,[3] one of the shaikh's disciples, who till now had sat in silence in the front passenger seat. We go on up in the semi-darkness of the stairwell, which my mother would have called a "climb." As we stand in the empty apartment in the modest three-floor apartment building in a poor section of this teeming city of millions, we are hit with the clamminess and cold. In the smallest of the three rooms Murat sets my suitcase down and switches on a small electric stove. I have about two hours to complete the full Islamic purification, or *ghusl*[4] before the shaikh will come back to "put me in."[5]

The time has finally come. Once again he reminds me: you don't go into a *halvet*[6] for your own sake, Islam doesn't have monks and monasteries,[7] the retreat is only temporary, in order to serve the community, the *umma*, more usefully after you're out.

"Pray for peace in the world," He says: "you are entering upon your *çile* at a very eventful time." And then, finally, after some melodically recited prayers (*gülbenk*), the words: "*Yumuşak geçsin,*" "May it pass gently." Then the door to the room shuts, then the door to the apartment shuts, the key turns in the lock from outside, and I am alone.

[But bear in mind:] never does their flesh reach God, and neither their blood: it is only your God-consciousness that reaches Him. It is to this end that We have made them subservient to your needs, so

---

[3] All names except those of my immediate family have been altered for the protection of those involved.

[4] *ghusl*: ritual washing of the entire body.

[5] The putting-in was conducted according to the tradition of Hoca Ahmet Yesevi (see the Glossary of Islamic Names in the Appendix, p. 209ff).

[6] *halvet* (solitude) or *çile* (forty days): Islamic retreat.

[7] "But as for religious asceticism—We did not enjoin it upon them: they invented it for themselves out of a desire for God's goodly acceptance." Quran 57:28.

2

that you might glorify God for all the guidance with which He graced you.

Quran 22:37

A thin, hard cotton mattress is my one piece of furniture. I look around me at the room that will be my home for the next forty days, almost six weeks: The window is blocked off by a torn curtain with olive and yellow stripes, and there's kitschy-looking wallpaper, striped, cream white with rose blossoms, like a German bedroom of the 1950s; it's coming off the wall in places and flopping down loosely. In one corner, on top of an empty plastic bag from a department store, I have laid out my few possessions: my toothbrush, toothpaste (my son Timur quickly tucked in a tube of his own which he considers much better than my "mediocre" brand), shampoo and hairbrush and an electric hair-dryer. In another corner stands the suitcase with my clothes and a change of bedding. My towel and bathrobe are hanging on the door from long nails set in above its little frosted-glass window. Right beside my mattress, on another plastic bag is the Holy Quran, along with the books by the two thirteenth-century authors that the shaikh has also approved for me: Hz. Mevlâna[8] and Ibn 'Arabi.[9]

On a nail above my mattress, I have hung the calendar my daughter Amina painted for me; in Arabic calligraphy she has written: "*Bismillāh ar-Rahmān ar-Rahīm*"[10] and the hadith[11] "Strive for knowledge from cradle to grave." Then the dates of the next forty days. . . . "Just turn the calendar over when you get sick of it," she said. On the other side is a copy of a poster that she just brought back from her year abroad in France: two hands holding up a wet

---

[8] Hazrati Mevlâna Jalaluddin Rumi (1207-1273). See also the "Glossary of Islamic Personages" in the Appendix, p. 209ff.

[9] Also known as "*as-Shaikh al-Akbar*," "the Greatest Shaikh" (1165-1240).

[10] *Bismillāh ar-Rahmān ar-Rahīm*: "In the name of God, the Compassionate, the All-merciful," the opening lines of every sura of the Quran, words which in Islamic countries are recited at the start of practically every function.

[11] *Hadith Qudsi*: non-Quranic words of God, which, alongside the Sunnah, the mode of action concretely practiced by Muhammad (Peace be upon him) are considered in Islamic tradition to be obligatory for an exemplary life.

and extremely indignant cat dripping with water and shampoo. She's added a dialogue balloon to make the animal say: "Have fun learning!!"

I'm thinking about the other animal, the one that gave its life for me today[12] and all the steaming red blood that flowed across the white marble. We had driven in the thick of Istanbul's afternoon traffic to Eyüp to perform the requisite ritual sacrifice. I must have looked pretty helpless surveying the thirty or so sheep crowded together under the canopy. In any event, Recep, another of the shaikh's disciples, decided for me: "This one here!"

The rest goes very quickly: three legs are tied together, the animal is weighed and then taken out to the place of sacrifice in a wheelbarrow. "Who is assuming the governance (*vekillik*)?" asks one of the attendants. I just nod, afraid that I'll burst into tears if I say a single word. But to no avail. "Then say so," the man demands, holding the sharp knife ready. Somehow I manage to force out the requisite words. The attendants recite the prescribed prayers.

"You must touch the sheep one last time, you must consciously make contact with it one last time," the shaikh had said. I lay my hand between the animal's soft white ears. It looks at me very calmly and peacefully, still chewing on the last blades of grass that hang from its muzzle. Why is it still chewing? Doesn't it know it's about to die? Or does it know, this close to death, about other things of a completely different nature?

As I step back, an attendant slits the throat with one swift cut. The head is bent back, and the bright red blood comes pulsating out into the white marble channel provided for the purpose. Another attendant is standing there with a hose, ready to clean up. One of the men dips his finger into it and makes a bloody mark on my forehead. The clumpy flakes of snow that the rain has turned into come sailing into the place of sacrifice, driven by the strong east wind, and mix with the blood and water as they flow steaming through the marble channel to become ONE with the earth once more.

---

[12] See "Blood Sacrifice," p. 113.

And somehow I've managed to get this far without crying. When, I wonder, does life end? The animal made no sound, and it trembles only in spurts, remaining motionless in the intervals between. Then, finally, staccato movements of the legs, three tied together, one free in the air. Eventually the attendants conclude that life has given way to death. They cut the rope, and the three legs spread out. The skinning goes unbelievably fast: they use a tire pump to blow air between the hide and the flesh. Then the hide is neatly removed from the body in one piece. The small, young animal is, or rather was, a male, as I now see. In a few minutes it's hanging on a meathook, with its guts hanging on another hook and the hide lying in the corner. Would I like some of the meat for myself? Again, fortunately, Recep answers for me: no, the animal, hide and all, will be donated to the poor.

All this is as unreal to me as the almost empty plane flight of the night before. Observing as if from a distance, I wonder what I, a scientist from a twentieth-century, Western, industrialized country have to do with this ancient, archaic ritual. Slowly we walk out, and I'm glad Recep also says nothing, that we can be silent together. We're almost outside when a little old woman, miserably dressed, comes shuffling up to us. She sees the fresh blood-mark on my forehead, clasps one of my hands in both of hers and touches it to her forehead and mouth, smiling and murmuring, "*Allah razi ol-sun*" (May God accept it.) Then she hurries on through the icy, gust-driven snow and rain to the adjoining soup-kitchen to get her portion of sacrifice meat.

I think how often in the supermarket I have dropped a cellophane-wrapped package of meat into my shopping cart: the flesh of animals that were slaughtered with no prayers, whose blood was not returned to the earth, and for whose death the responsibility, the "governance," was not assumed consciously by anyone at all.

Day 1

Istanbul'u dinliyorum, yemyeşil. . . .
I listen to Istanbul, so green, so green. . . .

Getting up as the *ezan*[13] sounds; ritual washing, *namaz.*[14] Trying to read the Quran. For some reason I'm real tired, all worn out. The exhaustion of these last weeks and months? The house is full of sounds, layer upon layer of "humanness." Must have fallen asleep. Terrible: that's not what I'm here for. And that sheep died for me. Forty days! On the one hand, so long. On the other hand, is it even enough? Try to pray but how? "May I use this special time wisely; let the sheep not have died in vain, not to mention all the other people who are making all sorts of sacrifices so that I can do this! May I prove worthy of all this." Outside, the sound of an icy mixture of snow and rain beating at my window. It seems cozy somehow, in spite of the spareness of my cell.

"Istanbul'u dinliyorum, yemyeşil. . . ." (I listen to Istanbul, so green, so green. . . .) How long ago that was! I recall the first lines of that poem my brother and I had to memorize for Turkish class back then. It's been a long time since Istanbul was "green," but "listening" to it still has its rewards. A city full of sounds, familiar and yet here in Üsküdar also strange. A major part of my teenage years was spent in Nişantaş, one of the more well-to-do sections of the city, with completely different sounds.

What does sound the same, both here and there, are the animals: the cats, who make a considerable ruckus fighting over the garbage in the cans and whose love scenes are almost equally noisy and intense; the countless pigeons cooing in the city's many mosques; the dogs; plus the calls of the street-vendors.

---

[13] *ezan*: the call to prayer that is heard in Islamic countries five times a day, indicating the hours of prayer.

[14] *namāz*: Persian-Turkish expression for *salāt*, the Muslim prayer ritual. See also "Methods of Sufi Schooling," p. 141ff.

Much is different here in Üsküdar. And the house itself is so much less soundproof. Noises come from everywhere: toilets flushing, the rattle of cold ashes being shaken out of the stoves, outside the beating of carpets and the sounds of many, many children out playing. This instead of the central heating, vacuum cleaners, nursemaids, and day-care centers of Nişantaş! Yes, it's a good quarter-century later that I now "listen" to Istanbul once again.

But listening isn't what I'm here for. The idea is to turn inward and leave the outside world behind for a while. I have to laugh at the thought that obviously everybody gets whatever circumstances they need. Most people considering a *halvet* are scared at the thought of spending almost six weeks in absolute silence and solitude. That never frightened me. I love tranquillity. And drawing inward is a strong tendency of mine, one of my time-proven coping strategies. So it only makes sense that *my* cell should be the one with all these noises! And on top of everything, the television! At home I can easily escape, we have a big house with sound-proof walls, and the TV is in its own little room. But here! The next-door neighbors obviously have their TV right up against the wall that divides us. And as for the programs they watch, they don't seem any too choosy, because it's going from early morning till after midnight. And roaring loud!

Actually the family's pretty loud itself. Somebody's always fighting with somebody: mother with father, mother with daughter, daughter with little brother, father with daughter, daughter with friend. I feel like an "auditory voyeur." As for these weeks, I will in a way be sharing their private space, while they know nothing of my existence.

Another circumstance custom-tailored just for me: I'm a cleanliness freak. And getting washed is complicated here. Next to my room is a tiny little bathroom. As in many Turkish dwellings, a shower has been put in as an afterthought, spraying out from above the toilet into the little room itself. It's heated by an ancient hot-water heater, pretty well rusted through. It takes an hour and a half of heating-up time so you can take a five- or six-minute shower. While it's heating up you mustn't turn off the thermostat, that apparently causes a short circuit. In addition, you can't use any other electric appliances during the heating-up time, or the whole system gets overloaded. That means I also have to turn off my little heater till the bathwater is ready. My room takes just a few minutes to get icy cold; obviously the walls have little or no insulation. But then, this quarter of the city has been without water since this morning, so showering is already out.

Knowing Istanbul conditions, when I got here yesterday, I took the four large empty Coca-Cola flasks that I found lying around and filled them with water. So for the time being I don't have to worry about drinking water. And the necessary ritual washings can be performed using sand if there is no water. That must be quite convenient if you live in the desert, but I don't have any sand here either. Going through the motions and having the right intention will have to be enough!

The ritual prayer, the *namaz*, is another of those things. I've actually never been very thorough about fulfilling this duty, which is one of the fundamental commands, one of the so-called "five pillars" of Islam. Now's the time! I reach for my scarf and feel a little silly. Is there any need for that if I'm here alone in my cell? If I were performing the rite in public, then of course I would follow the tradition. But who can see me now? From the Islamic point of view the answer is clear: Allah always sees you! Still feeling a little stubborn, I think, "Well, as He was the one who created me naked, surely my uncovered hair can't be that bad!"

On the rational plane my logic is entirely satisfying. But it doesn't feel right to me at all. And I'm not a person with an ingrained horror of breaking taboos. So what's the matter? I don't know, but I decide to put my scarf on. It feels right. But I can't stop poring over the "logic" of it all. Finally, I have a solution that satisfies me: Rupert Sheldrake's theories[15]! That's it, the "missing link"! When I get back out, I'll have to discuss it with him.

---

[15] See "Observations on the Theory of 'Morphic Resonance,'" p. 117ff.

Day 2

So what exactly should I do all day long? The instructions given me are really only guidelines, with much room for interpretation. Eating, for example. Basically, an Islamic fast is to be observed, the same familiar kind as for the month of Ramadan: from before sunrise to after sunset, no nourishment, no water, no nothing. But by night during the fasting-month you can eat as much as you like of whatever. During the *halvet* I'm allowed to eat a "handful of dates," and I've also been given a small store of olives and a plastic bag full of apples. How many dates in a "handful"? I try it out and decide: six to eight, depending on size. The supplies of olives and apples are easier to look over: I can eat about eight olives every night and an apple every three days. Then everything will last me for the forty days. By night I can also drink whatever I want, as long as it's Istanbul tap water!!

I can also read: the Quran, Hz. Mevlâna and Ibn 'Arabi. Two audio cassettes have also been approved for me, with *ilahi*[16] and sung *zhikrs*[17] on them. My son Cengiz gave me his Walkman to take with me for the purpose. And then there's the five daily ritual prayers[18] and the *zhikrs*. But now, what combination of these activities, and what should be emphasized? That also seems to have been left to my own judgment. Reading has always been one of my favorite pastimes anyway, so that would not be any sacrifice. Besides which, it also fits better with my cognitive approach to the world. From the psychological point of view, the human tendency to prefer the familiar, thus reinforcing it still more, is widely known. By that logic, if I want to open myself to any new experi-

---

[16] *ilahi*: dialogue with God in verse or prose form, spoken or sung.

[17] *zhikr*: repetition of the names of God or the formulas of prayer; an old dervish exercise in which various prayer formulas are repeated rhythmically like mantras, accompanied by movements of the head and/or body. (See "Methods of Sufi Schooling," p. 141ff.)

[18] The Islamic ritual prayers (*namāz*) are not prayers asking God for something (*du'ā*), but proceed in a fixed and detailed order of words and movements. (See "Methods of Sufi Schooling," p. 141ff.)

ences I have to do the opposite of what would naturally occur to me. Which means: *zhikrs*.

The shaikh has prescribed seven *zhikrs* for me. "The first two days," he said, "do a lot of *Estağfirullah*[19] and *Bismillahi*,[20] then do all of them on the remaining days." So how much is a lot? Would two hours be a lot? Or six? Maybe ten? At our meetings in the Frankfurt area, *zhikrs* generally don't last more than an hour. I'll start and see what happens.

He has also advised me to take notes on my experiences each day.

Day 3

Two days now without water. This morning the light doesn't go on. I run with my candle through the empty apartment looking for another bulb. When I come back, the old one's working again! A pointless detour? How often in our lives do we make such "detours"? Maybe the point is to recognize them as such?

I sense feelings of gratitude for everything around me: the water I drink, my handful of dates, the warmth of my little stove, my clothing. This morning I once again(!) fell asleep reading the Quran. How can that possibly happen? The neighbors always have

---

[19] *Estağfirullah*: plea for forgiveness of one's own faults, a "purification mantra" that precedes the other mantras. The sense of it is: as a human being I have only a limited time to live in this world. All knowledge that I acquire here is relative and transitory, and so I am subject to errors. In God the Creator lies perfect, unchanging knowledge. And so I ask God's help in correcting my faults, that I may achieve perfection through Him.

[20] *Bismillāhi*: abbreviation of *Bismillāh ar-Raḥmān ar-Raḥīm*: "In the name of God, the Compassionate, the All-Merciful." This mantra is considered the key to understanding the Sufi tradition. The sense of it is: Whatever I do, I undertake it in the name of God, the Compassionate, the Merciful. He has all the most beautiful names (that is, qualities) and still cannot be grasped using names.

the TV on at a deafening volume till midnight! What a lesson in tolerance for me!

Already the zhikrs are turning out differently today than yesterday or the day before. Somehow I'm "standing on the sidelines," watching as "useless" thoughts crowd their way in and then dissolve when I "look at them." The *zhikr Allah* makes me cry. And why shouldn't it? Cry some more; the truth is, it's been years and years since I've had a good cry.

In the evening, footsteps in the apartment outside my room, then there's a key in front of my door. That must have been Yusuf, the shaikh's older brother. He's supposed to make the rounds once a day, looking after me from a distance. Yesterday and the day before he apparently didn't make it. If I'm in any kind of trouble, I can leave a note for him. But the shaikh recommends that I make such contacts only in a real emergency. Also, I should only break off the *halvet* in a situation where there's really no other choice. He himself would only come to get me out in the gravest emergency. As a precaution, my address wasn't given to either the German or the Turkish side of my family; after all, they were all dead set against my endeavor. So now I have my own key, which makes my "confinement" more symbolic in nature.

Day 4

If you are a friend of God, fire is your water.
Hz. Mevlâna

The third day now without water, my hair was probably never so dirty in my life! I've already lost a fair amount of weight. Now the *zhikr Bismillahi* also makes me cry! Once you allow yourself to cry, the tears keep coming. Actually I'm not sad at all, in fact it's comforting. "*Allah'ın dediği olur.* (And He knows all that is on the land and the sea; and not a leaf falls but He

11

knows it.)[21] Really no one can do anything to me, unless it is meant to happen, so it's really just a matter of realizing that, of slowly drawing aside the "veils" and seeing things as they really are.[22] Peace and tranquillity prevail as I think that even my own intentions will only lead to the ends that He allows: actually everything is so simple, so comforting. And tears so soon again? What looks like pain is in fact grace, Hz. Mevlâna's "tricky reversals" of pain and pleasure, of intention and result! So that's what that means. Do I have the strength to bear this "grace of being called"? And already my intention, my reason for this *halvet* in the first place, is changed, transformed. This already on the fourth day! *Alhamdulillah*[23]!

When the pain comes, the veil of forgetfulness is ripped asunder.

Hz. Mevlâna

What had I really intended with this *halvet?* I think back. About six months after my Teacher[24] had accepted me as a student, he had said, just by the way, one evening in a restaurant: "On the path you will lose whatever is dearest to you." My first thought was, "O my God, my children!" And yet spoken of so calmly and so by the way, the whole thing seemed so monstrous, that it therefore couldn't seem real. I quickly changed the subject. For the next two years I had actually succeeded in driving that horrible remark out of my consciousness.

When it hit me, in January of 1990, it was like lightning out of a clear blue sky. It wasn't about my children, it was completely different from any picture I could have painted for myself. It was on

---

[21] *"For, with Him are the keys to the things that are beyond the reach of a created beings perception: none knows them but He. And He knows all that is on the land and on the sea; and not a leaf falls but He knows it. . . . "* Quran 6:59

[22] Well-known request of the Prophet (Peace be upon him) to Allah.

[23] *Alhamdulillah*: Allah be praised, all thanks be to Allah, praise be to God.

[24] Meaning my "real" Teacher, with whom—in contrast to his predecessors or the shaikh who made my *halvet* experience possible—I have an initiatory commitment; see, "The Person of the Teacher," p. 126ff.

"another level" of being, so unreal and unbelievable that it was all the more horrible for being so ungraspable, which made me all the more helpless in the face of this experience. But at the same time I knew, with the deepest knowledge that I'm capable of, that this was "it," that what he had predicted was here now.

My own reactions were also ungraspable for me. While on "this" level I went about my daily tasks, pure and simple, as if nothing had happened, I made the decision over the next few weeks, with difficulty, to live on. My pain was of a dimension that till now had seemed impossible to me: "unearthly." When it became so strong that I feared or hoped that it would literally tear me apart in a moment, that I would maybe become psychotic, just in that moment I would land somehow on the "other side." The "other side" was a stultified feeling of endless numbness. What at first seemed like relief was a devilish mechanism. It gave my organism the rest it needed to be sensitized to the horrendous pain all over again.

Existence as a whole was completely pointless. What I experienced could not be shared with anyone, because on "this" level nothing had happened. But the absolute worst was that, at just that moment, my Teacher became completely unreachable.

I recovered only very slowly. I felt like an empty dead shell, a marionette acting like a thinking, feeling human being. The feeling of unreality spread out across everything. I felt like an extraterrestrial among earthlings, whose joys, sorrows and needs I could no longer share. My teacher had once said in another context that one must sometimes simply act as if it was real. That's what I did.

What made it all even more unreal was that evidently nobody noticed a thing. One patient said to me during just this period: "Your smile always gives me the courage I need to go on. It shows me that there's at least one person untouched by fate, who always has a stable and happy equilibrium." My God, was everything really only *maya* or appearances, as Far Eastern spiritual traditions teach? So I simply went on, hour by hour, day by day. Finally I was so suffused by the senselessness of being, so burned out by the unreal pain, that even the thought of ending my life made no sense any more.

Then sometime during that summer, on a flight to Berlin, I noticed that it would be OK with me after all if the plane didn't crash. I realized that a part of me had obviously been waiting for such an "externally imposed solution": an accident, a fatal illness, anything. . . . But on this flight it became clear to me that even that didn't interest me any more; I might as well just go on living, it made no difference.

Over the course of the year the ungraspable pain now in a somewhat weakened form had wrapped itself around the one thing I could grasp: my desperate desire to be in touch with my Teacher once again. But my many letters went unanswered, when I called I only got to "talk with" the answering machine, and other friends of his who wanted to see him for various reasons all came to the conclusion: he seems to have vanished from the face of the earth.

Professionally, everything had worked out for me strangely positively. I had no interest in anything any more, including myself. And that caused my lectures, for one thing, to take on a new dimension. Now that I was free of the wish for success and recognition, both made their presence felt ever more emphatically almost inexorably, as it seemed to me.

But inside, what began as a "deathly calm" of indifference had gradually given way to an increasing obsession with getting some news of my Teacher. Could he have actually abandoned me? The actions of a teacher, when it comes down to it, are not for the student to understand or judge. A wretched inner condition of drivenness, which nothing could soothe. It was like the "thirst" of Kahlil Gibran: "Isn't the fear of thirst, when the well is full, the one thirst that is unquenchable?" Each day I feverishly waited for the mail, knowing at the same time that there would be no news. For a while I had a little bit of equanimity on Sundays at least, since there was no mail to be expected. But then my obsession began to expand: after all, a call, a telegram could come anytime. . . . Who knows, maybe now, maybe this very minute. . . .

14

How is it that you have seen and found when you are suffering, and now you don't see? Since it is because you suffer that you see, suffering is sent upon you and made your master, that you may remember God.

Hz. Mevlâna

A life of being on call. Just about the most pathetic thing about it was knowing how endlessly far afield this condition had taken me from what my Teacher really expected of me. Meanwhile winter had come, and almost a whole year had passed, and my own forces, my own capacities had not been sufficient to cope in any constructive way with the blow dealt by my Teacher. Gradually the thought of a *halvet* began to take shape within me.

A patient once told me about a friend of his. The man had had cancer in a stage where, medically speaking, there was no hope and no treatments. In a last, desperate act of will the friend decided to fast until either he, the cancer, or both died of starvation. The cancer had given up first, and now the friend was healthy. A *halvet*, being the most drastic spiritual exercise I know, struck me as the only way I might conquer an obsession that was resistant to every treatment method known to me from psychotherapy.

When waking up from error and negligence is given to someone, that is the grace of God and a clear gift.

Hz. Mevlâna

Only the fourth day! And everything, everything is different already! There never has been the slightest reason to despair. An almost euphoric inner jubilation: nothing can happen, unless He so wills! That applies to teachers too! Teachers (including mine!) are just tools for a higher purpose. How could I ever be so blind as to confuse the levels so totally? My unbelievable misery was based on nothing but my own shortsightedness! Not to mention my failure to observe ancient Sufi principles: "With trust and patience the journey is half done."

The teacher is an object for the student to practice on. The whole of existence, the Creator, Allah, whatever you choose to call it, is too ungraspable for an untrained person to work on directly. That even applies to trust and patience, which must first be acquired in relation to the teacher before they can be transferred to Allah. How little I had of either one! Acceptance of whatever a teacher does had obviously been nothing but a theory for me! If I had really accepted and trusted, deep inside, the entire excruciating obsession of this last year would never have been! What a change of perspective, what a liberation to see my limited, petty reality "dissolved" in an immeasurably greater one!

That must be what Hz. Mevlâna means when he says:

When they show obedience, they must be so obedient that they obey no matter what he [the teacher] may do, and they mustn't look to their own reason to aid them, because they may not be able to understand what he does by use of their reason; yet they must still obey him.

These efforts start making a pathway that "grace" can travel on.

When it is granted to someone to awaken from error and negligence, that is the grace of God and a pure gift. . . . Grace is like a spark of fire. The spark is a favor from God, but when you lodge it in a scrap of wool and nourish it and let it grow, that is giving thanks for the favor bestowed and reaping the rewards of the gift. You start out with the gift and end up with the grace and the reward (FmF, p. 120-21).

Jubilation wells up within me. The *zhikr* "*Alhamdulillah*" which the shaikh didn't even prescribe for me, bursts unbidden from my lips just like that! It feels like a bubbling spring, joyously pushing to the surface. How right Mevlâna is and how incredibly fast it all goes! To think what my reasons were for starting this *halvet* in the first place! To get rid of my petty obsession. And now! A first tiny spark of the realization that so much more is involved!

16

I actually don't like the word "grace" very much at all. But what else do you call it? This incredible freeing, this inner lightness after all these months of pointless suffering, how can you call it anything but "grace"?

> It is pain that a person is guided by, and he will make no efforts towards the goal if it contains no pain, no passion, and no yearnings of love.

Hz. Mevlâna

But actually, what leads me to the conclusion that the pain is pointless? No, that tormented time was obviously very necessary to prepare me for this breakthrough! Not suffering as an end in itself (that would be highly un-Islamic!), but suffering as a catalyst[25]— something all the ancient literature is full of. How else can it be understood, when Hz. Mevlâna sums up his entire spiritual development with the words: "I was raw, I got cooked, I have been burned up." Or the well-known saying of the Prophet (Peace be upon him): "Die before you die!" That's what my Teacher must have meant when he said that on the path one would lose whatever is dearest. It really did feel like dying: "Seeing the light of the fire in the lamp is physical science; but burning up in the fire or the light of the lamp is religious science" (FmF, p. 361).

Over and over the same metaphor of burning up, running like a scarlet thread through Sufi literature. The best-known picture is surely that of the moth and the flame, expressed by Hz. Mevlâna as follows:

> If there was some creature like a moth but which could get along without the candlelight and didn't go swooping into the light, that wouldn't be a real moth; but if the moth did go swooping into the candlelight and the candle didn't burn it up, that wouldn't be a real candle. Likewise, a person who can do without God and makes no effort is not a real person at all, but if God were within his grasp, that wouldn't be God. . . . And it is God who consumes a person

---

[25] See "Methods of Spiritual Schooling: Do They Make You Well or Make You Sick?", p. 156ff.

and annihilates a person, and no understanding can grasp Him (FmF, p. 96).

I let myself just drift from one *zhikr* to the next. The *"Alham-dulillah"* gives way to *"La ilāha il Āllāh,"*[26] and a completely different level of experience comes into play: ideomotor movements.[27] It makes me laugh that here, amid the deep experience of a *halvet*, I should be reaching for a technical term from psychology. Be that as it may, my head, all by itself with no voluntary action on my part, starts to execute the traditional movements. Stronger and stronger, faster and faster, at first from right to left, gliding smoothly, then simply up and down, up and down. A trance-like feeling sets in, as if my body, to the melancholy sound of the *ney*,[28] were floating out over the vastness of Anatolia.

---

[26] *La ilāba il Āllāb*: the Islamic profession of unity: "There is no God (no idol or fetish) but the one God." He is ever-present and eternal.

[27] See the "Glossary of Medical and Psychological Terms" in the Appendix, p. 000.

[28] *ney*: reed flute, the most important musical instrument of the Sufi tradition. "It sings the song of yearning to be united," as Hz. Mevlâna indicates in the prefatory poem of his *Mathnawi*.

Day 5

There are so many people doing things. Their goal is one thing and God's purpose is another.

Hz. Mevlâna

Upon waking up, a major shock: I have noticeably gained weight! During a period of fasting in isolation! It's my own fault, I did the wrong thing with the best intentions: the day before yesterday I had started to have second thoughts about my drastic weight loss. After three days I was already noticeably skinnier. Since my normal weight of one hundred twenty pounds is already on the thin side for a height of five feet, six inches that concerns me.

It is after all a basic principle of Islam not to hurt yourself, not to make yourself sick. Fasting during the month of Ramadan is not a duty for those who might be harmed and not helped by it, such as those who are sick and weak or extraordinarily overburdened, or travelers or menstruating women.

For that reason I had stuffed myself with lots and lots of dates though I wasn't very hungry at all. But I didn't want any false asceticism to endanger my health and my chances of completing the *halvet* as well. But gaining this much weight! Obviously part of it is that I'm not moving at all except during prayer times. And dates are full of calories. But how embarrassing! Gaining weight during a *halvet!* I wonder how many dates are right for me. "A handful" is such a vague indication.

I start again doing the assigned zhikrs. What is the right proportion here, I wonder? I should do a lot of zhikrs, but what is a lot? My usual approach to life is intellectual and cognitive, whereas zhikrs work on a completely intuitive level. Here we are dealing with other dimensions in which "reason is bondage" and where the idea is to leave it behind. Only temporarily, to be sure; since in many situations a clear, well-functioning mind is a valuable gift. But here. . . . Ibn 'Arabi says: "The creature known as a 'human,' however, is limited [in his perception of God] by reasoning, rumination or a faith that is too dependent upon authority" (FaH, p. 36). On the last evening when I saw my Teacher, he had shaken his head and said:: "You're still going through your head, not through your heart. But the thing is, that's the very way in which you have mastered your life; that's how you've survived." The idea is not to shut these faculties off but to make other additional faculties available.

When I get to the point where I usually stop doing the zhikrs, I decide to keep going. Perhaps some intuitive states that have not been much available will open up for me at the point in the *zhikr* where I turn away from the decision-making processes that normally guide me.

At some point I realize that I have fallen asleep again. I feel simply pathetic; the expression "maggot in the lard" comes to mind. A *halvet* where you gain weight and fall asleep in the middle of the ancient holy exercises! I am close to despair. I keep thinking about the sheep that gave its life for all this. The whole thing is not a joke, not a whim or game, it is in the truest sense "deadly serious," at least as far as the sheep is concerned. And the Persian Gulf crisis! That's what I was supposed to pray for, for peace in the world. So did war actually break out? The world outside is so unreal.

My despair over my inappropriate conduct grows. And now—on top of everything—am I starting to dissolve in self-pity and wallow in my contrition and guilt? There's really only one thing I can do: go on.

And after a while, at some point, liberation sets in. The effort to do the zhikrs well, to do them correctly, has disappeared, dissolved in the hopelessness of the realization of my incapability of anything that can't be done by intellect or willpower. All of a sudden they are no longer exercises to achieve something else. They simply *are*. A state of deep well-being envelops me, simply that. It feels "complete" somehow, all-embracing, and there is also a noticeable physical component besides the spiritual-psychic one.

Once again this reversal! It was precisely my failure that created the inward state that opened the door to something greater. A little later, I read in *Fihi ma Fihi*:

> So we absolutely know that the author of all acts is God and not a person. Every action that issues from a person, good or evil, is undertaken by that person with some intention and based on some principles. But the true meaning of his actions is not as limited as he supposes (p. 319).

That seems to apply to my date-gobbling and my falling asleep pretty well.

Already I've noticed in the last few days that I always read in my books the very thing that applies to my inner processes. The Islamic view of coincidence is that there's no such thing. Jung's synchronicities? Or am I "reading the meaning into the text" as people generally do with mass-media horoscopes? I decide to keep an eye on this process.

When I look back on my life, it was always the difficult times that in the end make possible some further development. And each of the teachers I encountered (or who were sent to me?) in the course of these past few years was also related to some painful experience. And they all disappeared from my life but in every case the disappearance was only temporary. They all came back in a different form. Why should it not be the same way with my Teacher? "Don't grieve," writes Hz. Mevlâna: "anything you lose comes round in another form" (OS, p. 46).

> We have put a substance into you, a seeking, a yearning, and we are guarding it; and we aren't letting it get lost, we're bringing it to a certain definite place.

> Hz. Mevlâna

How did it happen in the first place that "teachers" came into my life?[29] In the gentle floating state of well-being that envelops me

---

[29] See "The Call to the Path and its Consequences," p. 163ff.

now, the past suddenly seems so logical, so consistent, directed towards this goal from the very beginning.

In my family we never talked about religion. More emphasis was placed on using "common sense" as a guide and acting "humanely." We didn't need a church for that. Nonetheless, now and then we still came in contact with the Bible. There was a God who spoke to people. That was the deep yearning of my childhood, to have such a dialog. But all my childhood prayers went unanswered, and finally God went the way of the Stork, Santa Claus, and the Easter Bunny.

But the inner quest continued. My naive childhood faith gave way to all the "isms": communism, altruism, humanism, atheism. Religion, which I had experienced only as empty dogma, was dismissed as "the opiate of the people" or as "necessary structuring help for people with weak moral-ethical principles and no very palpable conscience." My family, with affectionate derision, referred to my questings as my "social vein."

My life's goals, after all the disillusionment, were finally very simple and pragmatic: a good marriage and four children, for whom I would be the ideal mother. Then, as I found my marriage devoid of the intellectual exchange so important to me, the more I began to get more and more involved with the three children that we had finally managed, with some trouble, to have. Then one day when my eldest son was about seven or eight, he said to me: "Mama, can't you go find something to play with for yourself so we can have a little peace?"

Suddenly I saw myself, years later, as a middle-aged woman clinging to her increasingly independent children—God forbid that should happen to my children and me! But now what should I "play with"? I still had my high-school diploma around somewhere, and there was a university not too far away. It took more than a year before my husband approved my study plans. The university was so different from school, which I had never liked. I became an inspired and eager student. That must have been what I had been looking for all this time without even knowing it: intellectual stimulation, acquisition of knowledge!

Arranging my courses around my children's needs, I put in long but happy hours studying away. My life seemed fulfilled, good. My inability to share any deeper experience with my husband, the re- alization that children aren't possessions but are only entrusted to us as a "loan of life"—none of that scared me any more. I had man- aged to compensate, to turn frustration into creative action.

Just when everything was okay, just as the quest had ended, strange "states" (hal)[30] started "finding me out." Isolated states that at first just stood there disconnected in a row. In my view of the world, one dominated by logic and reason, they had no contextual frame to lend them significance.

> At some point the states were joined by persons—teachers, as I later called them—who either seemed to cause them or lent them signifi- cance. Often both at once. And what a motley crew of teachers it was! An atheistic hypnotherapist, an American colleague said to be "far out" even by California standards, a centuries-dead Islamic saint. There was a common denominator to them all: each one managed to break another big chunk off my "intellectual shell." Each time it was painful. Each time there were lasting changes as a consequence. Finally my whole picture of the world was over- thrown.

> . . . they are like people who are being called from too far away.
> Quran 41:44

All at once, in this soft, floating state, there on my cotton mat- tress, I see the "big picture," see the consistency in everything that happened, yes, and it all had to happen the way it did. The seem- ingly unrelated events were simply different manifestations of the same, one, underlying power. Suddenly I understand Hz. Mevlâna's words:

> God's joy moves from unmarked box to unmarked box,
> from cell to cell. As rainwater down into flowerbed.
> As roses up from ground. (OS, p. 46)

---

[30] See "The *Halvet* in Transcultural Comparison," p. 179ff.

In Ibn 'Arabi (FaH, p. 57) I read shortly thereafter:

Thus, for example, the rainwater is a single reality which however varies in taste according to the soil that it goes into; for that reason, some of it is sweet and mild and some is salty and bitter, but the water remains water under all these conditions without deviating from its essential character, even when the gustatory sensations that it evokes are different.

How could I have been so blind for such a long time! And how comforting for now, for the future, to know about the contexts of the One underlying Reality. To *know* that the fundamental Islamic principle of *tauḥīd*[31] the principle of the unity behind the multiplicity, also manifests itself clear as day in my own existence! How could it be otherwise?

At every crucial time, somebody or something always came into my life to keep the development going that now has culminated in the "journey on the path." So it didn't depend upon the individual people, upon the teachers. They were only tools of this superior, purposive power known as Allah, which my naive childhood notions of God had given way to. Not only had the tormenting obsession with seeing my Teacher again disappeared as if by magic, but now I even had a rational explanation for the fact!

At some point the *ezan* draws me out of this trancelike state. But not completely. The ritual prayer opens itself to me more and more, every sentence of the *fatiha*[32] is so full of meaning, so full of life!

I suddenly understand what it means that the essence of the whole Quran is contained in the *fatiha*. Ancient, holy formulas which I recite with an ever greater sense of awe.

I am filled with an ever-deepening sense of happiness. I guess all unhappiness comes from holding on, from insisting that things must be the way we ourselves imagine them. And the key to this deep inner peace, which is so precious, lies in the readiness to accept. My Teacher said one time, "You may 'wish,' but you mustn't

---

[31] *Tauḥīd*: profession of belief in the eternal God.

[32] *Fatiha*: the "opener," that is, the first and most often recited sura of the Quran.

'need.'" So why is it so hard when it's really so simple? May I never again lose this insight, never again let the real goal out of my sight.

In the Quran I read in the Sura *Al-Fath* (48:1-4):

> *Verily, O Muhammad, We have laid open before thee a manifest victory, so that God might show His forgiveness for all thy faults, past as well as future, and [thus] bestow upon thee the full measure of His blessings, and guide thee on a straight way, and [show] that God will succour thee with [His] mighty succour.*
>
> *It is He who from on high has bestowed inner peace upon the hearts of the believers, so that—seeing that God's are all the forces of the heavens and the earth, and that God is all-knowing, truly wise—they might grow yet more firm in their faith. . . .*

"Peace in the heart." It's been over a year since I've gone to sleep feeling so relaxed, so quiet and full of peace. This *halvet* was the best idea I ever had!

Day 6

There's water again! What a pleasure, getting washed! I very consciously perform the ritual aspects of this purification. Inside and outside influence each other, and that goes for inner and outer cleansing. The one-and-a-half hours with no heater makes my room noticeably cold right away. I snuggle under my thick quilt to read the Quran. Soon even my fingers are chilly. Fasting makes a person freeze more easily. Though the shower water really is nice and hot, the bathroom itself is unheated. As soon as it's done, back into my cell to squat under the covers drying my hair. Then finally I can turn my heater back on. By ten minutes later it's already noticeably warmer. Once again I feel deep gratitude for everything that surrounds me. *Alhamdulillah!*

Still having a lot of trouble concentrating today, though. My thoughts keep drifting away from the *zhikr* formulas.[33] My satisfac-

---

[33] See "Methods of Sufi Schooling: Do They Make You Well or Make You Sick?" p. 156ff.

tion and gratitude gradually turn to frustration. I'm only just realizing how surprisingly easy it's been for me to "stick to the subject" till now. Today my thoughts turn outward: Has war broken out, I wonder? I even try to understand the thundering television set next door. But the rumbling lets only fragments of clarity get through. The word *savaş* (battle, war) comes up repeatedly. But are they only talking about the threat of war or are they really talking about war having broken out? At the same time I'm upset with myself: far from making an effort to turn completely inward, I'm consciously trying to listen to the outside world! And the zhikrs still won't go the way I want. I think about my son Timur flying back to Germany today. "Have a safe flight, my *Aslan*[34]," I send my good wishes along with him. Who will pick him up, I wonder? Which college did he get into? Why for heaven's sake can't I keep my "body and soul" on the exercises today? My frustration turns to helplessness. What in the world do I have control of if not the most personal thing of all, my very own thoughts?

I resign myself and turn to *Fihi ma Fihi*. Reading is always my salvation, I'm in my element there. What a person, this Hz. Mevlâna! What a gift to express so much transcendental wisdom in a way that is so accessible! And so relevant, despite the intervening centuries! Once again, the very thing I read is tailored to my own inner developments:

> A person assumes that he will drive out blameworthy characteristics by his own labor and struggle. When he fights very hard and has exhausted all his forces and means and is in despair, then God says to him: "Did you think that this would happen through your power and activity and intelligence?... Seek forgiveness for these thoughts and imaginings. For you flattered yourself that the thing would be achieved through the use of your hands and feet and not that it would be achieved through Us. Now that you see that it has come to pass through Us, seek forgiveness, for He is forgiving." (FmF, p. 151).

---

[34] Aslan: "lion," an endearment used by Turkish mothers for their sons.

This must be my *nafs ammara*,[35] my "evil-instigating soul": my arrogance! How tricky! After all, usually conquering one's *nafs ammara* involves withstanding temptations of every kind. Since "iron self-discipline" has not been a problem at all for me for a long time, I assumed I had conquered my *nafs* long ago. Naturally, Sufi authors in every century have warned against just this: there is rarely anything so suspect as the assumption that one has already succeeded. . . . That is one of the many well-known traps along the path. Knowing about the traps apparently affords only limited protection from them.

That must be it, my *nafs ammara* must be my arrogance. The tricky thing about it is that the form this arrogance takes accords perfectly with normal indications of "psychic health"! My assumption that the outcome of many things simply depends on me, on the extent of my involvement, the thoroughness of my planning, my readiness to stay "on the ball". . . . From a psychological viewpoint, just fine! From a Sufi perspective, intense personal effort is indeed indispensable, but the outcome of things cannot be causally traced to it at all. The outcome is in other hands.

The whole story is actually even trickier. When I don't succeed at something, as a matter of course I also assume responsibility for the failure: I should have prepared more carefully, should have been willing to put in a greater effort, etc. But really, even this total assumption of responsibility for failures is presumptuous! What a devilish trick! And psychologists are virtually pre-programmed to fall into this trap.

At some point the *zhikrs* start to go better. They say that nothing removes the "rust of the heart" as well as zhikrs. I obviously still have a lot of polishing to do. Good thing there are such old and time-tested methods of doing so.

In the course of the next few hours, changes in my bodily awareness noticeably increase. Actually, this is a continuation of

---

[35] *nafs ammara*: quintessence of human cravings, the lower self that spurs one on to excesses (cf. Quran 12:53).

processes that began the summer before and for which I have no explanation.[36]

Nor had the shaikh spoken further about them, but only recommended attaching significance to such phenomena and patiently awaiting further developments. Neither fearfully nor with too great an eagerness, simply remaining open. So now things are going forward!

Last summer I had spent many evenings alone on my patio, giving myself time to think my situation over. As a bird whose flight I was observing suddenly made a steep descent, I felt it very clearly and directly inside my own body. A feeling almost like the pulling at your gut when the rollercoaster suddenly goes steeply downward. I explained this curious perception to myself as synesthesia or an "overlapping of representational systems," which means for example a visual experience also being experienced kinesthetically.

I had just about forgotten it again, when a few evenings later, something similar happened. I was lying on my back looking up at the treetops overhead as they moved softly in the wind. Suddenly I clearly felt this swaying movement in myself too. This time I consciously abandoned myself to the novel experience. Then the auditory plane even came into play as well: I heard the *zhikr* "Allah ya daim"[37] inside me, in harmony with the movement in the trees and within me. Then the experience gradually went beyond "me," that is, beyond the boundary represented by my skin. It was as if an invisible substance was all around me, swaying softly along, together with me and the trees. Finally I had no very concrete sense of where my "boundaries" actually were; in any event "I" extended far beyond my skin.

Some time later I also started experiencing certain sounds kinesthetically, such as church bells and the sound of the *ney*. At the same time, an intense trembling arose in my whole body. Now and then it became so intense that real-live twitches and jerks occurred.

---

[36] See "Accompanying Physiological Phenomena," p. 131ff.
[37] *Allah ya daim*: "Allah, the continual."

It was strange the way it happened just like that, without being brought on by the usual stimuli like cold, anxiety or excitement. It was also distinctly visible to those around me. Friends were starting to tease me, saying I must have become an alcoholic in my old age after all.

In the course of the following months the trembling had become progressively more delicate and finally turned into a vibration that sometimes pulsed through my body like a current. Now and then there also arose an inner pressure against the top of my skull, or sometimes a feeling as if my lower pelvic cavity was filled with a bubbly, champagne-like liquid. In most cases all this activity took place inside the space enclosed by my skin. Then it went beyond "me" again, joining me to my surroundings and often coming in waves. All these perceptions were very pleasant, and after a while I learned how to "turn them on" voluntarily. Actually, it was more of a case of letting it happen, since for the most part these processes seemed to be proceeding continuously. Consciously registering them seemed to be more a matter of awareness.

Now, over these past few days, during the zhikrs, these perceptions had gotten noticeably stronger, as if my body was surrounded by a kind of bubble filled with some substance of slightly greater density than air. For want of a better expression I started thinking of this as my "air body."

On one of my cassettes was a rather long *ney* instrumental. Now, inside this "air body," I begin to "float" along with the music. This proceeded with the feeling of a great inner vastness. The air body, to my amazement, was a bit skittish: sudden loud noises of the neighbors made it "pull back" (while my "bodily body" remained at peace), a little like a snail when you gently touch it.

Once again my theoretical knowledge provided no frame of reference to arrange these experiences in. So I simply abandoned myself, with great interest, to what was happening.

In the course of the afternoon I am badly frightened, all of my "bodies" at once: the doorbell rings and rings and rings! I hear several men loudly arguing, then they start pounding on the door like men gone mad. Let's hope the lock holds! It just doesn't stop. Who in the world can that be? Who knows that I'm here?

It must have lasted five minutes by the time they give up and go away. My heart is in my throat. To my amazement it takes a long time before I have completely calmed down again. In general I'm not really the anxious type at all. And after all, what could these men want? Maybe they're not looking for me, but the landlord. How come this happening has affected me this much? Somehow my little confinement cell seems to me to have been "desecrated" by this raw violence poured out on the door with such fury. How safe I had felt, how sheltered. I only realize this now that my solitude has been violated. What if they come back and actually break the door down? I decide to get in touch with Yusuf after all and I write him a note. As he makes his evening rounds I hear his steps pause; he must be reading my note now. Then he leaves, but this time he turns the key twice in the lock. Somehow I feel safer again.

This evening there appears to be a special report on the Persian Gulf crisis on TV. At any rate they keep talking and talking, as if reporting the news, and the word *savaş* keeps coming up. Has war really broken out now, I wonder? Oh, I hope not, I hope not, that could mean breaking off my *halvet!*

With considerable horror I catch myself in my thoughts. My *halvet!* Instead of worrying about all the people affected in the event of war, I'm thinking about my *halvet!* How could I ever be so self-centered? I am utterly disheartened. Have I learned nothing on the path, not even the slightest little bit?

The words of a dear friend come to mind. Since he had already experienced the *halvet* twice, I had asked him what he recommended for this time. After thinking it over a little he said: "Have patience with yourself." How right he was! What choice do I have but to patiently accept my insufficiencies? And I actually thought I had conquered my *nafs ammara* already, just because I have no problem refraining from all sorts of things!

Late at night I am once again overcome with profound gratitude. My, how complacent I had gotten these past few days! Instead of looking upon the unexpectedly prompt arrival of these heartening new understandings as the grace that it was, I was actually ascribing it to my own actions! This when I'm not even able to keep my thoughts where I want them! But at least I'm beginning to get acquainted with my presumption. I also become more clearly conscious of the extent of the grace of these last two days. So I finally fall asleep with a calm feeling of gratitude, rather than the discouragement that preceded it.

Day 7

Stay with us. Don't sink to the bottom
like a fish going to sleep.
Be with the ocean moving steadily all night.
not scattered like a rainstorm.
Hz. Mevlâna, OS, p. 53

As of today, I have been in my *halvet* for a week already. How quickly the time has gone. It is kind of amazing that things have not fallen into a routine even though the rhythm of the times of prayer and the limited choice of activities determine the almost identical progress of every day. The inner experience obviously goes so deep that each new day seems eventful to me and completely different from the days preceding.

During the night I had a pretty bad scare: wrested from sleep by a noise outside my door, I saw my little heater slowly dying out. It went from the usual reddish glow of the heating filaments to a bright white and then out completely. I thought once more of the men who had tried to force their way into the apartment, and my mind turned to the kind of cheap mystery novels where the murderer cuts the electrical connections first before he overpowers his victim. While my heart races, I listen in what is now complete darkness. But all is still. And a few minutes later my heater suddenly goes on again. How comforting to see once more the reddish glow that has already become so dear to me. Probably there was a brief power failure, as so often happens in Istanbul. And the noise that woke me up must have come from one of the neighboring apartments. After all, you can hear everything in this place. My heart calms down as well, and I go back to sleep.

As I wake up this morning, I remember, with great urgency, a dream that must have been partly occasioned by the scary incident: I am deep down on the floor of the ocean. I wonder how much longer I can possibly last there without breathing. Somehow I realize that it's all right not to breathe, that drawing breath, for some reason, isn't necessary. Nonetheless, I decide I'd rather go up to the surface again. There's one last thing I have to take care of down here. I have to make sure that the corpse I'm leaving behind is resting comfortably. I do what I can and then I'm in a hurry for some reason, I have to get back up. I reach for my children and my purse and up we go. While I'm still surfacing, the dream becomes lucid, and I realize that my haste wasn't necessary; after all, for some reason I was able to exist down there without breathing.

Following the morning prayer, the dream continues to occupy my mind. It is clear to me that the corpse was my husband Mehmet. The metaphor of the ocean is a common image in Sufism. The sea is Being in Itself, in all Its endlessness. The spiritually developed person, in the images of Hz. Mevlâna, is one who has "sunk," who lets himself be moved and carried along by the ocean. Someone who neither swims purposely himself, insisting on his own will, nor simply lies at the bottom of the sea like a "sleeping fish."

Mehmet looked to me like the "sleeping fish," resting there on the bottom. If it isn't possible to wake him, then in any event I try to make his continued sleep comfortable before I take the children with me and go. Couldn't I really have done anything more for him? And how distant I am from Hz. Mevlâna's condition of the "sunken person" myself! Not only that I stubbornly insist on steering and surfacing instead of abandoning myself to the sea, no, I even have to take my purse with me! This seems to me to symbolize my over-attachment to worldly things. There's still such a long way to go!

"Figure how to be delivered from your own figuring" (OS, p. 78), writes Hz. Mevlâna. But how? If I could only "go through my heart"! In fact I don't even know what that means. How can I accomplish something that I don't even know what it is? Feeling pretty discouraged, I go back to the *zhikrs.*

In doing the *Bismillahi* there is once again a noticeable alteration in bodily feeling. My head glides back and forth with incredible ease, as if on ball-bearings. It finally gets to be like it's floating, like it's not joined to my body any more. Images present themselves as well: a still night in the vastness of Anatolia, a simple little mosque by starlight, gentle mountain ranges that stretch out farther and farther, all the way to Mecca.

At some point the voices of children playing outside invade my ears once more. They're playing war. "I'm the enemy, I'm Saddam Hussein!" "No, America is the enemy!" Little boys with the names of prophets and saints: Mustafa, Ahmet, Yusuf, Yunus, Ibrahim, ʿAli. Gradually they've become familiar to me. I also hear a girl's name now and then: *Ayşegül,* "Aisha Rose." Āʿisha was the favorite wife of the Prophet (Peace be upon him) in his later years, known for her intelligence, education, quickness of wit and eloquence. El Zubeir said of her: "I know of no one who has as much knowledge of theology, medicine and literature as Āʿisha." Even today, in Islamic countries, this woman who fought in battles and wars and sometimes even publicly contradicted the Prophet (Peace be upon him) is the model of an "emancipated" woman.

"Just keep it up, little Aisha Rose," I think, letting my thoughts go outward again. Does the children's game of war mean war has actually broken out?

Shortly before 10 p.m. I hear Yusuf's steps again. This time he knocks gently on my door. When his steps have died away, I open. Rice soup! In a little Chinese bowl, with hot, milky water and about two tablespoons of rice on the bottom. The bowl fits exactly in the hollow of my hand, like a little bird in its nest. For a while I just enjoy the warmth streaming out of it and am surprised to find that I'm not more starving than I am. I realize now for the first time that I'm not even thinking about food any more. During the first few days that wasn't so. Finally I eat the soup very deliberately and find that a little salt wouldn't have hurt; but I'm grateful for having something hot. The other thing I suddenly realize is that tonight my neighbors aren't watching television!

Day 8

In the morning, the *ezan*, actually a choir of muezzins, is particularly lovely. Because of the widely differing starting times it continues for almost twenty minutes. It's supposed to start when "with the naked eye, you can tell a white thread from a black thread by the dawning light." Evidently all the muezzins who call out within earshot of me have very different levels of visual acuity.

The temptation to just go with the sound and lie there till the last one finishes is very great. But that's dangerous, I could easily fall asleep again. So at the first sounds of *Allahu akbar, Allahu akbar,*[38] I make a point of jumping up to perform the ablutions. The unheated little bathroom and the ice-cold tap water wake me up fast. I think of the contemporary author As-Sufi, who speaks of the "sweet shock of cold water," which forms a line of demarcation between daily profane activities and the time when the believer consciously steps before his Creator.

Today for some reason I'm crying a lot again. I have also suffered a major relapse: my obsession makes itself conspicuous again, overshadowing everything else! And I really thought I'd outgrown that! But I think that would be too simple, such a sudden change after being stuck for so long. Hz. Mevlâna says: "There is that in me that has to be told fifty times a day, *Stop hunting, step on this net*" (OS, p. 58). I suppose that's how it is, the relapse is something that tells me: Stop hunting, it doesn't work the way that you imagine.

The power fails for an hour. How quickly it gets noticeably cold! And again the tears come. I sense my helplessness. It's so simple for this obsession to take hold of me again! In the chill air I roll up under the covers with my copy of *Fihi ma Fihi*. And once again, the very passage that I come to seems tailored to my situation:

---

[38] God is most great, God is most great.

Fishermen don't pull a big fish out all at once. If the hook is in his gullet, they pull on it to make him lose consciousness and get weaker and weaker. Then they let go, then they pull again till it gets very weak. And even when a person has gotten Love's hook in his throat, God pulls him in by degrees, so that this useless faculty and the blood within him come out slowly, slowly. . . . *God squeezes and lightens up.* (p. 202).

The Quran mentions over and over that signs are there for those who "are endowed with understanding." And Muhammad (Peace be upon him) himself prayed, "Show me things as they really are!" I wonder how many more signs I need before I can actually see.

What a faithful traveling companion Hz. Mevlâna is! His words give my experience a framework, they give meaning amid what might otherwise be my overwhelming incomprehension of the processes that I find myself in the middle of. On the other hand, some of my inner discoveries I am undoubtedly only making by virtue of his words having leveled the ground for the realization in question. So in fact it's circular: I experience with the help of his words, his words give my experience meaning, etc. etc. Maybe it's even a kind of spiral which provides my gradual realization with the structural framework it needs? "Words drive the seeker to seeking and idlers to weariness," says Hz. Mevlâna. (FmF, p. 313)

At some point my tears stop. In the middle of the *zhikr* "*Allah ya hayy, ya qayyum*"[39] (Allah, the Living the Ever-Subsisting) super-intense ideomotor movements set in. It practically yanks my head this way and that, and then later up and down. Then at some point, all at once with practically no transition, the deepest tranquillity, inner peace. And colors. Patterns that appear before my inner eye and disappear again. . . . A huge eye with long, thick lashes appears, looking at me motionlessly. In the Sufi view humanity is the pupil of the eye through which Allah observes Himself. . . . I look into the eye before me; who is looking at me through this eye? The thought, "I'm in a trance," drifts through my mind.

---

[39] *Allah ya hayy, ya qayyum:* The Living, the Self-Subsistent.

Day 9

. . . for, behold, all falsehood is bound to wither away.

Quran 17:81

The unpredictability of each day's progress has become almost predictable: days that begin in banality often end with important insights. Days that start promisingly mostly end up quite the opposite!

Feel pretty weak physically, spend part of the morning drifting back and forth between sleep and exhaustion. Put my contact lenses in for a change, to keep my eyes used to them. My, how seeing more clearly also helps the everyday world out there to invade once more! Concentrating on the essentials immediately becomes harder. So what is supposed to happen when the *halvet* is over? How will I protect these new insights then from the obviously overpowering grip of the everyday world? "Prayer protects," says the Prophet (Peace be upon him). Can I maybe keep myself safe if, in the times to come out there, I really perform the five daily prayers? Or maybe these constantly present quasi-electric bodily sensations will serve to remind me of the real truths? Forty days is such a short time to do so much lasting work. I just have to have faith.

And suddenly the obsession is gone again, as if it just lifted off of me and left me. *"And say, the truth has come, and falsehood has disappeared. Behold, the false is quick to fade,"* so I read in the Quran (17:82).

Day 10

I s the obsession really gone? I don't dare to test it. I don't allow any thoughts in that direction. I'd rather occupy myself with the *zhikrs*. Today I spend a long time doing them. Outside the children are playing War again.

How the days turn around and collide with themselves! Today I didn't think I'd have much to write about. Most of the day went its way quite unspectacularly. But then late in the evening!

During the *"Bismillahi"* zhikr, quite unexpectedly, I am suddenly stricken with love for Muhammad (Peace be upon him). I can really only describe it in terms of being hit. Naive pictures of hearts pierced by Love's arrow seem like an appropriate description. I cry more than ever, still doing the *zhikr*, but it feels totally different than ever before. The love I feel is so deep it hurts.

What a man, this Muhammad! How did we humans ever deserve to have him sent to us? How can we ever prove worthy of this blessing? All at once my thoughts go "straight to God." Normally He (She? It?) is too ungraspable for me to get any farther than abstract considerations. Now all at once, there is an indescribable direct access there! And I am struck down all over again, overwhelmed by a wave of the most ardent love for Muhammad (Peace be upon him), His messenger. And right away, almost in synchronization, this "direct connection" to Allah is there again, to Allah, *ar-Rahman ar-Rahim*, the Most Compassionate, the All-Merciful. My sense of this immeasurable mercy is so lively that an immense joy pulses through me, making me cry more and more. Tears of a very different sort! No, it certainly wasn't something we earned, having had a person like the Prophet (Peace be upon him) among us. It is clearly the result of absolute mercy, the purest all-mercifulness.

My thoughts—and actually it's not thinking anymore; rather, it's perceiving—leap from Muhammad to Allah to Muhammad to Allah. . . .

Finally this back-and-forth gives rise to an inner circulation. Then the movement that my body has been carrying out as if on its own to the accompaniment of the *zhikr* also becomes circular. To-day it is in Ibn 'Arabi that I afterwards read what I have perceived:

> But the person who carries out the circular movement, for him there is no starting-point and no goal; in consequence, he partakes of perfect God-realization and it is to him that all words and wisdoms are revealed. (FaH, p. 25).

Insh'Allah!

It takes a while, longer before the full extent of the miracle that has happened to me today becomes accessible to my conscious knowledge as well. I've often thought about one of the basic re-quirements of Islam: one must *love* the Prophet (Peace be upon him). That always struck me as an impossibility. The way I understand "loving," it's a feeling that develops in the course of contact with another being on the basis of certain shared experiences. How can I feel love for somebody who lived so long ago? With whom I could never have had any contact? A command to show respect and deference towards the Prophet (Peace be upon him) would have seemed appropriate to me. But love? My intense involvement with the historical Muhammad had indeed taught the greatest admira-tion for this extraordinary person well and good. But the Islamic command to love him, a person long since dead, struck me as im-possible, illogical, unthinkable.

Only now do I see how correct the word "un-thinkable" is for this command. Of course love isn't something that could ever be achieved by thinking, by an effort of the will. When it "hits," that is pure grace. Could that be what is meant when my Teacher is al-ways talking about "going through the heart"? Understanding what that means is still impossible for me. But all at once I have been allowed to have the direct, living experience of the "unthinkable."

One of the guidelines of Sufism is: "The person who tastes, knows." If for example someone has sucked on a lemon even once, the taste will give him enough immediate knowledge that the mere memory of it is sufficient to initiate physiological processes like salivation. The knowledge born of experience is of an exact kind that could not be acquired even by years of theoretical study of all the characteristics of lemons. It is the *'ayn al-yaqīn*[40] in contrast to the *'ilm al-yaqīn*.[41] The limits of reason! Only when they fall does the extent of them become visible! O Muhammad, teach me the way of the heart, the way of poverty! "Let me be prey in this lovely hunt, let me step on this net!" (OS, p. 58, 78).

Some time later, I reach for the Quran. The Suras 93 and 94 find me. I read over and over:

> *Thy Sustainer has not forsaken thee, nor does He scorn thee. . . . Has He not found thee an orphan, and given thee shelter? And He found thee lost on thy way, and guided thee? . . . And [have We not] raised thee high in remembrance? . . . verily with every hardship comes ease! Hence when thou art freed from distress, remain steadfast, and unto thy Sustainer turn with love.*

Quran 93: 3, 6-7 and 94:4, 6-8

Alhamdulillah!

Day 11

> If you are a friend of God, fire is your water.
> You should wish to have a hundred thousand sets of mothwings,
> so you could burn them away, one set a night. . . .
> One molecule-mote-second thinking of God's reversal of comfort
> and pain is better than any attending ritual.
> Hz. Mevlâna, OS, p. 76

During the *zhikrs* a sudden vision: my whole body is in flames, every single cell burns clean with holy fire. Even my by now quite pronounced emaciation feels good. "If the brain and belly are burning clean with fasting / every moment a new song comes out of the fire," says Hz. Mevlâna (OS, p. 42).

During the *zhikr* "*Hayy Allah*,"[42] Muhammad's (Peace be upon him) entirely unmediated love hits me again. Once more he has suc-

---

[40] *'ayn al-yaqīn*: certainty experienced through inner vision.
[41] *'ilm al-yaqīn*: certainty acquired intellectually.
[42] *Hayy Allah*: "Allah is the Living One."

ceeded in circumventing the limitations of my understanding. And again I cry, more and more.

At some point the tears of joy that come from this painfully intense experience of love turn to sadness, indeed despair. It stays that way. For the first time in this *halvet* I go to sleep at night without seeing my sorrow change into a renewed consolation or trust.

It occurs to me that in the course of the past few days I have prayed passionately for "a hundred thousand sets of mothwings" (OS, p. 76). After all, once it's necessary to be consumed like the moth in the flame, then you need wings upon wings, wings to burn. . . . Is this despair, for which today for the first time no consolation comes, perhaps the answer to my prayers? What could "mothwings for burning" be made of but pain?

Day 12

About 4 a.m., with the *ezan* still to come, I wake up, the words of the Quran ringing like a voice inside me: "*Verily, whenever kings enter a country they corrupt it.*" (27:34). When the "exact knowledge" begins to supplant the "relative knowledge," then a person's existing structures are simply too narrow, they must break apart to make room for the new realization. Just as a snake must molt to grow. . . .

I must have fallen asleep again. At the sound of the first muezzin I leap up, as I do every morning. It takes a few seconds before I realize that I'm lying on my mattress again. Everything's spinning.

Only when my eyesight clears again do I realize that it must have dimmed. I also notice that I'm bracing myself against the doorway to the bathroom. So how did I get here? The last I remember is that when I tried to stand up I fell back on my mattress.

The every-morning choir of muezzins is still sounding forth. Looking down I see my blood dripping slowly but steadily out of me. It mixes with the little puddle that always forms on the slightly concave cement of the bathroom floor.

I keep holding on and just watch for a while. Actually it looks just like the blood of the sheep that died for me, when it mixed with the snow and rain and the water from the hose cleaning up. "*Kurban olayĭm*," comes to mind, words from an old Sufi song, "Let me be the sacrificial animal. . . ."

My period had already started seven days ago. What to do? If it's Ramadan, you're simply freed of the fasting obligation; you just make up the days later, making them an "appendix" to the holy month. That doesn't work with a *halvet*. When the forty days are up, they come and get me out. The shaikh hasn't given me any rules of conduct in this regard. I didn't even think to ask. In Ramadan it makes no difference to me, what's three or four days? As long as I can eat in the evenings, that will do me. But now I'm already very much weakened and pretty emaciated. A loss of ten percent of body weight is enough to affect menstruation. That's probably why my period has already lasted twice as long as usual. The weakness that increases from each day to the next is no doubt also attributable to the same cause.[43]

I'm standing in the *qiyam* or starting position of the prayer ritual. All of a sudden I'm not sure any more whether I performed the required washings. How can I not remember what I just did? Or maybe didn't? Then I'm really jolted: it's worse than that, I didn't just forget that I performed the ablutions according to form, I real-

---

[43] Menstruation caused other problems as well. During this time neither the ritual prayer is to be executed nor is the Quran touched or recited, for "*none but the pure can touch* [*it*]." (56:79). I was conscious of offending against these commands of the *Sharia*. Why I did it is hard to explain. The entire *halvet* seemed to me like one great purification; I had the subjective feeling that once I was sealed in, I was in an uninterrupted state of spiritual purity. In the *Mathnawi* it says that the prayers of the menstruating are accepted.

When I reported this to the shaikh afterwards, he said nothing further about it (preaching morality after the fact is not his style). But for my second *halvet* I got the instruction to keep away from the Quran during this time but continue with the *zhikrs*. I assume that's on the basis of the Quran's instruction to remember Allah always and everywhere (". . . *people whom neither* [*wordly*] *commerce nor striving after gain can divert from the remembrance of God.* . . ." 24:37).

41

ize now that I've completed the ritual prayer as well. Sure enough, I'm done, the final position matches the starting position.

Maybe I really will have to break off the *halvet*. One mustn't knowingly harm oneself. . . . Why won't this period ever end? Why didn't the shaikh say anything? Am I still "all there" mentally? How can I judge that? I read Ibn 'Arabi. He's extremely complex. It's comforting to see that I don't understand him any worse than usual. I can't have lost the whole of my reason quite yet. "*Kurban olayım,*" so be it, and let myself be the victim, if that's the way it's supposed to be.

I notice that cleanliness is still a high-ranking need. I put my boiler on so I can wash my hair. If things should turn out that way, let them at least find me clean. Sounds melodramatic, but so what.

Before the *halvet* started, the shaikh had asked me to write a declaration and keep it with me, stating that I was going into this of my own free will. For some reason, I don't know why, I wrote the declaration in English. Just in case, I write it out again in Turkish and put it in a conspicuous place by the door. The only real source of danger I see here is my little heater. If I keeled over again and my hair got too close to the uncovered heating filaments, that could end very badly. As a precaution, I decide to crawl on all fours and give the heater a wide berth when I go into the bath for the ritual washings. After all, if anything happens to me here, no one will notice at first unless I write a little additional note on the subject quickly!

And suddenly another relapse! This obsession seems to have a life of its own, one that is stronger than I am. It doesn't strike me as at all improbable to suppose that it will continue to exist in some form in case I die here. It's overwhelming in its power. I resign myself and start reading *Open Secret,* which I normally don't do till just before falling asleep. After all, it isn't Hz. Mevlâna speaking directly, only "Versions of Rumi" filtered through the perceptions of his translators. Still. . . .

Only One is worth chasing with your living.
He can't be trapped. You must throw away your lovetraps
and walk into His (OS, p. 75).

I just have to accept not only the fact that this spiritual schooling hurts a lot, but also the fact that it lasts however long it lasts. It doesn't end just because I think that's enough! I have to stop putting up inner defenses against it.

The secret really lies in the acceptance. As soon as I'm able, as soon as I can consciously "walk into His traps" that must be the inner peace, the repose of the heart that Islam speaks of. The true meaning of the word *Islam*, "surrender," which has the same etymological origins as the word "peace." Peace in surrender to the divine will. Really it's so simple. How can I just make this insight manifest, how can I "remember"?[44]

Day 13

When the time comes for the things he has read and conceived to come to be, his belief in his Creator and his love and his intoxication grow even more intense.

Hz. Mevlâna

My period has let up a little overnight. I'm also feeling stronger already, and the nagging pains I've had in my abdomen and back these past few days are also gone. *Alhamdulillah!*

As I come out of the bathroom, two big black cockroaches are sitting on my bed, waving their feelers pensively back and forth, almost like a *zhikr*. "*All creatures sing God's praise, you just don't understand them,*" so it says in the Quran. I catch them and carry them into the room on the other side of the apartment. Before too long one of them is back again, and then so is the other. They must prefer the warmth of my cell. Again they obligingly let themselves be caught. This time I take my key, and when everything is quiet in

---

[44] From the Islamic viewpoint all knowledge is already present. It doesn't need to be "acquired" but rather "remembered."

the stairwell, I quickly unlock the door and put them both outside. Somehow I'm in a hurry to get back to my cell.

I suddenly realize that my Teacher *had* to act just as he did. If he had yielded to my need for contact, my desperation would never have built up to such a degree that it would have brought me here into this *halvet*. Deepest gratitude, love and even joy overwhelm me. Love, becoming more and more jubilant. Fortunately, my Teacher won't let me sabotage myself in my ignorance, he is implacable. Was it Hz. Mevlâna who said, "With a teacher a journey of a thousand steps becomes a single step"? In her introduction to *Fihi ma Fihi*, Annemarie Schimmel describes the "severity" of traditional teachers:

> On the long hard road that faces the disciple he needs a guide, the shaikh, for it is dangerous to wander alone. The prophets and saints are the soul doctors who can successfully diagnose the sicknesses and weaknesses of the soul, and if a person entrusts himself to them with no questions, they can heal them as well. However, their healing methods are sometimes quite severe. They show the wanderers that they must "die before their death," that they must completely lose their own being. . . .. (p. 41)

The thoughts that crowd their way in during the zhikrs, which I previously thought of only as a disturbance, now have a function: their contents show me in which areas principally my *nafs ammara* is still active: complacency, arrogance, self-importance! These indicator thoughts rise up before my inner eye looking like rust specks on an otherwise clear mirror. "There's a way to polish each and every thing and get the rust off it. What polishes the heart is the *zhikr*," says the Prophet (Peace be upon him).

The various zhikrs start to take on distinctly different "colorations": "*Hu Allah*"[45] flows on into me, soft and warm, almost like dark honey, like nectar. "*Hay Allah*,"[46] on the other hand, has

---

[45] *Hu Allah:* "He," the most perfect form of address, the holiest sound in Islam, the first sound in the cosmos. This *zhikr* is considered "the key to the other dimension." When the gate is reached, it opens to the sound "*hu*."

[46] *Hayy Allah*: "the Living One."

something very active, joyous, energetic about it. Something like the quality of "*Ya Aziz*,"[47] which sounds so triumphant, incorporating the active element of Islam. "*Allah'*" sounds simply comforting, all-embracing.

More and more I am starting to sense Allah behind everything. Not just in birdsong, but even in the roar of airplanes flying over the city and in the tooting of foghorns on the Bosphorus. When I was a young girl, I had a room with a view of the Bosphorus. My desk stood in front of the window, and while doing my homework I often watched the great ships passing, brightly illuminated, heading towards the Black Sea.

Back then in the sixties, when my brother and I were growing up in this city encircled by seas, you could still swim everywhere. Vacation lasted from May to September and helped to make up for the enormous scholastic demands of the German School of Istanbul. My father had been transferred to Turkey as a chief physician to the German consulate to build a program of preventive medical examinations for so-called "guest workers" [Turkish immigrant workers in Germany]. How differently my life would have turned out if we had stayed in the "high North," in my home country, dear old Schleswig-Holstein.[48] What a blessing that it didn't go that way! And how consistently one thing has led to another! More and more clearly I see the "hand that guides the pen."

Day 14

Two weeks already. How the time passes. Feel a bit stronger physically. I'm also less inclined to dizziness and fainting. If I just get up in the morning very slowly, in stages, so to speak, then it works fine. I also don't feel that it's necessary any-

---

[47] *Ya Aziz*: "the Mighty One," one of the ninety-nine Most Beautiful Names of Allah.

[48] Schleswig-Holstein is that part of Germany bordering Denmark, a very peculiar narrow strip of land separating the Atlantic from the Baltic Sea.

more for me to crawl around the heater on all fours. I walk carefully, but on my feet again.

But inside I feel somewhat dull today, numb, uncaring. No pain, no joy. Cut off from everything, perceiving as if from a distance. This being cut off is actually worse than being connected in the most intense pain! Hz. Mevlâna says (OS, quatrain 674): "You don't have 'good' days and 'bad' days. . . ." My abdomen is strangely swollen and very hard, but it doesn't hurt. Hunger-swellings could hardly be the explanation at this point. In doing all the *zhikrs*, which involve specific breathing patterns, have I swallowed air?

Outside it's snowing. After evening prayer, soup! This time there's lots of rice in it. Although I eat very consciously and with pleasure, when my bowl is empty I think, what is the big deal? Perhaps a hint about the relative unimportance of worldly needs? "Everything is perishing but His face" (28:88). What an austere day!

This time, thinking about Hz. Mevlâna makes me cry. I'm sure I haven't cried so much in the last thirty years together as in these last two weeks. But why not? Who could I be disturbing here? I decide to perform, very concretely, one of the old exercises, the "The Way of the Dervish": "When the *nafs ammara* is in a mood to complain, at that point one should work against it, expressing such exaggerated gratitude that you acquire yourself some love. Lying while saying, 'Thank You' is a way of seeking love from God." (FmF, p. 366). Thanking, perhaps, for having already outgrown what in fact I'm still dealing with?

So I start in as fervently as I can, giving thanks that my obsession has already been taken from me. The first thing I notice is that this exercise leads to an intense pain of greater and greater severity. I feel Allah's presence near me, feel more veils lifting. How much better the pain of the presence than the indifference of the isolation! I'd want more and more pain, till I'm burned completely and utterly clean, like the *ney* that is passed through the fire till its tone comes forth full and pure. I'd like more and more pain till finally I stay "open." I think of ear-piercing. While the ear heals, you have to keep turning the new earring so that it doesn't become ingrown, to make sure a hole is really formed. This turning hurts as long as the ear is still trying to close itself. Only when the hole stays open voluntarily does the turning not hurt any more at which point it also isn't needed any more.

I ask for more and more pain. It feels so much more right than the dead indifference that preceded it. I also sense more and more distinctly that the process of transference from Teacher to Allah[49] is going on, realize that the actual goal of my obsession is the presence of Allah. If I could only remember that always. If the veils will just keep from closing again. All at once I also understand Hz. Mevlâna's seemingly paradoxical verses: "In pain I breathe easier," "When I'm ruined, I'm healed." (OS, quatrains 1131 and 1115). The normally gentle, pleasant "currents" inside me have become, as they did at the beginning of last summer, a violent trembling of the whole body. Could that be what Hz. Mevlâna means when he says:

> So it has become clear that trembling and passionate love are needed on the quest for God. Whoever doesn't tremble must be the servant of those who do. No fruit grows on the trunk of a tree, because trunks don't tremble close to the ground, it's the tips of the branches that tremble (FmF, p. 346).

Would that my trembling could always make me remember. How many are the veils of forgetfulness! There suddenly opens before me a deeper meaning to two other guiding principles of Sufism: "It is not enough to give thanks for the rose or for its thorns, one must give thanks even when there is no rose there at all," and

---

[49] Ruzbihan (d. 1209) points out that what the pupil experiences as "transference" is actually a deeper level of the knowledge of love. According to Ruzbihan's teaching, "human and divine love do not stand in opposition to each other as a dichotomy that forces the mystic to choose between them. They are two forms of the same love, the text of one and the same book, but one must learn how to read it (that is, how to read with the 'eyes of light'). The transition from one to the other does not consist in transferring love from one *object* to another, because God is not an *object*: God is the absolute *subject*. The transition from one form of love to the other consists in the *transformation of the subject*, the lover, the *ashiq*. The whole of Ruzbihan's teaching tends toward precisely this direction" (Corbin, 1989, p.117, emphasis in original). Henry Corbin, *Die smaragden Vision* (The Emerald Vision), Munich, Diedrichs, 1989. German translation by Annemarie Schimmel.

"Hell is sweet for the unbelievers, since it teaches them to be aware of the presence of Allah. And nothing is sweeter than His presence."

Day 15

S till got my period, feel my strength coming back, though. If I'm slow and deliberate about changing my sitting or lying position, the feeling of faintness remains manageable. Outside, tender little snowflakes fall. They're starting to stick to the unbeautiful surface of the junkyard outside my window, "powdering" it clean. Looking out the window is not an activity conducive to turning inward. So every* morning after prayer I allow myself just one quick look through a big rip in my curtain.

This *halvet* is a brainwashing par excellence! I notice that my speech is being "Quranicized." Expressions like *insh'Allah*, "if God so wills," or *Alhamdulillah*, "God be praised," intrude more and more into my thoughts. Not surprising: cut off from all outside distractions, one becomes much more receptive to the limited stimuli available. Since these consist exclusively of the holy writings of Islam, the resultant "Islamic brainwashing" is a natural consequence. Anyone who goes into a *halvet* "neutral" is guaranteed to come out a Muslim. Anyone who enters as a Muslim comes out a "Muslim squared." Should one perhaps for ethical reasons warn Westerners by making this brainwashing dimension insistently clear to them in advance?

But then on the other hand, who would get into something like this unless they had at least some closeness to the Islamic way of thinking? And anyone like that should find it's very good for them; the result for them, as for me, should be a powerful strengthening and firming up of knowledge that previously was only present in cognitive form. Anyone who doesn't accept being "manipulated" isn't going to place trust in a traditional path or teacher anyway.

I am grateful for the combination of authors allowed me. The often drastic analogies and ecstatic love-words of Hz. Mevlâna find their opposite pole in the calm, scholarly tranquillity of Ibn 'Arabi. So I'm getting a balanced, harmonious brainwashing that I can surrender to completely in deep confidence.

My belly is still hard and swollen.[50] I decide that from now on I'm going to do the *zhikrs* silently, to make it a "*zhikr* of the heart." In the course of the day this leads to a new dimension of experience. First, the air body definitely gets denser. It seems almost as if this invisible shell I feel around me is now filled with a syrupy substance. The more I surrender totally to this feeling of swinging back and forth in time to the *zhikr* against the mild resistance offered by being in this substance, the more intense is the body-and-soul feeling of marked well-being. At some point it becomes impossible to overlook something: this intense well-being has an erotic component. Is that part of doing *zhikrs*?[51]

I start paying more attention to these feelings. During the *zhikr* "*La ilāha il Āllāh*"[52] it becomes very noticeable. And the deeper my concentration upon this ancient holy formula, the more I get into it, "body and soul," the more pronounced these extremely pleasant sensations become. Somehow sexual, and yet in many respects very different. For one thing, it's not an arousal in the sense that it "wants to get somewhere," there is no "goal" to reach, it's "already there." It's closer to the feeling right after orgasm, this floating afterglow of well-being. It's also noticeable that these sensations are in no way limited to or focused on the genitals but are felt flowing through the entire body, on up into the head, where a gentle, sensuously pulsating beating starts to develop under the top of my head. Another thing: this "aspect of eroticism" (what else should I call it?) doesn't distract me from the *zhikr* at all. On the contrary: the more exclusively I concentrate on the object of meditation, the

---

[50] See "Accompanying Physiological Phenomena," p. 131ff.

[51] See "Spirituality and Sexuality," p. 167ff.

[52] As mentioned above, the Islamic profession of faith: "There is no god but the one God"—that is, God is the only reality, which is immanent in all appearances and transcends them and reveals them.

ancient holy formulas, the pleasanter the sensations are and the pleasanter the sensations, the more exclusive my concentration on the *zhikr*.

What to do? Is that as it should be? No one prepared me for this, nor have I read anything about it in classic Sufi literature. Finally, in my doubt-filled ponderings, I recognize once more my old acquaintance, my *nafs ammara*. It is pure arrogance to attempt to decide what is supposed to be part of a *halvet* experience and what isn't. That's making an end-run around reality, because there it is, beyond all question; and what is, can only be because it's supposed to be; otherwise, after all, it would not be so! Once again my presumption in attempting to divide Allah's One World into right and wrong according to my human estimation! How far I still am from *wahdat al wujūd*![53]

Why does it seem right to accept the intense pain the traditional exercises evoke almost every day, but not the pleasure? My hesitations are surely based on the parts of me that bear the stamp of the West: remnants of the traditionally anti-sexual attitude of the Christian churches. Islam is anything but anti-sexual; sexuality is holy. The ancient writings even use explicitly erotic language to give an allegorical description of union with Allah, the Beloved. Allegorical.

Trusting in the system of Sufism, this ancient, time-tested method of becoming spiritually conscious, I decide to continue going with my immediate experience, uncensored, accepting whatever develops.

And already I've fallen in a trap all over again. It occurs to me how careless and messy my kids are about handling the mail. What if my Teacher were to write to me now, of all times, when I'm in the *halvet*, and what if my kids drop the letter someplace? With horror I realize how strongly my thinking is marked by secondary causes! Again I'm seeing the pen and not the hand holding it! If the

---

[53] *Wahdat al wujūd*: the unity of the whole of existence. On the Sufi path, this realization, the direct experience of the *wahdat al wujūd* constitutes the goal of the quest.

hand wants a message to reach me, how is the untidiness of my kids going to prevent that? How blind I still am, how thick the veils are that still block me from seeing primary causes! But at least I catch myself faster and faster going down what I now realize are the paths of error. Before, I really still believed that trains of thought of this nature, involving twisted chains of causality, had a reality behind them.

Why can't I be done with the nonsense? Especially with such excellent guides along the way: Muhammad (Peace be upon him), who practiced the way of the heart, the way of poverty: "*Faqri fachri.*"[54]

And Hz. Mevlâna, who left an abundance of "road signs" behind in his writings. He shows the way so clearly:

Try to lose. Don't do anything
for power or influence. Run into the mind's fire.
Beg and cry and come walking on your knees. (OS, p. 78).

With that in mind I should simply wish for any such letter to get lost. . . . But how hard that is for someone not generally inclined to self-destructive behavior.

---

[54] "My poverty is my pride." The Sufi concept of "poverty," also sometimes called "emptiness," refers neither to material poverty nor to intellectual poverty in the sense of intellectual weakness. This spiritual "poverty" consists in recognizing the manifold forms of outward appearance for what they are and becoming aware of their ONE inner essence. For a person, it means being "extinguished" in regard to everything concerning his individual interests (*fanā*) and living on in the ONE (*baqā*). It is the highest state of existence a person can reach. It is a most humble submission to the first cause—and thereby its incarnation as well. The hadith *An-nawafil* describes the state of such a "poor man": "... And my servant continually comes nearer to me by doing additional works until I love him. And when I love him, I am the hearing by which he hears, and the sight by which he sees, and the tongue with which he speaks, and the hand with which he grasps."

Day 16

I t's still snowing lightly. Hordes of children are playing delight-
edly in the junkyard. For a few minutes I break my rule against
peeping out of the window to get a look at them. It is so moving! The kids in this poor part of town own only the most insufficient clothing. Most are wearing sneakers in what is by now a
pretty thick layer of powdery snow. One even has plastic bath
slippers! No one has gloves, only a few have caps or scarves. Jack-
ets or thin windbreakers are all they have to keep warm with. No
one has equipment like skis or sleds. Without having anything,
they play with an abandon of the purest, exuberant joy. Joy over
the falling snow, joy in the romping of their own small bodies.

And Ayşegül is with them again. Her laughing stays with me for
a while until I dissolve into the *zhikrs*. I am catching myself earlier
and earlier at the point of falling into the same old traps I know so
well. I also realize that I have only one fear left: that the veils could
come down in front of me again, that I could find this more direct
access to the One Truth barred again. In fact, there's nothing
worse. If I could just always keep conscious of it. But no doubt
there will still be many times when I get lost in petty pseudo-
worries, such as that I'll never see my Teacher again. At times like
those, Muhammad (Peace be upon him) shows me the way of love. I
sense that with astounding clarity, wishing that the *zhikrs* may polish my heart clean so that I can perceive this way of love! *Fanā*[55]

---

[55] *fanā*: disappearance of ego-consciousness, loss of being.

and *baqā*[56] are truly the only goals I have left. The "only ones"! What immodesty! What greater thing could be given to a person? How can I just protect this knowledge of the only important goal? My new perceptions seem to me like tender, fragile little plants.

The erotic sensations streaming through my whole body become more and more intense the deeper I penetrate into the *zhikrs*. Can something like this maybe lead to orgasm, I wonder? So what if it does? What do I care?

Day 17

It's still snowing, the soft little flakes are sticking where they fall. In the meantime, the little ones have converted some old cardboard boxes into sleds. My period finally seems to be over. The *zhikrs* are becoming more and more meaningful. In addition, however, there is a noticeable tugging sensation somewhere around the heart. Could this really be the "polishing of the heart" manifesting itself physiologically? In that case, this expression might be more than the metaphor I took it for.

In the late evening, till almost midnight, the young men of the neighborhood take over the street bordering the junkyard property. They've made a sledding course and are zooming down it with the greatest enthusiasm. No cars are driving there anymore, no doubt it's too slippery. I wonder, does the entire traffic pattern of Istanbul still break down the way it used to, anytime there's snow on the ground? Such an evening comes to mind, it was a long time ago. As Mehmet, then my fiance, and I came out of the movie theater, a sudden snowstorm had plunged the traffic into trackless chaos. After struggling for hours to get seats on one of the few still functional public transportation conveyances, we finally managed to get to his family's house in Yeşilyurt, at the other end of this sprawling city. The much shorter way to my family's house, because of the steep hills of Istanbul, had become utterly impossible.

---

[56] *baqā*: resting in God after a preceding *fanā*.

Day 18

The *zhikrs* are becoming even deeper; in the truest sense of the word they are taking on "substance." This is where the inner peace unfolds, the peace described so beautifully by Islam as the tranquillity of the heart. My head moves inside a column formed by my air body. Then I get the feeling that every back-and-forth motion of my head is spraying strings of this substance all over the room. Like water spraying from the hide of a wet dog when it shakes itself. Except that these strings have some kind of life of their own that draws them out farther and farther into the universe. Right above the heart region is where you feel it, as if pulling open curtains (veils?) on either side. With the steady, broad-stepping movements of a skater's legs—right, left, right, left . . . . So is this the "polishing of the heart"?

Sometimes it feels as if I'm penetrating directly into the syllables of the holy formulas, into the sound that echoes silently within me. The greater the awareness, the more intense the experience is. The *zhikr* is showing me how to do *zhikrs!* The old precept comes to mind: "At first you act as if you're doing the *zhikr.* Then you do the *zhikr.* Then finally the *zhikr* does you." All at once I perceive this steering process as one of the "signs" of Allah: "*He is closer to you than your jugular vein.*" Where can one perceive Him Who is immanent and transcendent if not in one's deepest insides? The signs of which the Holy Quran speaks are "*on the horizons and within yourselves.*" Is that it? "His Heaven and His Earth cannot contain Him," says Islam, "only the [shiny, polished] heart of the believer has room for Him."

Suddenly it becomes painfully clear to me. There's really only one way: absolute surrender, absolute giving-up of wanting-for-oneself. The voluntary giving-up of "whatever is dearest." In the words of Hz. Mevlâna: "to take the step toward the lion *in the lion's presence*," to "jump into the fire," to "fall into the trap."

The Lion

So the reports of a lion reached every corner of the world. A man amazed by the rumors made his way to the forest from a faraway place to see the lion. For a whole year he endured the rigors of the journey, traveling from waystation to waystation. When he got to the forest and saw the lion from afar, he stood still and couldn't go a step closer. "What's this?" they said to him. "You came all this way out of love for this lion. This lion has the trait that if a person boldly comes up to him and strokes him lovingly, he will not hurt that person or do anything to him; but if someone is fearful and anxious, then the lion becomes furious at him; indeed he attacks some people meaning to kill them because they have a bad opinion of him. That being so, you've given yourself a year of trouble. Now that you've gotten close to the lion, you stand still. What kind of standing there is that?" No one had the courage to go a single step farther. They said, "All the steps we took up to now were easy. Here we can't take a step farther." Now, what Omar[57] meant by faith was this step, taking a step in the lion's presence toward the lion. This step is extremely rare; it is the part of the elect and God's close friends alone. It is the real step, the rest are only footprints.

Hz. Mevlâna, *Fihi ma Fihi*, p. 206

---

[57] One of the four "Rightly-Guided Caliphs" (ruled 634-644) and companion of Muhammad (Peace be upon him).

The dearest thing I still have is not anything that I possess: it is my despairing wish to see my Teacher again. I make several approaches to sacrifice this. I feel as if I am once again about to die, till I finally succeed in praying never to see him again.

The pain is as burning and fresh as if a whole year had not passed. At some point, much later, the terrible pain ceases all at once just for a second, and I experience the deepest and richest tranquillity of the heart that I have ever felt. Hz. Mevlâna's "poorhouse of not wanting," this must be it. Now I have given everything, I have nothing left. Will I ever be able to stop crying? Only three weeks more, then they'll come and get me out. I wonder whether I can get myself back together by then.

And yet these few seconds of such a qualitatively utterly different, such an indescribable feeling of the peace of the heart are enough to strengthen me in the assumption that I'm on the right track. So I go on and on, until, between the tears and the exhaustion, I no longer know for sure whether I'm asleep or still praying. Absolutely empty and spent, I pull myself off my mattress sometime toward morning to perform the washings for the night prayer that still remains to be performed.

In front of my door, I find a little sack with some olives. Dear old Yusuf!

Day 19

I feel only emptiness, burned-out, endless emptiness. No traces of this indescribable inner peace, the "poorhouse of not wanting," that had come in the night for a few seconds like a beam of light through the cloud-cover of pain: I still keep wanting to decide for myself which way to go. I still have a lot to learn before I become the Sunken One who is moved along by the currents of the ocean. What I lack is "Islam," plain and simple, in the truest sense of the word. Really, that is everything. The absolute surrender of a truly Sunken One must be a profound peace. . . .

Day 20

It's good when you're helpless all the time and see yourself as helpless under all circumstances, even when you have power, as well as when you are powerless. For above your power stands a greater power, and in all conditions God has you overpowered.

Hz. Mevlâna

I give up, declare myself helpless, admit to myself my complete helplessness. I have to face the fact that even my greatest voluntary offering of renunciation the night before last has brought me nothing. I realize that in this matter I was also making my own plans, was "figuring my own figuring." Yes, Ibrahim[58] brought the sacrifice of that which was dearest to him. But he did so out of humblest obedience! In no way had he decided on his own say-so that he would bring his son Ismail* as an offering! He knew his place better than that! I feel completely trapped in utter helplessness. I have nothing more to give, nothing more to do. My scheming reason, always trying to take control for itself, has finally and conclusively cornered itself in a hopeless blind alley. I can't go on.

Hz. Mevlâna says:

All your persecution, your misfortune, and your disappointment come from this understanding. This understanding is a shackle to you: you must get free of understanding to become anything at all. . . . Understanding is good and useful for just long enough to bring you to the King's gate. Once you reach His door, then submit and cut yourself off from understanding, for in that hour understanding is harmful, a regular highwayman (FmF, p. 196).

But how? I don't even understand how to begin not to use my understanding. Perhaps that is the root of my abyss-like helplessness?

---

[58] Ibrahim corresponds to the Biblical Abraham, and Ismail rather than Isaac was the sacrifice.

If one stands before the "gate" and knocks and says, "It's me,[59]" one can't get in. Only when one can say, "It's You," is admittance granted. For there is no room for anything but Allah. Only someone whose being has been lost in Allah can exist in Him after this *fanā*, can experience *baqā*. "Break the pitcher and become the ocean." But how? I have exhausted my expertise. I can't do anything more except pray to be able to speak of myself as "It's You," to acquire true *Islam*. "Allah hears who praises Him," goes the ritual prayer. When something can't be achieved by effort, will, logical thought, strategic planning, etc., what's left but prayer? (And trust in one's teacher . . . and patience. . . .)

For the first time I understand the deeper meaning of the old Sufi instructional tale, "The Essence of the Student's Role." Up till now this portrayal seemed more like a *koan* to me. After all, viewed from the rational plane, the student couldn't win. Whatever he did turned into a paradox. But that's just it! His shaikh was capable enough to structure his learning situation so that he experienced, no matter what he did, the essence of the student's role: giving up his own plan-making will. Obviously the student, just like me, had confused good will and enthusiasm with surrender. He won at the point where he just couldn't win! There was a teacher who didn't allow his student to sabotage himself. . . .

At some point the thought comes to me that my helplessness is the answer to my prayer! For days I've been praying to be delivered from my self-important plans, to become the Sunken Man, to acquire true Islam. What could one imagine that the fulfillment of such a wish would be like, if it didn't take the form of a "capitulation into helplessness"? I have received just what I prayed for, only I didn't imagine it being like this! Apparently I don't have all *that* much understanding left.

"Your Lord will spread His mercy over you and show you a comforting way out of your plight," so I read in the Holy Quran before falling asleep (16:17).

---

[59] Cf. "Since You are Me" on p. 60.

The Essence of the Student's Role

The tale is told of Ibrahim-i Khavvas, that once when he was still a disciple himself, he wanted to be taken on by a certain teaching-master. He went in search of this wise man and asked for permission to become one of his students.

The teacher said: "You aren't far enough along."

As the young man stubbornly insisted, the master said: "All right, I'll teach you something. I'm just about to set off on a pilgrimage to Mecca. Come along."

The student was overjoyed.

"Now that we are traveling-companions," said the teacher, "one must lead and the other obey. Choose your role."

"I will obey, you lead," said the student.

"I will lead if you know how to follow," said the master.

The journey began. As they rested one night in the desert of Hijaz it started raining. The master stood up and held a blanket over the student to shelter him.

"But I should do that for you," said the student.

"I command you to allow me to shelter you this way," said the wise man.

When daylight returned, the young man said, "Here we are starting a new day. Let me be the leader, and you obey." The master agreed.

"I'm going to gather twigs to make a fire," said the disciple.

"You mustn't do any such thing, I'll gather them," said the wise man.

"I command you to sit there while I gather twigs!" said the young man.

"You're not allowed to do that," said the teacher, "because it isn't in line with the conditions of being a student for the follower to allow himself to be waited on by the leader."

And so at every turn the master showed the student most vividly what being a student really means.

At the gate of the holy city they separated. When the young man came upon the wise man some time later, he couldn't look him in the eye.

"What you have learned here," said the older man, "is something of the essence of the student's role."[60]

"Since You are Me"

A certain man knocked at his friend's door: his friend[61] asked: "Who is there?"

He answered, "I." "Begone," said his friend, "'tis too soon! At my table there is no place for the raw.

How shall the raw be cooked but in the fire of absence? What else will deliver him from hypocrisy?"

He turned sadly away, and for a whole year the flames of separation consumed him;

Then he came back and again paced to and fro beside the house of his friend.

He knocked at the door with a hundred fears and reverence lest any disrespectful word might escape from his lips.

"Who is there?" cried the friend. He answered: "Thou, O charmer of hearts."

"Now," said the friend, "since thou are I, come in there is no room for two I's in this house."

Hz. Mevlâna[62]

---

[60] From I. Shah, *The Secrets of the Dervishes*, p. 54.

[61] "Friend" and "Beloved" are Sufi concepts of God.

[62] *Mathnawi*, I, 3056-64, translated by Annemarie Schimmel in *Mystical Dimensions of Islam*, p. 314. Unless otherwise noted, all other citations of Schimmel are from *Mystische Dimensionen des Islam*.

Day 21

Only new love carries love along,
when she chooses a better dearest darling.
Gurgani

I'm fairly calm, I don't understand anything anymore. There's nothing more for me to do but do what was assigned to me: *zhikrs*, prayer, some reading. "*He will show you a comforting way out. . . .* " Really, all I can do is pray for this. Because what such a way out of my plight might look like, that is veiled from my eyes.

Ibn 'Arabi writes:

One can only protect oneself from a thing through the thing itself. . . . So one protects oneself from iron with iron. Correspondingly, the command of Muhammad ordains the following prayer: 'I take in Thee my refuge from Thee!' Grasp that! (FaH, p. 116).

So pain is healed by pain, love only by a still greater love. . . . "Jump in the mind's fire," says Hz. Mevlâna. No more defenses! Only one goal, one prayer, makes any sense: true *Islam*, peace in absolute surrender.

Day 22

Why organize a universe this way?

Hz. Mevlâna

First thing in the morning, I turn off my little heater to heat up some shower water. In the face of the cold that immediately sets in, I plan to survive as usual: huddling under my blanket reading the Quran. I have taken the conditions involved in heating water here as an occasion to broaden the limits of my tolerance in matters of cleanliness. It's been four days since I washed my hair. But now enough is enough, my normally fluffy-clean hair is dangling in strings over my face and irritating me with every movement.

After three-quarters of an hour of cold, there's another power failure. Oh well, I can keep reading by candlelight. It's getting colder and colder. Finally, after a good two hours, I notice that the TV next door is on again! But my lamps are still dark. Why don't I have power? I check the hallway and try the lamp there. No light there either! Finally it dawns on me: the power failed while my boiler was heating up! And after all, they told me that you get a short-circuit if you shut off the boiler while it's heating up! Evidently the boiler couldn't tell a power failure from a manual shutoff. . . .

Above the door to the staircase are four large porcelain knobs that look like fuses. Holding my candle, I climb up onto a wobbly three-legged stool that was in the kitchen and start fiddling with these antediluvian fuses. I keep climbing down and trying the light. Nothing! Finally I give up. Now my cell is not just cold but also dark. Only the holes in the curtain let a few beams of dreary February light come in. In the course of the slowly passing day I get colder and colder. That must be because of the fasting. I'm already very thin. My hipbones protrude like in pictures I've seen of cows in India. I put a second sweater on over the first one. Finally, I spread my winter coat on top of my blanket.

At first the new severity of my conditions seems like a lesson in endurance. So be it! As my ears get colder and colder, I put my scarf on. How miserably uninsulated this house is. The tragedy of third-world countries in microcosm: poverty resulting in insufficient insulation, resulting in increased energy consumption, resulting in increased poverty. . . .

What makes me so sure in the first place that this is a lesson in endurance? Perseverance or steadfastness, characteristics that can be gained through inner discipline, aren't my problem at all. No, this is very clearly an exercise in surrender, in unconditional acceptance! A very concrete chance to practice what I have been praying so hard for: true *Islam*!

As soon as I cease my inner resistance against the cold, as soon as I accept my situation as a learning opportunity, it feels much better already. I consciously begin to "expand inside" instead of "contracting." The cold becomes more bearable. In *Open Secret*, p. 44, I read: "I want that moment again when I spread out like olive oil in the skillet." What a wonderful image! I simply let myself spread like olive oil in the skillet. My inner tension passes, peace fills me. I also have a better understanding of what could be meant by Hz. Mevlâna's saying that "there are no good days and no bad days." Precisely what is bad about today leads to something good, to further awareness.

So the day passes by, and I wait patiently for Yusuf to free me eventually from being stuck in the cold and the dark. I catch myself hoping he won't wait till 10 or 11 p.m. to come, as he sometimes does. And of course there was that one time, the first two evenings, when he didn't come at all. . . . There I am again, looking out for myself, making my plans! And this though I can see that the harshness of the circumstances is helping me to perceive. So what do I do. . . ? Just hope it's over soon! (And how did the people during the Second World War in Germany, on top of everything else, ever get through the winters with no heat?)

It's good that Allah evidently has endless patience with the insufficiencies of His creatures. (My own patience with myself is rapidly decreasing.) Of course one might naturally also wonder why the Creator made His creatures like that. "Why organize a universe this way?" (OS, p. 79). But that's just where the freedom and dignity of human existence lies: "having the gift of discernment," it is up to us to choose "the straight path." Hz. Mevlâna describes people as creatures made of angels' wings with an ass's tail tied on the back. Angels and beasts reach perfection through their unknowing nature. The former can do nothing else but give praise and glory to God, the latter can do nothing else but respond to their impulses. But the human being, in between the two, is free. If he chooses the "straight path," he rises higher than the angels; if he chooses "the path of those who have earned disfavor," he is "more going astray than cattle." *They are like cattle—nay, they are even*

less conscious of the right way" (7:179), says the Holy Quran, which
is also known as *"Al Furqan,"* the Discerner.

Hz. Mevlâna writes:

> Some [people], however, are still at war, namely those who feel
> pain and worry, complaint and longing in themselves. . . . Those
> are the believers. The saints are waiting for them, to bring them
> up to their own level and make these others more like them (FmF,
> p. 151).

Now my hands are so icy that I'm having trouble turning the
pages of my book. I take off my scarf and wrap it round one hand,
the other I warm between my thighs. That must be the warmest
spot in this apartment. I cover my ears with my hair (if only it were
clean!). Freezing is really terrible! Every time I keep wishing it was
already over, the lovely metaphor of the olive oil comes to my aid.
As soon as I "spread out like the oil in the skillet," let myself relax,
I'm all right again. *"For God takes away, and He gives abundantly,"*
so it says in the Holy Quran (2:245), and also: *". . . one whose
bosom God has opened wide with willingness to self-surrender unto
Him, so that it is illumined by a light that flows from his Sustainer"*
(39:22). That's also a very fitting picture. When I "expand," then
surrender comes, and through surrender and acceptance come the
wide open spaces of inner peace.

It's about 7 p.m. when Yusuf comes! I listen to him flicking the
light switch on and off a couple of times, then climbing up on the
stool. After a short time he jumps back down, then the apartment
door closes behind him and all is still.

Fifteen minutes later I hear him come back. This time there is a
clattering of tools, and then my light goes on again! To me it's like a
palace illumination, my 75-watt bulb! Thank you, dear Yusuf! I've
been freezing too much and for too long to heat up the boiler and
wash my hair at this point. Just enjoy the blessing of the little
heater! I'll get through this one more night with my stringy hair. I
feel in harmony with myself as I thaw out slowly, feeling right satisfied. I have survived it, *Alhamdulillah!*

Just then, without warning, comes the ringing and ringing of my doorbell, the yelling and the beating at my door all over again! I am startled out of my wits, my heart is once again pounding like mad. "*A'uzu billahi mina'sh-sheytani-r'rajim, bismillahi-r'rahmani-r'rahim,*"[63] the ancient formula of protection, passes my lips unbidden. I don't move, I scarcely breathe. Like a hypnotized rabbit faced with a snake, that's how I feel. Why doesn't one of the neighbors come to check on this? After five endless minutes they give up. Once more the door held!

Just as I was complacently thinking I had it made. . . . Even now I am still too blinded by secondary causes to see the hand that guides the pen. Did I really think my lesson was over just because I have power again? Later I read (of course!) in the writings of my faithful traveling companion Hz. Mevlâna:

> For people look to secondary causes. But to the saints it is revealed that secondary causes are but veils. . . . When they see some such thing, they know that secondary causes are a pretext and that the real cause is something else. . . . Secondary causes are a veil for ordinary folk to occupy themselves with. . . . Why do you forget all that? (FmF, p. 139).

Indeed, why do I forget all that? You keep thinking once again you've made it. How senseless!

Day 23

Rather it is more fitting in the view of the perfected mystic to humble oneself and ask God to lift the affliction from him.

Ibn 'Arabi

Early next morning, as I once again flick off my heater and flick on the boiler, I feel uncomfortable. Enduring in the cold and darkness wasn't nice at all. There I go again! My

---

[63] *A'uzu billahi. . . .:* "God protect me from it" ("I seek refuge in God").

fears! Why should it happen again? I have so much confidence to learn!

This time it only takes half an hour for the power to fail. At first I just can't grasp it. Once again I run through the apartment as the neighbors' televisions come on again, once again I fiddle with the fuses—it just *can't* be! Another long, long day in darkness and cold! How is it possible? I really did feel sincere gratitude for the privilege of warmth, of bathing-water of everything! And now that my speech is so Quranicized, I didn't even think things like "Tomorrow I'll wash my hair" without always, as a matter of course, adding an "*Insh'Allah*" to my intentions!

As all this goes through my head, I see the trap I've once more fallen into. Even just my asking Why proves my assumption of a causality that I could perceive! If there were really a causality that human beings could grasp, then Allah would be predictable, He could be manipulated. Didn't I learn *anything* yesterday?

Something pragmatic, at any rate! Once again I put on two sweaters, wrap my scarf around my hand, cover myself with my overcoat and think about spreading myself out like olive oil in the skillet. It also doesn't seem to be as bitter cold as yesterday, and actually I am about as contented as somebody could be in these unpleasant circumstances. At least I've finally learned a little bit, to accept, to "put a fair face on foul misfortune." But then I read Ibn ʿArabi ! Although he too sees "steadfast patience in the face of God's affliction" (FaH, p. 155) as an indispensable virtue, in his view "complaining of woes" is part of it! In fact he sees "withholding complaints about afflictions" as "bad manners and insubordination toward God's power." He describes a "certain group of Sufis" as "shut off from correct realization," because in their opinion "steadfastness consists in refraining from bringing any complaint." He points out that God praised Job for his steadfastness though he prayed for relief from pain. Ibn ʿArabi comes to the conclusion that "steadfastness consists in refraining from bringing one's complaint *to anyone but God.*" He ends his discourse on dealing with afflictions with the following advice:

But following the way of life suggested by this realization is an obligation that falls only on the educated servants of God, those who faithfully keep the divine secrets; for God has His stalwarts, whom He alone knows and who know each other. We have given you our sincere advice, so act accordingly and make your request of Him.

So there it is! Complain! Just when I was being proud of myself for putting fair face on foul misfortune! My old *nafs ammara*! I keep imagining that now I understand, now I've learned my lesson! It really is interesting how each person in the course of a *halvet* receives the lessons he or she needs. If only my hair was cleaner! It's been six days already!

In the evening I hear dear old Yusuf switch the light on and off again, I can almost imagine the look of incredulity on his face! Once again he goes away and comes back, again I hear the noise of tools, and I have light again. Just as before. Except this time I'm going to heat up the boiler right away and not wait till morning.

Minutes later I stand gaping in the bathroom: now there's no water!

Had I really believed all over again today that it was *because of the electricity* that I couldn't carry out my plan? Yes indeed, "secondary causes are a veil to occupy the common folk with. Why do you forget all that?" I can already see it coming: I will be "occupied" till I freely consent to remember. . . . Hz. Mevlâna writes:

> Thus secondary causes are like a pen in God's almighty power. The mover and writer is God. Until He wills it so, the pen does not move. You fix your gaze upon the pen, and do not say, "Well, there must be a hand for this pen!" You see the pen and think about it, but you do not think about the hand (FmF, p. 356).

So first I "complain" (completely unfamiliar to me!) in the sense of Ibn 'Arabi, then I spread out like olive and oil and accept. At any rate I have light and warmth! I turn to the *zhikrs*. In the night, when I am in deep absorption, there all at once comes another moment of recognition in which certain parts of my whole life are suddenly standing there in a meta-context right in front of me. As if all the little separate stones had fitted themselves on their own into the mosaic they were always intended for. My whole life long, from earliest childhood on, situations have been created for me to practice my ability to "feel longing"!

Because of post-war conditions in Germany, my parents were living at the time of my birth with my grandparents and my Aunt Püti. When I was one-and-a-half, my brother was born. This coincided with a severe illness on the part of my mother. So it came about that my aunt "took me over." My earliest memories go back to her, my earliest feelings of loving and being loved, of joy, fun, comfort and security—Püti was all of those things to me. When I was five, my aunt got married and moved away. At the same time my parents found a place of their own, and so we also left my beloved grandparents.

Many nights I used to wake up crying from nightmares that were always the same: I saw Püti right in front of me and still couldn't reach her. My mother would come to my bed and sit with me till I calmed down. Years later she told me how hard it was for her as a mother to console her own child for the "loss of her mother." I probably sensed that on some level; in any event I learned not to share my pain with others any more.

Similar scenes were repeated throughout my whole life, running through it like a scarlet thread. The love which I felt for some people was absolute, coming from the totality of my being. I loved my grandpa so much it hurt. I remember one evening when I was eleven years old. My grandma had taken sick, and Grandpa asked if I wanted to go to the opera with him in her place. They were putting on *Carmen,* and everything was very fateful, tragic and dramatic. Perhaps that was the reason? It occurred to me that grandparents simply are much older already. The grandpas of some of my girlfriends had died already. During this evening all my grief over Püti came alive again.

My love for Grandpa I felt with overwhelming intensity then, and the knowledge that I would also lose him eventually ripped my heart right in two. At the same time there was the consolation that he was very much alive, very near, sitting right there beside me. At intermission he bought me a soft drink. During the second act I managed not to cry by cuddling as close to him as the theater seats allowed. My beloved Grandpa! As we went back home in the darkness, I couldn't hold back anymore and told him of my fears. He put his arms tightly around me and assured me that he had no intention of dying, no, on the contrary, he planned to be around for a long time to watch me grow up. On one level I was consoled. On another level I knew perfectly well that there was nothing for it, he was going to die, too, just like all the other Grandpas. But it was enough for me to keep this pain locked away deep inside me, too, a pain that no one else understood anyway. After all, Grandpa was not only still alive but enjoying the best of health. I must have been a pretty strange child.

So it went in the course of my life, several times more. And every time I had the same experience all over again: other people didn't understand. Once, for example much later in my life, it wasn't about a beloved person, but a beloved country. Over the space of twelve years, America had become my adopted home-land, the only country that felt like home to me after my previous nomadic existence. So when my husband decided to return with us to Europe, I felt truly uprooted for the first time. As a child I had left Kiel (in the very north of Germany) behind; now more than twenty years later I was coming "back" to Bavaria (in the very south of Germany). I have never felt "at home" in any country since. I soon learned to keep my homesickness for America locked inside me too. Most of my associates thought I must be overjoyed to be finally returning to my "German homeland" after twenty some years. . . .

> Hear the flute's sound and what it has to tell.
> Hear how the pain of parting makes it wail. . . .
> It seeks a heart that knows separation's pain,
> To whom its parting grief might be made plain.
> Hz. Mevlâna

These and other experiences all stand before me simultane-ously, here in my little cell. And I suddenly grasp the meaning: from the beginning I have been prepared to feel a deep longing. My whole life long my *ney* has been singing its song of yearning.

How can one be made ready for that most basic longing of humankind, longing for the presence of Allah, if not by "practicing longing" with worldly things? I feel the pain of all the previous losses, freshly, as if it had all just happened. But back then the pain was clothed in despair and abandonment. Now there is a sweetness to it, I can't think of any other word for it. What I had experienced over and over again as deep pain was nothing but a preparation.

In that uncertain state between waking and sleeping, sentences of Hz. Mevlâna go streaming by me: "When a work has no pain and no passionate love in it. . . " "This new love, this greater love. . . " "Now that I know how it is, to be with You in constant conversation. . . "

I startle from sleep without knowing why. I see a fountain of sparks shooting out of my electric outlet along with little flames licking up toward the loose strips of wallpaper hanging above them. Bolting wide awake I wrap my thick towel around my hand, bat at the flames and pull the plug out of the fountain of sparks. It's half melted! Only one of the prongs is still on the plug, the other is melted into the socket! I really have to laugh. If somebody sat down and tried to think of things that could go wrong in the solitude of a closed cell, who would think of so many things? "Until He wills it so, the pen moves not at all!"

The warmth lasted all of four hours! My heater was plugged into the outlet with an extension cord, so the plug on the heater itself is still all right. But the room only has this one melted-down outlet. Maybe I could move into the other room? I go over to check, but the light isn't working. With my candle (good thing the shaikh gave me a nice long-burning one—from Germany!) I go back to take a look. The room has no bulb and no socket for a bulb, just a wire dangling from the ceiling. But that's all right, what do I need light for the rest of the night? The main thing is, I can plug in my heater! But then my glance falls on the floor. It's covered with dark spots. Holding the candle nearer, I see what it is: cockroach upon cockroach, lying beaten or trampled in their dried blood! Someone must have really gone on a murderous rampage. In that case, I prefer the cold!

Once again I put on several sweaters and even my overcoat. I wake up intermittently during the night when I shift in my sleep and my face falls on an ice-cold section of pillow not already warmed by contact with me.

Day 24

So grasp that in this world what He wills comes to pass.

Hz. Mevlâna

Right after prayer, in the still hesitant early morning light, I prepare to change my quarters. I have to get out of this room, not only to use my heater, but so that Yusuf can get in and salvage whatever can be salvaged. I'm still very stiff from the cold, it takes me a while to get moving.

Only now, by the light of day, do I see the full extent of the cockroach catastrophe. There must be eighty of these whom someone has obliged to depart from the scenes of this life. In the bathroom there's one of those little Turkish hand brooms made of straw. It's stiff enough to scrape the little corpses off the floor and sweep them up. But a rag to remove the dried blood with is nowhere to be found. But then there's no water anyway.

My cotton mattress is incredibly heavy or else I've really lost a lot of strength already. But I manage to drag it behind me into the small adjoining room. I also bring along whatever I really need for the rest of the day. My first room, probably because it shares a wall with the apartment next door, is a good deal warmer than this one, which stands between two empty rooms and has a completely uninsulated front window. For whatever reason, despite my brave little heater it just doesn't get warm. Who knows how much time I'll be spending here. . . .

Toward noon the key turns in the lock! Yusuf! Until now he's never come before evening before! Right away I hear his steps interrupted. He's looking from the front door to the door to my cell and it's open now. I can imagine his alarm, since in fact something like that could only mean trouble. Very slowly I hear him advancing towards the room. For a while he doesn't move, then he steps quickly out the door. No doubt by now he has seen the melted pieces of plug and the scorched wallpaper, and he probably also noticed that today the door to the other little room is closed, when usually it's open.

A half hour later the dear fellow is back. I hear him puttering around for quite a while. Then he leaves. I run right over to see: all fixed, good as new! By now Yusuf has come to seem like an angel in the flesh, again and again he rescues me from miserable situations! Besides that, he's an electrical engineer. How convenient! While I'm dragging my mattress back, I hear a loud whooshing, as my toilet tank fills up with water. Water!

Just yesterday I had read in *Fihi ma Fihi:* "God's way is not to deal with each problem singly and in isolation; one answer clears up all questions at once, and the difficulty is solved" (p. 94). What an excellent manifestation of this principle I have just experienced! When the "hand" so willed, all "pens" wrote at once: Yusuf, the electricity, the water. . . . How many-sided are the movements of the One as seen in all the facets of creation! These shimmering veils of secondary causes all point to only one Truth! How should we recognize the One if not through His expression in the many? "God the Exalted made these veils for a good reason. For if God's beauty showed itself without veils, we wouldn't have the strength to bear it and would take no pleasure in it," so Hz. Mevlâna explains this mode of action (FmF, p. 95).

This time, as I switch on the boiler, I feel very differently. I have no anxieties anymore, my confidence is now absolute. Not that I have confidence that it will work this time. No, almost the opposite. I'm going on the assumption that once again something might happen that not even the most creative person could have reckoned with. But I KNOW now that whatever happens will be just what I need for my next lesson! I could call it a "meta-confidence" independent of contents or of customary dualistic judgments of good or bad, positive or negative.

As the one-and-a-half hours pass by, I lie peacefully under my covers. An extremely pleasant floating state embraces me; it's almost as if I were being carried along by deep inner peace—a state of inner vastness and expansion.

I am so grateful... not just for light, warmth, and cleanliness—now I have it all at once—but much more for the grace of being allowed to have these direct experiences of the TRUTH, of being allowed to be on the Path.

And the neighbors argue, laugh, and cry as much as ever! It seems like new conflicts come up every day, only to be resolved and make room for others. . . . In my isolation I am freed of all that. For how long? Is it really so different at home with my loved ones? Less volume, certainly, but. . . . Hz. Mevlâna compares these endless ups and downs to a mill wheel:

> This speaking and silence, this sleeping and eating, this getting angry and forgiving and all these traits, they are the turning of a mill wheel. It is a mill wheel that turns constantly. . . . For these are the conditions of the world. Now that you know that, complain to God and grovel and ingratiate yourself and say: "O God, instead of this journey and this constant turning, grant me a different, spiritual turning, since all needs are met by You and Your generosity and mercy is all-embracing." When this goal is fully reached, there is *light upon light* (FmF, p. 284).

I am overcome with deep sympathy for this family, so trapped on its own mill wheel. Surely this is also what is described in Castaneda's books: "The world of people goes up and down and people go up and down with their world; as sorcerers we have no business following them in their ups and downs"

Toward evening, I feel shaky, as if I had a fever. Have I maybe caught cold over the last few days without my heater?

Day 25

Verily, none but the people who deny the truth can ever lose hope of God's life-giving mercy.

Quran 12:87

Healthwise things are better, but I feel sad. Will I ever reach *fanā* and *baqā*, I wonder? Only fifteen more days! But grace can come at any time, for "He has the power to do everything." I mustn't lose confidence. "Allah does not love those without hope," says the shaikh, and "Hope and fear are the wings of striving." Still the sins of doubt and despair sneak in. I wonder, will I ever see my Teacher again?

Day 26

I've hit bottom. Can't concentrate on the *zhikrs* any more, can't even concentrate on my books. Spend most of the morning between crying and praying.

Suddenly, at the height of my despair, I realize with absolute certainty that all my striving, which has taken so many different forms over the course of my life, was nothing but striving for the presence of Allah. The forms were nothing but veils. Although this sudden knowledge is unshakably firm within me, it is still only *'ilm al-yaqīn* or rational knowledge. Oh, if it could become *'ayn al-yaqīn*! If I could only feel in my heart what I now know so surely in my head. Let this be my only prayer!

In the evening, no water again! Perhaps this is the setting-up of some kind of security provisions for the time after the *halvet*, for the world out there? Please, may I always remember all these lessons every time I wash my hair!

Day 27

Today I feel completely different. I think I'm actually finally beginning to get my priorities in place, not just on the rational plane but on the plane of the heart as well. Let's hope that isn't just more self-delusion or one of the "light veils"[64]!

Sometime around noon, all of a sudden, with no lead-in or warning (there never is), there's an earthquake! And as always happens all the doors fly open and I hear the people yelling and running outside.

This is the first time I am not running with them but sitting behind closed doors listening to the sound of panic around me. A touch of panic comes over me too. I do have a key, I can unlock the door and follow my herd instinct by trying to join the others before the next jolt hits. But then the *halvet* is broken off and there's no continuing, no matter how understandable the reasons for breaking it off.

All this passes through my mind in a fraction of a second. And I stay. I even resist the temptation to at least put the key where I can grab it quickly. Even an earthquake is only a secondary cause, and the words go through my head, "... *and not a leaf falls but He knows it. ...*" (Quran 6:59). How can I tell myself I'm starting to perceive the hand guiding the pen if any real trial makes me run away?

As I sit there waiting for the next jolt, the idea occurs to me that I could at least crawl under my mattress. But in the same moment I recognize this idea as a cheap little back-door that I'm trying to keep open for myself. No, I will sit upright and wait for whatever may come. Again my heart is racing. After all, it's a very strange feeling when the earth is swaying under you.

Time passes. This is the first earthquake I've ever experienced that had only one jolt. After about twenty minutes I also hear the other tenants going back into their apartments, assuring each other

---

[64] Generally, "too great" an effort to acquire good qualities, allowing the seeker to be diverted from the quest so that he ends up forgetting the real goal.

that no doubt it's safe now. Oh, how can we ever know that? Truly we people are like bleating sheep. And how appropriate the word "herd instinct" is.[65]

A good half hour later the call to noonday prayer rings forth from all the minarets. I have to admire the muezzins, climbing up there so soon after an earthquake. My brother and I did this once when we were kids, it's so narrow and dark inside there! But perhaps for these men the knowledge I still have to struggle so hard for is already deeply interiorized.

My thoughts go back to my first earthquake. It was a relatively intense one, on "Republic Day" in 1964. We had the day off from school, and my brother and I were making stick figures out of chestnuts. When they fell over, we accused each other of jiggling the table. Then we realized, still not really grasping it yet, what was happening, what was involved! Paintings and ornamental plates thrashed around wildly against the walls. Our mother came running out of the kitchen and the three of us clung to each other standing in the doorway to the stairwell, which had been pointed out to us as a bearing wall of the building. It had been explained to us that when houses fall apart, the stairways are the first thing to cave in, whereas the bearing walls are often the only thing left standing.

We had a lovely penthouse apartment in a building of reinforced concrete. The next shocks were so strong and so distinctly felt here on the eighth floor of this trembling edifice that we were slammed onto the floor. I had the feeling that the entire house on both sides of us was hopping several feet up into the air and restacking itself floor by floor as it came down again. How could any structure withstand that? And we were sliding back and forth on the smooth floor, trying to hold on to each other, to the walls, to anything. The other tenants, more accustomed to earthquakes, had run right out after the first mild shocks. The yelling, stampeding,

---

[65] This bleating eventually stops. The wolf appears.
We run off in different directions, with always some thought of how lucky we are.
(Hz. Mevlâna, OS, quatrain 65)

and door-slamming will always be synonymous with earthquakes for me.

When the shocks were over, we also ran, the only ones left in the giant building. Down below, everyone had gathered under an old tree. We also joined them. I still remember how I looked up at the tall houses around us and wondered how much safer we really were here at the foot of these concrete monsters. But the gathering lent a certain security. The earthquake had been a powerful one, and it was a long time before one family after another went back in. The same with us. In the meantime my father had arrived; he had left the office and fought his way through the chaotic traffic to get to us.

That evening, my parents sat down beside my brother's and my beds and we looked at a geography textbook with handsome illustrations of distant countries. And I realized, as we were all trying to get interested in the book, that parents cannot protect us, that they are just as exposed as children. If not even the earth beneath our feet is firm, what is? By then I had already entered my long phase of spiritual disillusionment without the knowledge that I have today. So my principal conclusion was to question every type of security. Looking back later, I have often thought that was the day I grew up.

Day 28

A strange day. Nothing seems "to fit." I don't know what to do with myself, nothing seems to do anything for me. I have intermittent relapses of my obsession.

Outside it's raining; it's definitely warmer than a few days ago. In summer this miserable apartment must be an oven. May God stand by all future occupants, them and all the poor people of the world!

My expectations are concentrated on the soup, since tonight is the night for it. Yusuf is late today, he doesn't come till a little before 11 p.m. He comes and goes away again without bringing soup!!

I am amazed how little I care, even though I spent the whole day looking forward to a bowl of something hot! Half an hour later Yusuf comes back with the soup! Although I enjoy it very much, it means as little to me to have it as it did to do without it. Again I think that is certainly symbolic of all worldly needs. But why in the world does this obsession keep tormenting me over and over? Why in the world can't I "remember" what I supposedly "know"?

In the Quran I keep reading Sura Forty-eight over and over again: "... *so that God might show His forgiveness of all thy faults, past as well as future, and thus bestow upon thee the full measure of His blessings, and guide thee on the straight way, and show that God will succour thee with his mighty succor.*" (48:2-3)

And may He help me with powerful aid!

Day 29

Ocean music, not the sad edge of surf, but the sound of no shore.
Hz. Mevlâna

I'm not quite sure if I'm asleep or awake. Or is it what one would call a vision[66]?

I am a majestic stream, flowing toward its goal in serene tranquillity. Placidly, but surely, it flows into the OCEAN, mixes with its waters in complete naturalness, becomes ONE. There is no need to "knock on a door." Just flow, go home! The OCEAN is *Raḥmān, Raḥīm* through and through, all-merciful. Enveloping, inclusive, endless in its tranquillity. "Lovers don't finally meet somewhere / they are in each other all along" (OS, quatrain 1246).

The feeling of becoming-one/being-one is all-embracing, orgasmic. Later this feeling is completely gone again. Why doesn't something like that last? Is it a *hal*, designed to give me courage? I

---

[66] *See "The Authenticity of Mystical Experiences," p. 171ff.

have to practice patience. For days now I've been feeling a vibration in my whole body, in every cell of my being.

Day 30

In the early morning hours I dream the same sequence several times in a row. It's a strange dream, one not connected to seeing or hearing. Looking back I wonder what kind of sensory perception took place. The content was very clear: An old man shows me certain practices that will lead every cell of my body to start glowing, that will cause a little flame to burn in each cell, burning me all bright and clean. "Oil," he says without using words, "so bright that it gleams before it's even lighted."[67]

I wake up amazed that I have dreamed the same sequence several times in a row and that neither words nor images went along with it. What a strange way to dream!

I drift into the next dream: someone I can't see explains the previous dream sequence to me: "This old man is Muhammad (Peace be upon him). By his light the other lights are lighted. That's why your body has been vibrating." This time I wake up to the *ezan*.

I've definitely lost some more weight. The last few days my weight seemed to have stabilized. But today my belly is even more sunken in, you can see all the bones beneath the skin. Before the *halvet* I had thought that this inevitable fasting would have make a haggard old woman out of me. Once you're over forty. . . . I imagined wrinkly skin with hanging folds. To my surprise it has turned out very differently: the skin lies taught and firm on my bones. My thighs, for example, look more like those of a child—it's touching, somehow. And as for what my face looks like? At first I found it strange that this empty apartment had no mirror in it. Now that seems very suitable to me. After all, for these forty days I'm not supposed to see any people. So I'm not even seeing myself.

---

[67] Cf. Quran 24:35 (observation of Annemarie Schimmel).

The other thing is that I apparently have lost some more of my stamina. The last few days I had felt pretty strong. Only getting up in the morning required caution, I had to do it in slow-motion. After that I was okay. Today, though, I must have fallen asleep in the late morning. I dream that my closet has Mehmet's clothes mixed in everywhere. Carefully and conscientiously, but also determinedly, I separate them from my own clothing items and hang them in their own closet.

Today again makes more sense than the last few days. The ritual prayer has reached a new dimension. Ibn 'Arabi writes that when a person is alone at prayer, he should imagine Allah in front of him and the two angels that accompany each person behind him, and that they are joining in the prayer. I start to perceive this "triangle" kinesthetically, as if between Allah and the angels some kind of magnetic or electrical field has been formed and I am now inside the force field. As the day goes on it becomes more and more intense. Each time I pray, starting with the second *rekat*,[68] it becomes so clearly noticeable that it now feels like whisper-fine strands of rubber, amid which I perform the prescribed movements.

I have no interest at all in reading anymore. This although reading has been one of my favorite occupations my whole life long! But now I feel almost an aversion to it, in fact, to *all* cognitive activities. The intuitive approach is the only one that feels right. The zhikrs are qualitatively different today, most unusually soft and gentle.

Late in the evening a raging storm arises. The lights flicker from time to time. Will the power fail, I wonder?

---

[68] *rekat*: section of prayers consisting of one standing position, one bow from the waist, and two prostrations, together with the respective recitations that are prescribed to accompany them.

Day 31

I had intended to wash my hair, but once again there's no water. Well, not today, I think. But how do I know that it won't come back by afternoon? Everything is possible! Hz. Mevlâna writes:

> Then he grasps that all his fear and worry and regret was of no use. People have watched a hundred thousand times as their plans and intentions came to nothing and that nothing went the way they wished. But God brings down forgetfulness upon them so that they forget everything that has happened and pursue their own ideas and their own choices (FmF, p. 268).

Once more a day where nothing seems to fit, kind of a wasted day. In the course of intense prayer during the afternoon I am confronted again with the full extent of my helplessness.

My whole body is aglow with inner vibration, each cell with a life of its own, burning. Is it Muhammad (Peace be upon him) showing me the way of poverty, the way of the heart? Finally I feel burned out, exhausted. Mentally too: just completely depleted. Feel a deep indifference. Let each person do whatever he or she wants, I just want to find the "way home," the way to the OCEAN, the way into *fanā* and *baqā*. "Don't think of good advice for me / I've tasted the worst that can happen" (OS, quatrain 670).

Still no water. I've been reading the Holy Quran more and more. Curiously, it is not affected by my aversion to reading of the last few days. Quite the contrary!

A quiet, almost peaceful resignation takes the place of the dissatisfaction of these last few days, this feeling that nothing gains me anything: I am simply here to serve. What else? What gain is it supposed to bring me? I'm supposed to give!

"The only thing you can give Allah," so I once read somewhere, "is a heart polished to a shine." Fine, so be it.

Day 32

I dream that I'm sitting on the bottom of a deep still pond in crystal-clear water. I decide to surface and so, still sitting cross-legged, I start to rise higher and higher. Then the moment comes when I reach the surface, but without the slightest alteration in gravity, I just keep going higher and higher. Now I'm rising up in the air, as weightless as the air itself. Higher and higher, till I decide to come down again. Going down just as gently, once again I meet the surface of the water with no resistance whatever. I just descend farther and farther, with nothing to mark the transition. . . .

Even when I wake up, this incredible bodily feeling of weightlessness is still clearly perceptible. As if I had "really" experienced it. "Really?" In a way it wasn't like a dream, it was "more real" than dreams generally are. I wonder what would have happened if I hadn't switched into my conscious, anxious-to-steer mode of thought, which made me turn back. Where might I have floated off to? And how indescribable, this feeling of weightlessness, which, interestingly enough, was identical in both elements—a fact that surprised me even during the "dreaming" itself!

There's water again! Can I maybe manage to take a shower? While the boiler is heating up, I catch myself again in my little "back-door" thoughts. Do I really need five to six minutes of showering time? Maybe it's enough if I just heat it up for an hour?? When will I ever "remember" what in fact I "know"? I decide not to give in to my impulse to hedge my bets. Besides, I actually need at least that much time. Part of the Islamic ritual cleanliness requirements is shaving your whole body—except for the hair on your head, of course! And that takes a while. "When the hair in your pubic region is getting long, you are not properly prepared for prayer. As long as the length does not exceed the breadth of a barleycorn, you are perfectly shaved from a religious point of view," so Hz. Mevlâna explains the matter. This time the heating-up works fine, with no problems.

In doing the *zhikrs*, images arise again. This time I'm looking into myself. I see my heart as a crystalline structure, like the anatomical illustrations of hearts that one sometimes sees, consisting only of the network of veins. But instead of being blood-red, the network of veins is like glass.

All my stupid rational thinking, my anxieties, my stubborn planning, all that keeps me from "being mindful" of the One Truth, is visibly there, sticking on top like fragments of black olives that get caught between one's teeth. The *zhikr* "*La ilāha il Āllāh*" comes like a scouring brush and cleans and scrubs till all the black-olive fragments are removed. The rhythm of the back-and-forth movements of the *zhikr* is almost like windshield wipers. It takes quite awhile to get everything clean. Now the "heart" is a porous, gleaming structure open to the "winds of non-neediness," as Hz. Mevlâna says.

Now the *zhikr* "*Hayy Allah*" takes over and fills the crystalline structure with life. It turns into a shimmering gold-and-white formation, full of tender little golden flames. With quiet certainty the light of Muhammad (Peace be upon him) burns within me. Outside a soft, heavy rain is falling.

Following the evening prayer I am hit with a totally unexpected wave of the deepest concern for Mehmet. To put an end to the deteriorating situation at home, he has accepted a research assignment in the United States. He's supposed to start there in March. In contrast to me he just can't stand being alone. How lonesome he's going to be there without all of us! Why is it that we just couldn't give each other what we had hoped for from each other? All my prayers tonight, my deepest wishes, are for him. Don't let him be lonesome!

To me being alone is nothing, but now the thought that he could feel lonesome rips my heart right in two. My prayers for him are joined to the rhythm of the heavily splashing, falling rain.

Day 33

In this wind of non-neediness the atoms of the ashes of those hearts dance and shout and are intoxicated. And if the hearts do not see that their real life lies in this burning-up and being scattered to the winds, why do they long so passionately to be consumed by the fire?

Hz. Mevlâna

A voice in a dream says to me: "Your heart has already arrived. But you're still holding on."

For the last few days I've been feeling pretty weak during the morning hours. I have to execute the bows of the ritual prayer slowly. Today, once again, I don't know what to do with myself. If I can just use this special time correctly and not squander these valuable days!

As I pray, all at once an image is before my eyes, sharp and clear: I see Muhammad (Peace be upon him) sitting in a white Arabian gown. I see slender, fine hands, powerful, with a slightly tanned skin-color, and similar feet, bare but for brown leather sandals. I see no face or head; it's as if I'm too close to see it. But I see myself. He has me on his lap and presses me to his bosom, like my grandpa did when I was still a little girl. As I gaze at myself sitting there, I become younger and younger before my eyes. Finally I am once again the little girl with braids and pigtails that once, a long time ago, I used to be. I cuddle up close to him as I did to Grandpa, back then, and he wraps part of his costume around me. Only my hair is sticking out. What security!

I ask him to show me his heart, to teach me the way of the heart, the way of poverty. He opens his garment to show his chest, and his heart is like a gleaming, reflecting mirror, like an indescribably powerful silvery-white sun that burns up and destroys everything in its cool fire. It seems unbearable and at the same time irresistible. It turns every superfluous thing to ashes, burns everything empty and clean. I stay there for a long time, right in front of this glittering, all-penetrating light source, secure in his strong arms, kept safe. In manifold form and with heightened power all the feelings return that I felt back then during the opera *Carmen*: infinite love, pain, consolation. At the same time I sense my body in the here and now: thin, empty, hungry, twitching, shaking, vibrating in every single cell of my being—burning clean, glowing.

Day 34

... enter then, together with My other true servants—yea, enter thou My paradise!

Quran 89:29-30

These last days have seemed so much longer than at the beginning. From a certain point of view that is a good thing. If the idea is to serve, then surely the harder it is to serve, the greater the service is. But today the day passes faster again. I am made conscious of how endlessly valuable and irrecoverable every single *halvet*-day is that lets me stay a little longer in direct contact with the whole of the *silsile*.[69] Sometimes I think I can sense the *baraka*[70] of all the links in the "chain" that came before me. The countless dervishes, now mostly nameless, who experienced the same pain and the same sweetness of the Path before me, who lived through the forty holy days of the *halvet*, just like me. Oh, may I use this special time wisely! May I prove worthy of this living "chain"!

I now have, at least on the cognitive plane, the absolute certainty that the only road to freedom consists in really and truly transcending every last trace of neediness (obsession!) toward worldly things. Only then can one be weightless enough to "shout and

---

[69] *silsile*: "chain of the master," the spiritual chains of transmission of the Sufi order, which all lead back to Muhammad (Peace be upon him); also, the disciples of the Sufi order.

[70] *baraka*: God's blessing in the aura created by turning to Him; the spiritual infusion of grace that passes from the teachers to the pupils.

dance with the atoms of the incinerated hearts in the wind of needlessness," only then can one be porous enough to be one with the ocean. "Wind" and "ocean" are always there and ready to carry along the one who is ready to let go. One qualifies oneself or disqualifies oneself. The dead weight that absolutely must be left behind is the demands of the ego (*nafs*).

It isn't yet an *'ayn al-yaqīn*, but in any event it is an absolutely certain *'ilm al-yaqīn*. With each *zhikr* I now try consciously to become emptier and emptier. I have turned the vision of the "black-olive remnants" into an exercise: I change all my self-centered wishes, wants and needs into "olive remnants." With every back-and-forth motion of the *zhikr* I let the "spiritual windshield wipers" give it a thorough polishing.

Throughout, I pray fervently that with Allah's help the inner purity, the "emptiness" of Sufism, the "poorhouse of not wanting" may come my way. I pray to be able to serve better, till *fanā* and *baqā*, God willing, are my life someday.

And say: "the truth has come to light and falsehood has withered away: for, behold, all falsehood is bound to wither away!"

Quran 17:81

Day 35

Again a day that passes only slowly, where nothing fits. My, how the days alternate between what strikes me as good and what strikes me as bad. In fact they are neither. After all, who knows what purpose is hidden behind what events?

Zhikrs are difficult and frustrating. Now that I have practically no trouble anymore keeping my thoughts on the matter at hand, a completely unexpected and inexplicable complication arises: the air body has gotten so much denser with the passing time that the "substance" surrounding me is like a viscous mass. When I try to move my head from right to left, it's like trying to move the flat of your hand through water. The result is a fluttery, disordered movement. Or sometimes I just glide "on top" of it, like a stone thrown low and level so that it skips across the water's surface. In the extreme case the only thing that helps me is to lead with my chin, which then parts the "substance" like the prow of a ship parts the water. The *zhikr* "*La ilāha il Āllāh*" is the only one that works a little better, maybe because of its somewhat different underlying rhythm. Here I can actually use this "gliding effect," and the feeling arises of being carried along by large wings. But sometimes nothing at all works anymore, and then I am, in the truest sense of the word, stuck in this mass.

Soup! The last time, God willing.

Day 36

When you have reached this point, stand still and make no further effort. Reason is no longer in control here. When it gets to the shore of the sea, it just stands there, even though there is no longer any such a thing as "standing there."

Hz. Mevlâna

In a dream I encounter people of the white, red, and black races, living in mortal enmity with each other. "I" consist of nothing but "pure will" or "spirit." Wishing to help them, I take on a rather androgynous human shape. I go to their meeting and offer myself in exchange for peace. They accept, and I deliver myself up to them. To my surprise I survive uninjured. It is only the shape I took on that dies. And that is so unimportant that I only notice it, if at all, marginally and in passing. Hz. Mevlâna says: "Be melting snow." In this dream I begin to understand that that actually works.

During prayer a new state comes on. A kind of "largesse," an indescribable vastness, so great as to encompass the whole of creation. This immeasurableness simply flows right through me, no resistance or hindrance from "self-important demands" blocks the flow. A feeling of absolute weightlessness and transparency. The expression "emptied of self, filled with *hu*" is a living reality.

The afterglow of this experience stays with me afterwards for a while longer. Putting it into words as part of my notes is even harder for me than usual. The REALITY of things can't help the limitations of language. I have to remember not to hold on to anything. Every neediness is like a lead weight by which this incredible, living reality of freedom, of melting, of becoming One, of "dancing in the wind of no-need" is inevitably prevented.

When I get back out, I'll have to build myself back up with the greatest care. I intend to do this very consciously. When I start taking nourishment again to let my emaciated physical body come back to normal, I want to keep the other levels in mind at the same time. Nourishment isn't all that's important, equally important are the thoughts that once again are allowed to have access to me. After all this emptying, this is my big chance to consciously build myself in a new way on all levels.

> The quality of 'Absolute Certainty' is the perfected shaikh, good and true thoughts are his disciples. . . . Wandering, false, denying thoughts are the ones that the Shaikh 'Certainty' expels. Every day they get farther away from him and become more lowly day by day (FmF, p. 224).

Despite my physical weakness, I feel inexpressibly good. Once again this well-being is all-encompassing, definitely mental, spiritual, physical. There is also a feeling as if an important and difficult assignment has been carried out well. Redemption, relief. "When I break free from my several parts that will be through His boundless graciousness and my delight over His opening-up and His incomparable staying-open" (FmF, p. 234).

I am writing a few parting words to my children in my notes. When I am dead, whenever that may be, eventually my Mina is sure to read this. Then, not right after my death, she will find these words for herself and her brothers. Then they will know that everything is good the way it is.

It's Thursday night, and I feel even closer than usual to my Mina, my little Minch, my little Mini-mau, as I tell my part of that old dervish story. We had just started on it when she went to France to boarding-school. It's a Sufi "lucky story," which you must share with someone every Thursday while eating dates. Then you'll have luck!

Dates have a manifold significance in Islam. Among other things, they are the carriers of handed-down spiritual knowledge, as in the story of the initiation of Hoca Ahmet Yesevi. They are also the symbol of sharing, of generosity. The Prophet (Peace be upon him) says: "If you have enough dates for one, you also have enough for two." Telling a dervish story in the appropriate manner also stands for living one's life in the appropriate manner. Then one will have the "good luck" to live a life well-pleasing to God.

When we are far apart, Amina and I, one tells the first half, the other the second half. Somewhere or other, the two halves meet.

The Initiation of Hoca Ahmet Yesevi

At the start of his mission, the Prophet Muhammad (Peace be upon him) and his friends were persecuted for their faith. One day as they were fleeing, their provisions were exhausted. And so the Prophet (Peace be upon him) was asked to pray to God for nourishment. After his prayer the angel Gabriel appeared with a bowl of dates. As he handed the bowl to the hungry ones, one date fell on the ground. The angel said that this fruit was intended for a man who would be born five hundred years later. His name would be Hoca Ahmet Yesevi and he would live in Sayram (in what is now Turkistan). Since this date had now been manifested in this world, it couldn't be taken back again.

So the friends had a discussion about who should deliver this fruit. A loving person named Arslan Baba declared himself ready to take on this task, and so the Prophet Muhammad (Peace be upon him) placed the date under his tongue. There Arslan Baba kept it till one day in the town of Jessy he met Ahmet, who was seven years old. He was playing just then with a group of children the same age when he saw Arslan Baba. "Did you bring me the present?" little

Ahmet asked the old man. So Arslan Baba completed his assignment and became the child's first teacher.[71]

Soon Ahmet grew up to become a great spiritual leader with countless students. One of them was called Lokmani Perende. He in his turn was entrusted with the spiritual direction of a disciple named Mehmet Bektaş[72] . . . .

Day 37

Again a day where nothing fits! I'm slowly getting used to this regular back-and-forth. Surely it has a meaning. Perhaps it is a form of preventive hardening for the time after the *halvet*. So that I'll learn to accept with equanimity the good days and the bad days. Till I learn that neither one nor the other exists. . . !

I know with greater and greater certainty what I *don't* want to do: reading or any other purely cognitive activities. . . . I have such a craving for the direct closeness that only becomes accessible through intuitive approaches. Yearning for the way of the heart. Only how? All I can give is my defective *zhikrs*. The result is in other hands. I can't do anything but make an honest effort.

Reading the Quran, however, is something that amazes me. Besides the eight suras that the shaikh "prescribed" for me, I had planned to read the entire Quran. Doing it all in sequence is something I have done only once before in my life, as a thirteen-year-old. At that time I was beginning to get interested in the religion of the country where I grew up. Looking back, I can only say that it was mostly attributable to my persistence that I actually read the whole Quran through from front to back. As reading matter I simply found it boring and redundant.

---

[71] In his book *Divana Hakmet* (The Book of Wise Sayings), Hoca Ahmet Yesevi relates these events.

[72] Quoted according to G. Tucek, *Yunus Emre, "Seit ich mich selbst vergass. . . ,"* in *Gedichte und Leider.*

Two decades later, when I had become a Muslim, I began to feel awe for the Holy Book but precisely because it *is* the holy book. It had little to do with the contents. Even at the start of this *halvet* it ranked, as far as my interest goes, behind Hz. Mevlâna and Ibn 'Arabi. Now, however, and it amazes me, my desire to read the Quran gets stronger every day. Indeed, it has become a craving instead of a dutiful exercise!

Partly, no doubt, that is because I am slowly penetrating more deeply into the multilayeredness of the contents. But no way is it that alone. People always mention the magical power that the Holy Book has in the original Arabic, which of necessity gets lost in the translations. Of course no translation can ever be "authorized" in the religious sense. Despite all that, I am starting to feel this magic very clearly! It's almost irresistible. The book has a direct influence on my spirits. Like some kind of magic spell! By now I also have three "favorite suras," forty-eight, ninety-three and ninety-four, that I keep reading over and over. Reading the Quran isn't something cognitive anymore, it's a direct opening on an intuitive level.

Day 38

Oh You, the only Being! When I imagine my selfhood separate from You, it is only a sign of inattention.

Shebenderzadeh Ahmed Hilmi (1865-1939)

"An eye that does not see means a heart that feels no pain," so I read in Ibn 'Arabi (FaH, p. 155). Is the reverse also true, I wonder?

As part of the common currency of Sufism, the need to be "attentive" is emphasized. Attentive to what, and how? Somewhere I have read: "Being attentive means always keeping an eye on the context of all being." In other words, the hand and not the pen? Always to remember that, remembering one's own helplessness?

Today I scarcely read at all, with deepest yearning I crave direct heart contact. The day goes by, flowing, drifting, in a calm transitional state of being.

Soup! Even though it isn't Wednesday at all! Obviously the idea is to strengthen me for my emergence from the *halvet*. In truth we're getting towards the end.

Day 39

Several times in my dream, Beyazid Bistami's famous plea to God rises up before me: "I wish not to wish, I want not to want." Without words, without writing, without pictures. The plea is simply present in its essence. Insistently, over and over.

Today my patience with myself runs out again. The *zhikrs* are hard for me; during the water-heating cycle my anxieties about electrical matters resurface. What an endless amount I still have to learn. And there's scarcely any time left. My touch of desperation makes me impatient, and my impatience heightens my desperation. A bad cycle.

In the evening, soup again! Plus a beaker of hot tea sweetened with honey and even a piece of bread! Many unexpected gifts! To my amazement I have difficulty eating the crispy fresh Turkish bread that I usually love so much. It takes me almost ten minutes to eat that one slice.

The Prophet is that love and affection, which is eternal.

Hz. Mevlâna

Resignation sets in. In Sufism, despair and impatience count as sins. "With trust and patience the journey is half done," goes the saying. I haven't even succeeded in "clothing" myself in these basic virtues; how much of the journey is still undone! What presumption to pray for *fanā* and *baqā* If I could only *enter among His servants!* "Only"? That's presumption too! When, when will I learn?

92

Quite unexpectedly, Muhammad (Peace be upon him) is with me again. Not in the form of the old man of my dream, nor as the strong, protective middle-aged man of my last encounter. This time he has no human form. He's like a great endless cloudbank. Still, there is not the slightest doubt that it is him.

"I" see "myself" from behind, with arms and legs spread wide, tiny by comparison, flying toward this immense cloud bank. Drawn as if by a powerful magnet, falling in as if into the sea.[73]

Then "I" stop seeing "myself." Now there is only one perceiving. Inside this cloud bank I spread out farther and farther. My outstretched arms and legs at first get longer and longer, I am pulled in all directions at once. Then I come apart and dissolve completely in this fog that is purest love and mercy. As if a glass of tea were tossed into a great sea. The tea gets thinner and thinner till finally it's "tea-being" is lost in the "water-being," leaving only one sea water.

Having now become one, "we" spread out immeasurably, endlessly, farther and farther. "We-I-he" are so dissolved, so spread out, that we embrace the whole universe. But again, there can be no talk of "embracing," because that would imply boundaries, whereas love has no boundaries. The whole cosmos, in fact, con-

---

[73] Up till now, when it wasn't simple for me to put my experiences into words for my journal entries, this difficulty could partly be circumvented by the use of analogies, metaphors and, above all, quotations from Hz. Mevlâna. At this point it is no longer possible for me even to give indications that would make the actual experiential quality understandable on this level. To start with, there is the rather banal fact that all of the pronouns in question are out of the question.

"We" isn't right as this is correct only if there are at least two persons present. But "we" have become "ONE."

"He" isn't right, because this pronoun requires a dissociative mode of perception that is no longer available.

I see no possibility of expressing the state of being that is not "we" or "I" or "he."

Once again the most reasonable approach is to take refuge in quotations, in this case to the *ḥadīth*: "I have a time with God, where there is no room for any commissioned prophet nor any of God's closest angels." But this is completely impossible, for a greater presumption is scarcely imaginable.

sists of purest love. It is one single Being of immeasurable love and mercy.

As this state slowly ebbs, I know with irreversible certainty that it doesn't matter in the slightest if war really has broken out. Oh, if I could only make all the people who must then be suffering understand that there is not the least little tiniest reason to be sad! If they only knew that everything is Love!

But it won't be possible to make that understandable to anyone; I already don't understand it myself anymore as I am writing down my (whose??) experience. It seems monstrous to me to even think such a thing, let alone speak it. Still, I know with every fiber of my being that it is so. Is that maybe the *'ayn al-yaqīn* that I have been craving so much? How can I ever protect this knowledge and carry it over into my daily life? Everything is right just the way it is. There is really not the slightest reason to feel the need of anything or anyone. Not even Beyazid Bistami's need not to need any more makes any sense at all at this point!

I can only pray that I may be given the gift whereby some reflection of this immeasurable love that is Being may be manifested "out there." In Sufism one way to show love for God is to live in love for His creatures.

I have a time with God . . .

Annemarie Schimmel illumines the well-known *ḥadīth* as follows:

It is also to Muhammad that one of the best-loved Sufi sayings is ascribed: "I have a time with God . . . "—*waqt*, "time," can be precisely translated, using the expression of Middle High German mystics, as *Nu* (now, moment), for it is a time of the most intimate union, seeing as the person in question bursts through the bonds of created time and reaches the *nunc aeternum* (eternal now), a moment in which no room can be made even for Gabriel himself, even the highly honored angel of the revelation doesn't fit in here. Maulana [= Mevlâna = Rumi] sees in this saying of the Prophet (Peace be upon him) the secret of prayer, in which a person, wholly divested

94

of his own self, can have unmediated dialogue with God (Schimmel, p. 25)

But even the word "dialogue" that Schimmel uses implies duality and contradicts the notion of "being fully divested of one's own self" as well as the reality I experienced.

Guénon's effort to describe the indescribable corresponds better to my own experience:

> A person is not "absorbed" when he achieves "liberation," even if it might look that way from the standpoint of manifestation, since from that viewpoint the "transformation" looks like destruction; when a person makes the move into unconditional reality, which is then all that's left for him, then the opposite happens: he is, if we may use such an expression, spread out beyond all boundaries (which reproduces exactly the symbolism of steam spreading out endlessly in the atmosphere), for he has realized the fullness of his possibilities.[74]

In the eleventh century Al Ghazali not only expressed the impossibility of communicating the nature of this state, but also warned explicitly against any such attempt:

> After the ascent of the Gnostics into the heaven of truth, they are in agreement that in this existence they have seen nothing but the One, the Truthful. . . . For these ones multiplicity became utterly unthinkable, and they drenched themselves in the pure Oneliness and lost their reason in it. . . . That's why one of them said: "I am the truth![75]"

> Another said, "How lofty I am, how magnificent I am!" and "Under my robes there is nothing other than God"[76]

> But the words of those who are lost in love and in a state of intoxication must be kept secret and may not be passed on. . . . When this state prevails, in relation to the person who experiences it, it is called "extinction" or even "extinction of extinctions (in God),'" be-

---

[74] Quoted in F. Schon, *Den Islam verstehen.*

[75] Al Hallaj, d. 922, who suffered a martyr's death because of his estatic pronouncement "*Ana'l Haqq*" [I am the Truth (God)].

[76] Beyazid Bistami, d. 874.

cause his self is extinguished. For in this state he perceives neither his own consciousness nor his unconsciousness of his consciousness. After all, if he were to perceive his unconsciousness, he would have perceived his own consciousness. In relation to the person who finds himself in this state, this is called, in the metaphorical sense, "identity," or, in the language of reality, "union." Behind these truths stand secrets whose explanation, however, would take us quite a ways.[77]

The whole night through, the *zhikrs* have an incredible softness to them, they just flow along, they're like Hz. Mevlâna's "Ocean with no shore". . . . The *zhikr* "Allah, Allah, Al-lah" to my amazement, transforms itself into "Allah, Allah, All-love."

Later, in the middle of the *zhikr* "*Bismillāh*," there arises the peaceful immeasurability of the starry heavens over Mecca. It becomes an experience that is no longer what I know of as "*zhikrs*." The air body, which in recent days had given me so much trouble with its syrup-like resistance, suddenly carries me along! Fully set loose, weightless, freed, "I" float out of my inmost self into this endlessness. *Estağfirullah, Estağfirullah . . . .*

Day 40

Have We not opened up thy heart, and lifted from thee the burden that has weighed so heavily on thy back? And have We not raised thee high in dignity?

Quran 94:1-4

In my dream I hear the melody of the old song by Simon & Garfunkel "Like a bridge over troubled waters, I will lay me down. . . ." I see a great outsize construction site that encompasses almost the whole known world. And yet it all seems to be taking place in America. A field of vision of almost three-hundred-and-sixty degrees. An enormous bridge construction spanning Asia

---

[77] Al Ghazali, *The Niche of Lights*, pp. 24-25.

and Europe is already finished. The bridges to unite all the other continents are taking shape. It's my birthday. "This is your gift," says a voice. Even there in the dream I am conscious for the first time of the double meaning of the word "gift": "gift" in the sense of "present" and "gift" in the sense of "talent." Talent is purest gift. . . . Then Mehmet comes and gives me a birthday gift, a tiny morsel of a strange type of drug.

I wake up, everything is still dark. Sura Ninety-three goes through my head: "*In the night when it is stillest . . .*" So does the beginning of a poem that a friend in California once wrote for me: "Light a candle for darkness . . ."

I light the candle that was so often my only light, lie on my mattress and watch as the dimness of the fortieth morning gradually dawns. Then the chorus of muezzins starts up. All the way to Mecca, I think. I imagine the Earth from the viewpoint of the All, with living Islam encircling it in waves. The rhythm of the five daily prayers, which after all is determined by the position of the sun, moves like a ceaseless wave around the earthly sphere. If one could see all the people bowing, prostrating themselves, and getting up again, it must really look like concentric waves with their center in Mecca. For much more than a thousand years it has gone like this, across space, across time, yet spaceless and timeless . . . The soundwaves of the *ezan* also encircle our earth at all times. And I feel so secure, embedded in this great community.

Following the morning prayer I depart from my usual activities. Today, on my last day, I'm going to read my notes. At first with horror, then with amazement, I follow the process unfolding before my eyes. Just think what my reasons were for going into this *halvet!* And what unbelievable grace brought my selfish intentions in line with the real purpose of such an exercise! Hz. Mevlâna says:

> So we know absolutely that the author of all acts is God, not a person. Every action that comes from a person, be it good or bad, is undertaken by that person with an intention and according to some principle; but the real meaning of the actions is not as limited as he or she imagines . . . The full value of the action is known only to God, who arouses the person to the action (FmF, p. 319).

97

The Holy Quran speaks of *"Light upon light,"* but here "Grace upon grace" is visible! "Gratitude upon gratitude" overcomes me. These are tears of joy that well up in me now. How grateful I am for everything, grateful for the gratitude! And then, just as the *ezan* sounds for midday prayer, I come to "now." Forty days—what wisdom lies in the exact measure of this time interval. Forty days, no more, no less! I am so grateful!

All the gifts I received here are so infinitely precious. And so unsupported still, like tender, beautiful blossoms exposed without protection to the raw winds of spring. I feel flooded with gentleness, acceptance, confidence, inner peace. I ask for every protection for "the outside," to "remind myself," when the real tests come. May the veils never close again! May my *nafs ammara* of arrogance, self-centeredness be conquered by this love and mercy. How much was given me! May I have the power to pass something on, wherever I can, "like a bridge over troubled waters . . ." May the inner *halvet* continue on beyond the *halvet* itself!

Around 7 p.m. the shaikh is suddenly here. Outside, through the still-closed door of my room, I hear him melodically reciting prayers, as at the beginning. The *halvet* is "unsealed." In the part that he speaks in Turkish, he prays again for peace in the world and that my prayers may be accepted. Then he knocks, I open, and I see my first people in forty days. Murat is with him again, along with his little daughter.

I don't know what I'm supposed to do; I offer them the only seat I have, namely my mattress. He asks how I am, and I notice that I have scarcely any voice left. To think that something like that also disappears for want of use! The little one says, "*Ablaciğim*[78] you're wearing the same pantyhose you had on the last time I saw you!"

Again we sit in the small white car and drive through the evening traffic of Istanbul. The swarming streets seem overwhelming to me, though surely it's no different than it always is. The little one merrily engages me in conversation. I try to answer and notice

---

[78] *ablaciğim*: My dear little older sister.

something strange: I can't find the right verb forms! I mean to speak in present tense and hear myself using the future. Plus I can hardly understand what the others are saying. "They're speaking Turkish!" I think. And: "I speak Turkish too!" So why can't I understand?

At last, after two attempts, I manage to indicate what trouble I'm having. The shaikh says that will go away soon, for now I should just listen. So I listen some more to the little one, who has quite a lot to tell.

In the shaikh's dwelling, besides his beautiful, young wife, his mother is also waiting for me. After I have kissed her hand and touched it to my forehead, as is customary, she embraces me and strokes first my body and then her own. Being so fresh out of the *halvet* I still have some of the blessing clinging to me, and in this manner she partakes of it. I am given my first meal, rice soup with little mutton dumplings. Again it surprises me that I have scarcely any appetite after all the deprivation.

Then it is time to speak of my experiences. At first it goes badly. Not just that my voice won't work right as of yet, but also I still have these strange syntax problems. My thinking is crystal-clear, which only makes the discrepancy more noticeable. And where should I begin? After all, so much has happened! But the manner in which the shaikh listens compensates for a lot. I can tell from his nonverbal reactions which subjects he considers important. I can see from the brief questions he slips in that he understands what I wasn't even able to say.

What principally interests him is the several encounters with Muhammad (Peace be upon him). He asks me to describe them in detail and listens with closed eyes. The others sit in silence, even the little one is still. Gradually it gets easier for me to express myself. But the re-experiencing that goes along with this intense re-telling affects me strongly. Once again I start to tremble noticeably.

After two hours the shaikh decides that it's enough for tonight, or else I'll be overtaxed. "She has met her heart," he says to the others. Murat drives me back to my cell. The shaikh's wife had already prepared a bed for me, but for a less abrupt transition it seems better to me to spend one more night in the "solitude" I am now accustomed to. The word "loneliness," it occurs to me, is not in the least applicable, for whatever else I may have felt, I was never lonely. The PRESENCE one seeks in a *halvet* was always with me.

First Day Afterwards

At 7 a.m. I'm ready and waiting for Murat to pick me up. The little room isn't "my cell" anymore. Since the unsealing the atmosphere is completely different. I stand at the window with the curtains open for the first time. "My" kids aren't out playing yet, it's too early still. A few old men are coming back from the mosque.

While I'm standing there at the window I suddenly have the feeling that I'm sinking into the floor. It is so real that I am scared, I hold on tight to the windowsill and pick a spot on the wallpaper as a gauge to test if I'm really sinking. No, of course not! I have scarcely calmed myself down when it starts up again. Either I feel like I'm sinking into the floor or else that my bones are shrinking and I'm getting shorter. It's pretty unpleasant.

Since it doesn't stop, I sit down on my mattress and lean back against the wall. Where can Murat be? Now I feel myself pushing backwards on into the wall. Again it is so real that I stretch out my arms for something to hold onto and look back to convince myself that it's only an illusion. This observation, however, doesn't make it any better. I try walking up and down. Now it's as if my legs were of soft rubber: with every step I collapse. That, if anything, is even worse. I lie down again on my mattress and, perhaps because I already expect it now, the sinking-in doesn't concern me much. In my thoughts I do *zhikrs*, and now things get better. A feeling arises of rocking back and forth as if I were on an air mattress on a lake.

The comparison pleases me. As I abandon myself to the calm "motion of the waves," I wonder if the neurological effects of doing *zhikrs* have ever been investigated. Towards the end of the *halvet*, because of my need for intuitive approaches, I'm sure I must have spent from eight to ten hours a day doing them. This uninterrupted rhythmic back-and-forth motion of the head combined with the inner sound patterns must have its effect not only on the equilibrium centers but probably also on the entire central nervous system.[79]

Then, at quarter to eight, Murat is here. First he takes me to see Yusuf's wife, who cooked all my rice soups. She would like to share my first breakfast with me. Yusuf arrives, and I have no idea how to thank him for all his rescues. Both decline my thanks with the greatest firmness: helping somebody in a *halvet* means serving Allah. But Yusuf's wife asks me to come with her to see her mother, who is old and very sick. She's probably going to die soon and had asked to see me. I kiss her hand, and she also runs her hands along my body and then along hers.

We go to pick up the shaikh, and then we're on our way back to Europe. In the morning everything's tied up. Endless lines of cars are stalled heading toward the needle's eyes of the great bridges. Murat has bought several newspapers. "The latest on the Gulf War," he says, and hands me one. So there really is a war on. I try to read for a while and then give up. I notice that I haven't the slightest connection to it, I can't relate to it at all. "At least there's one person in the world who hasn't heard anything about the war," the shaikh says to me.

I was actually planning to fly back to Germany tomorrow. But now everything's going too fast for me. If I could just hear the *ezan* calling for a few more days before the West comes crowding in on me again. I'm going to try to change my reservation. "That won't be a problem," suggests the shaikh: "what with the war, practically all the flights are empty." He also considers a more gradual acclimatization to be a better idea.

I am to be "turned over" to my Turkish family in the shaikh's offices in the European part of the city. Many of the shaikh's circle of friends greet me happily, surprised that I'm "back so soon" in Istanbul. Only a few from the innermost circle know that I was in the

---

[79] See "The *Halvet* in Transcultural Comparison," p. 179ff, and "Accompanying Physiological Phenomena," p. 179ff.

halvet. I'm supposed to sit here for an hour and get used to people's comings and goings before my family can come to take me home.

"*Anneciğim*[80] don't say anything!" is all I can say as I see in my mother-in-law's eyes how horrified she is at my appearance. My brother-in-law handles me solicitously, as if I were an invalid. He takes my arm to support me! "I'm not sick!" I say, and notice that talking is still hard for me.

At my brother-in-law's place, in the fancy suburb of Yeşilyurt, I also get a shock when I look at my face in the mirror. Then I *really* get a shock when I step on the scale: ninety-seven pounds. . . . My mother-in-law complains about me, speaks ill of dervishes in general and the shaikh in particular and only then disappears into the kitchen to give Lütfiye, the maid, instructions for cooking my favorite dishes. I decide to go vanish in the bathtub. It seems I'm still sinking in whenever I try to sit still. During the bumpy car ride that wasn't a problem.

I consciously register the fact that my brother-in-law's bathroom, paneled in marble from top to bottom, is larger than my cell was. And with just a flick of the wrist, steaming hot bath water comes streaming in. Because of Istanbul's chronic water shortages, all the houses in Yeşilyurt have had their own cisterns for a long time.

My sister-in-law and my husband's aunt come to say hello to me. They all want to know what I have experienced. How can I explain it? For simplicity's sake, the conversation turns to my weight. Lütfiye brings me one delicacy after another. I have neither hunger nor appetite, but I do have the desire to gain weight again as fast as possible. Whenever I think I can't eat any more, I force myself to take at least one more bite.

A letter from my husband is handed to me. A sweet letter, full of concern, that makes me sad. So very different from the way Mehmet was when we took leave of each other. It's much more like the feelings I felt for him on that one night during my *halvet.*

---

[80] *Anneciğim:* my little mother.

102

Wouldn't it perhaps make sense for us to try again with each other? For twenty-six years, since I was fifteen, we've gone through life together, though more beside each other than with each other. . . Perhaps we see more clearly once the Atlantic is between us. If he comes here from America on vacation, or if I visit him there . . .

I get phone calls from my children, my parents, and friends. I assure them all that I'm just fine.

The Second Day Afterwards

It is necessary to exert yourself so much that you don't stay around, so that you realize what it is that will stay.

Hz. Mevlâna

In the dim light of dawn I lie awake. For the first time I feel miserable. How quickly worldly things regain the upper hand! Already my deepest experiences of the *halvet* seem almost unreal. Something Mina said on the telephone yesterday brought all my obsession right back. With all of its own special power and unique vividness, as if I had never been in the *halvet!* Will it torment me my whole life long, I wonder? Was it all for nothing?

Abdominal cramps have been keeping me awake for hours now. I have watery diarrhea, plus my period has started up again. Finally, the *ezan* sounds forth. Here in this lovely apartment on the Marmara Sea, one only hears a single muezzin, and even that one sounds muffled as if from a great distance. If I hadn't been awake already, I probably would have missed hearing him. I had intended to go downtown today to get presents for my family. Well, we'll see how it feels when I've been up a while.

Toward noon my mother-in-law insists on taking me to the hospital. My body can't keep the least bit of anything down, not even fluids anymore. Everything goes right through me, the cramps are increasing. In my haste to regain my normal weight I've accomplished exactly the opposite. My forced, indiscriminate eating of yesterday is taking its revenge. I refuse to go to the hospital, crawl back into bed. I'm not used to so many people or to daylight any more.

Later I come back and sit with the others. I see a fax from Mehmet lying there, my name leaps to my eyes. As I reach for it, my brother-in-law snatches it out of my hand. "That's from my husband," I say, amazed at his unaccustomed rudeness. "But it isn't for you," he says, "it's addressed to us." He puts the letter away.

When he goes out on business I ask my mother-in-law to give me the letter. When my brother-in-law comes back I thank him for his concern. He just didn't want me to find out in that particular way.

While I was in the *halvet*, Mehmet began a relationship with Lâle, a distant relative. Everything went very fast. She's going back with him to the States, they are to be married. "Lâle was a guest at your wedding," my mother-in-law say; "she was just a little girl then." I crawl back to bed, saying that I want to sleep.

Now "gift" is what we call anything that a person's imagination cannot grasp and that he cannot get through his head. For whatever is in a person's imaginative power is in line with his lofty striving and his capabilities. But God's gift is in line with God's capabilities. For that reason God's gift is what is worthy of God, not what is worthy of a person's imagination and striving. My gift is beyond all this !

Hz. Mevlâna

All of a sudden Muhammad (Peace be upon him) is with me again. Again this overwhelming presence strikes right to my heart, again there are tears upon tears, and finally tears of joy again. How could I ever be so dumb, how could I have doubted again, after everything that I now *know*? How could I have been so blind that I still didn't see the hand that holds the pen? Not to realize that so many of my prayers had been answered at once? "It isn't God's way to deal with each problem separately and by itself; *one* answer clarifies all questions, and the difficulty is solved. . . ."

How I had prayed that Mehmet might not be lonely in America! And that after the *halvet* my "inner *halvet*" might continue! And that

I might be given an opportunity to be of service by passing love and selflessness along! That my pain if necessary might persist until I "remembered" for certain. Truly, one answer "clarifies all questions, and the difficulty is solved." Lâle! Except *that* wasn't how I imagined it! Of course not! "For that reason, God's gift is what is worthy of God, not what is worthy of a person's imagination and striving!"

What unexpected riches I have been given just when I least expected! And at the same time I also have the direct experiential knowledge that I have not been abandoned, that the blessing of the *halvet* continues wherever I may be! "*Wherever you turn, there is Allah's face*" (Quran 2:115). "How should our religion leave someone alone, till it has brought him to the goal?" (FmF, p. 201). Oh, that I may prove worthy of this blessing!

> He has shown you all this so that you will be sure that other way-stations still lie before you.

> Hz. Mevlâna

For a long time I just lie there feeling the grace of deepest, most selfless love flooding through me, wave upon wave. "But His unlocking is not like His locking, for its kindness is indescribable. When I break free of my parts, that will be because of the endlessly subtle mercy and the delight over His unlocking and His incomparable opening-up." (FmF, p. 233).

Once I'm again in control of myself, I write a letter to Lâle. From my heart I wish her all the best with Mehmet. May they give each other what we weren't able to give.

The Fourth Day Afterwards

. . . and the morn as it softly breathes. . . .

Quran 81:18

This morning I still only weigh ninety-three pounds. But I feel so much better. The calm certainty that I am now permeated by·is so much more than I ever had. Yes, it will continue, step by step. "*Even thus, O men, are you bound to move onward from stage to stage. What, then, is amiss with them that they will not believe in the life to come?*" (Quran 84:19-20).

This afternoon the shaikh is expecting me one more time. He sends everyone else out. Then he speaks to me of the *silsile* whose *baraka* I felt so plainly during the *halvet*. He speaks of his own initiation, he talks about some of the shaikhs just before him. He tells how they lived and died. Then he shows me the objects that have been handed down along this living "chain" to him confirming him in this succession.

Finally he hands me a traditional object from this dervish brotherhood, which now comes down to me. "You have now met your heart," he says once again. Do I have any questions? Really only one: What can I do to keep the fruits of this grace, this direct knowledge, from slipping away again? To cherish and care for these little "plants of awareness"? To make them grow?

He explains about an old dervish exercise: "Every night before going to sleep, take a little time. Let the day that has just finished pass before your eyes. As you come to each of your actions, ask yourself if that was appropriate in light of your *halvet* knowledge. Thus, in the course of time, your actions will correspond more and more to this spirit, the veils will get thinner and thinner."

The object he gave me, which will fly West with me in my carry-on luggage tomorrow, will very concretely help me to "remember."

Bismillāhi'r-Raḥmāni'r-Raḥīm.
Have We not opened up thy heart,
and taken from thee the burden
that weighted so heavily on thy back?
And have We not raised thee high in dignity?
And, behold, with every hardship comes ease:
verily, with every hardship comes ease!
Hence when thou art free,
remain steadfast,
and unto thy Sustainer turn with love.

Sura 94: *Expansion*

وجود موسیقی انسانك خزینه عشقندن براسرار دهر

Commentary

Science is a dot, but the ignorant have made it many.

Hz. 'Ali[84]

One of the most distinctive features of the effort to illuminate the *halvet* experience from a Western scientific point of view is that a mosaic of the most various disciplines is required. The strength of the West, after all, lies in its reductionism, in its attempt to find, in each case, the "smallest underlying block of building-matter." Sufism, by contrast, has its source in the knowledge of the essential unity of all being. That explains why this section of commentary does not do what would be more in line with a scientific methodology: make strict divisions according to subject-matter or strictly separate personal experiences, comparisons with other experiences in the same direction, and analogies based on other religions or cultures or epochs, etc. The juxtaposition of two poems, one Western-reductionist and one Eastern-systematist, might clarify the difference in the mode of observation:

Flower in the crannied wall,
I pluck you out of the crannies,
I hold you here, root and all, in my hand,
Little flower but if I could understand
What you are, root and all, and all in all,
I should know what God and man is.

Tennyson

---

[84] Quoted according to Güvenç, p. 100. See "The Glossary of Islamic Names" for information on Hz. 'Ali and others cited below.

Listen to the reed and the tale it tells,
how it sings of separation:
"Ever since they cut me from the reed bed,
my wail has caused men and women to weep.
I want a heart torn open with longing
to share the pain of this love.
Whoever has been parted from his source
longs to return to that state of union."

Hz. Mevlâna[85]

Tennyson is aware of the fact that the totality of life is also manifested in one flower. But his way of trying to understand is to pluck
the flower and thus separate it from its context. He then analyzes
the half-dead plant "root and all," that is, he satisfies his intellectual
curiosity.[86] The first few lines of Hz. Mevlâna's *Mathnawi* put forward a similar theme. The difference is that this time the separation
becomes a catalyst for the realization of a greater, indivisible context. The same differences of perspective between West and East
become apparent in the mode of observing human existence in
general and the resulting assumptions of Western and Eastern developmental psychologists in particular. Lately there have been attempts by scientists working in an interdisciplinary mode to
compare the theoretical concepts of human growth and maturation
processes that underlie the Western and Eastern world views.

Wilber[87] arranged Western and Eastern forms of therapy on
various "levels of consciousness." These in turn depend on the
"boundary of identity" that people—unconsciously—draw for
themselves. In his five-level model, ego therapies and psycho-
analysis are on the second level, gestalt therapy, bioenergetic
analysis and Rogers work are on level three. The fourth "level of
consciousness" is represented by transpersonal therapies such as
the work of Maslow and Jung. Eastern methods such as Sufism,

---

[85] *The Mathnawi*, vol. I, 1-8, trans. Helminski in *Love is a Stranger*.
[86] Cf. Arasteh, *Toward Final Personality Integration*, p. 54.
[87] K. Wilber, *Wege vum Selbst—Östlicher und Westliche Ansätze zum Persönli-
chen*.

Taoism, forms of Buddhism and Hinduism, but also esoteric Christianity and Judaism, reside for him on the fifth and highest step. (In this model each level includes all the levels below it.)

Shafii juxtaposes the steps of development of the ego psychologies with those of Sufism. Both Freud's four stages and Erikson's eight stages are correlated with his own nine stages of Sufism with the result that they end up falling between levels two and six on the Sufi scale. (The first level of the Sufi scale consists of the more encompassing concept of the unconscious.) That means that at the point where, according to the Western ego psychologies, a person has achieved maturity and become "self-realized," for that person, in the Sufi view, the process of "truly becoming human" (*Insān al-Kāmil* [88]), that is, self-transcendence, is just beginning. The goal of Sufi psychotherapy, based on its systemic mode of observation, is accordingly not the Western ideal of autonomy, of independence, but the conscious acceptance of mutual dependence—i.e., "interdependence"—rather than independence." In the human maturation process, therefore, the Sufi tradition, instead of Western self-realization, strives for *transcendence of the self*.

The question suggests itself as to why the (more recent) Western psychologies, in their stage models of human development, stop where the process of "becoming human" in the Sufi view is just starting. Partly, no doubt, this is made inevitable by the above-mentioned differences in underlying world-view. A way of seeing that has been limited to the material plane at least since Descartes and Newton is necessarily more limited than one that presumes the immanent and transcendent oneness of all being. Besides that, in my opinion, there are also purely pragmatic reasons: the higher stages are never going to be reached by most people. That is shown in a Sufi "classic" of the thirteenth century. In 'Aṭṭār's *Conference of the Birds*, a giant swarm of birds sets out to find the mythical bird "Simurgh" (self-transcendence, direct realization of

---

[88] *Insān al-Kāmil*: a person in whom the potential capacities have become full reality, a perfected person.

111

the existential oneness of all being). At the end of the difficult journey through the "seven valleys" (seven stages of development), there are only thirty birds (in Persian, *simurgh*) left who reach the goal of "becoming whole," the level of the *Insān al-Kāmil*.

One of the familiar strengths of Western efficiency is its tendency to occupy itself principally with what is feasible. Why invest a lot of energy in something that only "thirty birds" will ever accomplish? But the same strength that makes possible miracles like organ transplantation is, from another viewpoint, a weakness, precisely because of its self-appointed limitation to what is materially graspable. When the higher levels of being human are not even available in a certain culture even in the form of a theoretical concept, they also can't really be aspired to. Existential meaninglessness then abounds.

Though attainable only for the few, the holistic concept of the *Insān al-Kāmil* can still be seen as an inspiring ideal. According to Shafii (p. 241):

> *Insān al-Kāmil* is a hope-inspiring ideal which encourages the best in humanity. It is the guiding light which can help human beings transcend the fragmentations of the past, dualities of the present, limitations of culture, and preoccupations with the self. Awareness of the potential for becoming an integrated human being and genuine endeavor on the Path of Reality, itself, stimulates psychological and spiritual integration. Although one may not reach the ideal, just being a traveler on the Path and having the goal in mind can be a source of continuous encouragement, development, and hope.

Or, as Hz. Mevlâna says:

> Just as a bird that tries to fly to heaven, although he never reaches heaven, still he distances himself from the earth more and more with each moment and flies higher than the other birds (FmF, p. 284).

Blood Sacrifice

Anthropological investigations show that the tradition of ritual blood sacrifice goes back to the beginnings of humanity. At first, almost everywhere, living people were sacrificed; later, animals took their place. In a thirteenth-century text, Ibn 'Arabi describes this using the example of Ibrahim, to whom it was permitted to sacrifice a sheep in place of his son Ismail:

> How should the ransom of a prophet come about through the slaughter of a sacrificial animal? And how should the bleating of a ram replace the ordered movements of a person? God the Magnificent declared the ram to be magnificent out of concern for us or for it, I don't know which consideration was uppermost. . . .
>
> Oh, if I could only know how the lowly individuality of a miserable ram can make its essence serve as a replacement for [a human being, who is] the Deputy of the Merciful One! (FaH, p. 36).

In many cultures, blood sacrifices were then completely replaced by symbolic rites. In the Catholic Mass, for example, the hosts and wine symbolize the eating and therefore the blood sacrifice of the body of Jesus.

In Islam this development has not taken place, ritual animal sacrifices are offered then as now. But that should not lead to the conclusion that only the concrete level exists. A basic principle of understanding Islam is that of simultaneous validity on various levels at once, at the very least on exoteric and esoteric levels.

The task of recognizing the existence of these various levels is made more difficult for the outsider by the fact that the same thing can represent all levels at once. Distinctions become recognizable only to the degree of the observer's own capacity for differentiation. Wilber[89] points to similar difficulties in the work of most modern anthropologists, who for example failed "to ask the crucial questions about the differentiation of the 'Great Mother' and the 'Great Goddess,' because they do not distinguish between sign and symbol, exoteric and esoteric, alteration and transformation."

For every religious rite, according to Wilber, can function as a *symbol*, thus bringing higher levels of reality into play that transcend the average mentality and reveal supraconscious impulses. Or else it functions simply as a *sign* and thus confirms and reinforces only the earthly plane of reality. Which of these functions rites are effective in depends largely "on the psychological state of the individual who confronts them and the understanding that he or she brings" (*Chakras*, p. 162).

The same lines of thought are clarified in the Quran, the Holy Scripture of Islam: "*He it is who has bestowed on thee from on high this divine writ, containing messages that are clear in and by themselves—and these are the essence of the divine writ—as well as others that are allegorical*" (3:7); "*And thus it is that God propounds parables unto men, so that they might bethink themselves of the truth.*" (14:25)

Here also it is pointed out that the interpretation of parables, that is, the esoteric contents, is not open to everybody: "*And so We propound these parables unto man: but none can grasp their innermost meaning save those who are aware of Us.*" (Quran 29:43). In the thirteenth- century Hz. Mevlâna clarified this issue as follows:

> The Quran, which in its endlessly multilayered beauty appears like a "double-sided brocade," is comparable to a woman's breast: the baby and the lover both take pleasure in it. Both pleasures are good and proper, the only difference is in the capacity for understanding, that is to say, in the level of development (FmF, p. 272).

---

[89] Ken. Wilber, "Gibt Es die Chakras Wirklich?" (Do The Chakras Really Exist?) in J. White, *Kundalini Energie* (Kundalini Energy), p. 163.

In the case of blood sacrifice, the Quran does not content itself with parables for the "knowing ones"; instead, it points explicitly to the non-material, transcendent level: *"But bear in mind: never does their flesh reach God, and neither does their blood: it is only your God-consciousness that reaches Him."* (Quran 22:37)

Now then, why is a *halvet*, a pathway to consciousness transformation, initiated with a blood sacrifice? In the anthropological view, ritual sacrifice symbolizes "the death of the separate ego to make possible the resurrection in Unity; that is, sacrifice the immortality of 'I' and discover the immortality of all being" (Wilber, in White, p. 169). As an initiatory rite, the *halvet* corresponds to the structure, "death, retreat, rebirth," which can be found in the form of similar rites in all traditional cultures.[90]

The necessity of "dying" as a prerequisite for transcendence finds expression in the well-known saying of the Prophet: "Die before you die."

One dies when, by Allah's will, one's borrowed time ends. One's material being—which is called life—ending at an appointed hour, loses all its character and qualities both good and bad, and nothing of him remains. In their place Allah comes to be. His self becomes Allah's self; his attributes become Allah's attributes.

That is what our Master, the Prophet of Allah (peace and blessings be upon him) meant when he said: "Die before dying."[91]

In the case of the *halvet* it is once again a ram that dies in place of a person, as in the example from the Quran of Ibrahim and Ismail. What dies in a person (ideally), namely *fana*, is the tight holding-on to individuality that keeps that person from having an actual experience (*baqa*) of the underlying unity of creation (*tauhīd, wahdat al wujūd*).

On the esoteric plane, blood sacrifice is at once a symbol of transformation and an auxiliary aid to transcendence. On the exoteric plane, it serves as a jumping-off point for exercising the Is-

---

[90] Cf. O. van der Hart, *Rituals in Psychotherapy*, pp. 39 ff.
[91] Ibn 'Arabi, *What the Seeker Needs*, p. 37.

lamic virtue of generosity by donating the meat to the poor. From a psychological perspective, the feeling of obligating oneself to undergo the rite of the *halvet* and the urgency of the proceedings are both strengthened by the drastic and irreversible character that the conscious killing of a living being has. As in observing any other such rites, it would also be inappropriate in this case to judge ritual sacrifice only according to its outward form, since the same outward form makes different statements according to the developmental state of the perceiver.

Observations on the Thesis of "Morphic Resonance"

It is only since becoming acquainted with Rupert Sheldrake's thesis of the "morphic field" and "morphic resonance" that I have had the vocabulary to make many aspects of the Sufi experience understandable to Western ways of seeing.[92] Over and above that, it provided me personally with plausible explanations for certain decisions that I made (for example, wearing a head covering during ritual prayer), decisions that appeared to be, not logically, but intuitively correct. What follows is my brief attempt to summarize these hypotheses so provoking from the viewpoint of current science.

Sheldrake's theses provide even non-mystics with at least cognitive access to the experience underlying all esoteric traditions, the experience of the absolute oneness of all being. Sheldrake himself declares that he has "nothing new to say, nothing that all the spiritual traditions have not said many times before."[93] His contribution, for Westerners, lies in making this "eternal knowledge" accessible to the testability requirements of the scientific method and

---

[92] Rupert Sheldrake, born in 1942, biologist, lives in London. He studied natural sciences at Cambridge and philosophy at Harvard. Upon his return to Cambridge he was named a fellow of Clare College and a research fellow of the Royal Society. There he researched the development of plants and the processes of aging and regeneration. In addition he has carried out research projects at the University of Malaysia and in Hyderabad, India. I thank Dr. Sheldrake for his conversations and correspondence concerning my *halvet* experience.

[93] Personal communication, 1990.

thereby also accessible to the "rational knowledge" that most people in industrial nations at first require.

Sheldrake starts with the assumption that there is such a thing as a "morphic field," similar to gravitational or electromagnetic fields. This can be understood as a "thought-field of nature" in which all the happenings of the universe are recorded, including thought forms and gestures. The brain and nervous system can be thought of as "receivers" for the information written down in the morphic fields. (This is analogous to a radio that produces no music of itself but functions as a receiver for the appropriate radio waves.) Transference or transmission of knowledge takes place through the process of "morphic resonance." It is a kind of passing-along across space and time that does not make use of either genetic inheritance or learning processes. Instead, an organism "hooks in" to the channels or grooves left by other members of the same species over the course of time. From this point of view, laws of nature are "habits" that have been so stabilized by constant repetition that we perceive them as "rules and regulations."

If one wishes to share a certain group's knowledge or experience, one must "get into resonance" with that group's "grooves" in the morphic field. The more often a process is repeated, the more distinct its grooves. So if one wishes, for example, to take part in a certain spiritual experience, it makes sense to turn to the most frequently practiced rituals of the tradition and carry them out as exactly as possible according to form. Any deviations, such as attempts to "modernize" ancient practices, disturb the resonance and thereby reduce the effectiveness. The more exactly the rituals correspond to their traditional forms, the more effectively one will have access to them.

Ibn 'Arabi repeatedly points out that it makes sense to preserve certain "worldly" (that is, tradition-bound) forms, regardless of the fact that a person's "level of realization" may already be that of the "oneness of all being":

> The Gnostics, on the other hand, who know the true state of affairs, give the appearance of rejecting these manifestations [idols], which

are objects of veneration; for their rank in the orders of knowledge is a reason for them *to fit in with the demands of the given situation.* . . . Furthermore, the "perfected person," irrespective of his knowledge about this question,[94] holds to the custom of praying facing the Holy City of Mecca *as regards the outward form.* . . . (FaH, p. 148, 64).

More simply and therefore more clearly the same thought is expressed by Hz. Mevlâna:

But the normal way is that everyone who reaches this position [of high spiritual development] devotes his life and works to striving and virtues. That is for the sake of making it possible for average people to rely on them and their words. For the average person's glance does not penetrate the interior; they see only the exterior, and since average people follow the exterior, then, using the exterior and its power to bless, they can find the way to the interior (FmF, p. 286).

In this way the framework is created that enhances the possibility of having certain kinds of experience. Sheldrake makes the underlying mechanism plainer with an analogy from the sciences:

[Morphic] fields embrace and include the individuals within them, as magnetic fields embrace and include the particles of iron which they organize into characteristic patterns. The individual insects are within the social morphic field, just as the iron particles are within the magnetic field. From this point of view, trying to understand the social morphic field from the basis of the behavior of isolated insects would be just as impossible as trying to understand the magnetic field by taking iron filings out of it and studying their mechanical properties in isolation. . . .

In a similar way, social morphic fields can be thought of as coordinating . . . all patterns of social organization. . . . The members of a traditional tribe for instance, are included within the social field

---

[94] That means that no one conception of faith can be considered the "one true" faith, for *God is too all-embracing and great to be grasped by any one system of belief to the exclusion of all others. For He says: "Wherever you turn, there is God's countenance"* (Quran 2:115).

of the tribe and the fields of its cultural patterns. These fields have a life of their own, and give the tribe its habitual patterns of organization, maintained by self-resonance with the tribe itself in the past. Thus the field of the tribe includes not just its living members, but its past members as well. And indeed, all over the world, the invisible presence of the ancestors in the life of the traditional social groups is explicitly recognized.[95]

The description just given is one possible way of imagining the influence of the long-dead saints of the various traditions as well as the influence of the entire chain of handing-down (*silsile*) that one is "linked into" through the initiatory agreement with a shaikh. Such a "link" can be seen as a deliberate "clicking into" a certain morphic field.

The idea of replicating certain practices in a manner as true to tradition as possible does not however mean that outward forms must likewise be kept unchanged in the course of a spiritual tradition's history. In Sufism, according to Shah, one can assume the opposite: experience shows that schooling institutions that maintain a rigid continuity of outer structures quickly turn into "empty shells," to "petrifications of once living processes":

> All such entities are temporary forms. When they have completed their effective lifespan, others take their place.
>
> The outward form or husk may, however, persist and contrive to perform social or other comparatively less significant functions. The inheritors of these forms seldom, if ever, realize that the entity is "organically dead."
>
> This is why almost the last place in which to seek the continuation of a transmission such as the one being discussed is in apparently well-established traditionalistic bodies.[96]

Shah considers these processes of disintegration to be natural:

> Were it possible to attain the object in a systematised way, the means to do so would have been enunciated and recorded many thousands of years ago: just as the laws of ordinary material stability

---

[95] Rupert Sheldrake, *The Rebirth of Nature,* p. 95 ff.
[96] Idries. Shah, *Learning How to Learn,* p. 223.

and performance are recorded and employed in physics or in applied arts.

Further, he regards this as one of the most important functions of spiritual teachers:

> This is the major perennial reason for the cyclic emergence of living teachers. It is they alone who can restore harmony and balance in circles and individuals which have sacrificed these things in the search for continuity and reassurance in the hope of stabilization.[97]

In a traditionally carried-out *halvet* every "inner" detail agrees with tradition as exactly as possible: rituals, reading material, food/fasting, structuring of time. . . . (By following the Islamic times of prayer, for example, not only is one brought into "morphic resonance" with the other people who have performed and are performing these prayers, but since the prayer times depend on the position of the sun, one is also brought into harmony with the larger rhythms of the cosmos.)

In the case of my schooling, the outer framework in accord with the considerations outlined by Shah above was flexibly adapted to the demands of Turkey's political development: an empty little apartment replaces a Sufi *tekke*. The offices (both inside and outside Turkey) of the shaikh who made possible my *halvet* experience are likewise not immediately recognizable to outsiders as Sufi institutions.

The complaint is often made about esoteric traditions that while they speak of the "underlying unity of all being" and the "one God," they nonetheless insist paradoxically as it would seem that their adepts follow the direction laid out by the teacher in question to the exclusion of all others. Why this exclusion of other religions, which are presumably of equal worth in the light of the "oneness of all being"? And why are seekers always warned against moving along several spiritual paths at once? (This is a widespread phenomenon among the seekers in the "New Age" movement, this so-called "guru-hopping.") Going by the explanatory model of mor-

---

[97] Ibid, p. 228.

phic resonance, however, this purity requirement common to the old traditions appears quite sensible: if access to direct experience, that is, to mystical experience, is based on principles of resonance, then a synthesis of dissimilar paths hampers or prevents the "sinking-in" to the existing "grooves" that make such an access possible.

Perhaps the experiences in all esoteric traditions that are perceived as visions should be understood as a sudden access to the "resonance" of past events. This would also explain why the visions always unfold in the metaphors, images and forms of expression of the respective traditions that gave rise to them regardless of the fact that the phenomena in question are obviously universal and therefore above all sectarianism. In an Islamic *halvet*, accordingly, an "archetypical" encounter with Muhammad (Peace be upon him) or Hz. Mevlâna is more to be expected than an appearance of Buddha, for example. Also, just the fact that descriptions of "encounters" with holy persons are found over and over in all spiritual traditions seems only to be expected in the light of "morphic resonance."

Perhaps the requirement—so hard to accept from the Western point of view—of "dissolving" into one's teacher (*fanā fi'sh-shaikh*), sometimes described as "spiritual osmosis," represents nothing more than a perfect "plugging in" to his "receiver mechanism," which facilitates greatly the student's ability to achieve "direct access." That could be the "shortcut" that is meant when one says that in Sufism "a journey of a thousand steps becomes a single step" with the help of a teacher.

Also, in this view, the subjectively perceived transition from the stage of *'ilm al-yaqīn* (rational knowledge) to *'ayn al-yaqīn* (sure inner knowledge) could consist in successfully "sinking in" to the "grooves," gaining access to the actual experiential dimension of what one had known only theoretically before.

The basic requirement of Sufism to acquire the virtues of trust and hope, from the viewpoint of morphic resonance, can be interpreted as a method of connecting to "positive" currents. If, on the other hand, one falls into the sins of hopelessness and doubt

("*Verily, none but people who deny the truth can ever lose hope of God's life-giving mercy.*" Quran 12:87), one is following in the tracks of all those who have ever practiced those non-virtues.[98] In Islam God has "ninety-nine Most Beautiful [known] Names," that is to say, attributes. Among them are names that from a Western viewpoint would not necessarily be understood as beautiful, like "The Taker-Away of Honor and Might" *(Al Muḍḍill)* or "The Imposer of Justice upon the Unjust" *(Al Muntaqim).*[99] Allah, immanent in all and transcending all, necessarily contains every kind of attribute, "good" and "bad" insofar as one judges on the dualistic basis of human thinking. The Quran, however (17:110), gives this direction: "*Say: 'Invoke God* [Allah], *or the Most Gracious [Ar Rahman]: by whichever name you invoke Him.'*" Notice, *Ar Rahman,* the Merciful, instead of *Al Muḍḍill,* for example, the Taker of Honor and Might. One could take the position that calling on a certain name that is a certain facet of the reality containing all facets enhances the "resonance" with that quality.[100] In that case, as it says in the well-known Quranic tradition, "God's mercy has precedence over His wrath."

Ibn 'Arabi repeatedly points out that God corresponds to the image that one makes of Him: "I am the way My servant thinks of Me" *(ḥadīth qudsi).* That means that one calls forth the things that one believes in:

---

[98] Even in Western psychology one speaks of the "self-fulfilling prophecy" (SFP), when circumstances arise that the patient fears or expects and seems to have thereby "conjured up." This can also happen in either a "positive" or "negative" direction. For that reason, in cognitively oriented therapeutic processes the patient's expectations are worked on. There is ample empirical evidence that this process exists. How it functions is explained in different ways—according to the respective orientations of different schools. Perhaps one further thesis should be added to those that have been advanced: the thesis of morphic resonance.

[99] My thanks to Prof. A. Falaturi for his correction of the inexact translations of these names current in much of the literature. Still each of the "Names" can be understood in more than one way. "The Misguider" and "The Avenger" are also commonly found.

[100] See also , "Methods of Sufi Schooling—*Zhikrs,*" p. 141ff.

But each person forms his conception of the Godhead only by creating it in his own interior; therefore, the religious conceptions of divinity only exist insofar as people make them [for themselves], and therefore such people see only their own selves and what they have created within themselves. . . . But whoever sets God loose from these limitations will never fail to recognize Him and is familiar with Him in every shape He may transform Himself into, and God gives him as much of His own self as suits the shape in which He manifests Himself, up to and including an infinite amount. For the forms of divine manifestation have no boundaries where a person must stop. . . . Consider then the different levels people are on regarding the knowledge of God! For this knowledge is identical with this ranking in the eyes of God on the day of resurrection (FaH, p. 179, 63, 71).

Thus Sheldrake's theses make possible a Western-scientific mode of observing many "common" esoteric experiences independently of any particular religious orientation. People whose mystical experiences have become the basis for "direct certainty" need no scientific explanations, for "there is a boundary drawn where reason must halt, while the mystic who achieves direct certainty through ecstatic experience may pass beyond" (Ibn 'Arabi, FaH, p. 162). Yet for all that, such rational attempts to understand are also sensible in the Islamic view, since the Quran calls on us to do scientific research. *(The signs are there in nature.)* The underlying premise is that the more things a person comes to realize through empirical investigation, the greater his realization of God will be; after all: "*In time We shall make them fully understand Our signs through what they perceive in the utmost horizons of the universe and within themselves.*" (Quran 41:53)

In addition, it is interesting to relate the thesis of morphic resonance with the respective conceptions of the unconscious that prevail in the psychology of Sufism and in Western psychology. Although Jung's concept of the "collective unconscious" goes beyond Freud's individual approach, it is still conceived with a human range of experience in mind. The mode of observation in Sufism *(waḥdat al wujūd)* is much more inclusive: it includes Jung's concept, but goes beyond human experiences of past, present and future. The unconscious forces also include those of the animal, vegetative and inorganic levels of being, in addition to human, spiritual and universal states. This approach is not in any way limited to fantasies, dreams, illusions and primitive forms of thought processes; it also includes the organic and psycho-spiritual relations between humanity and nature and thereby the universal reality *(al haqq)*.[101]

Sheldrake's theses are in harmony with Sufism even as regards transcending human realms of experience:

> In the human realm such a concept already exists in Jung's theory of the collective unconscious as an inherited collective memory. The hypothesis of morphic resonance enables the collective unconscious to be seen not just as a human phenomenon, but as an aspect of a far more general process by which habits are inherited throughout nature.

---

[101] Cf. Muhammad Shafii, *Freedom from the Self.*

The Person of the Teacher

The true teacher knocks down the idol that the student makes of him.

Hz. Mevlâna

On all paths of spiritual training known to me, the teacher is of central importance. He or she embodies the teaching as a living representation of the tradition. He or she helps the student to grow beyond the boundaries of self. Since each person can only, by definition, operate *inside* his or her current limits, outside intervention is indispensable to make the "breakthrough." My Teacher depicted this state of things with the following analogy: "You can give yourself first aid, putting a bandage on a wound. But you can't operate on yourself."

The fundamental changes that the path requires in the student's world-view and behavior resemble a major operation. The very personality features that the student holds the tightest to, with which he most strongly identifies himself on this level, are also the ones that prevent the student from fully becoming what he or she potentially is.[102] "It is necessary to make so great an effort that you are not left standing, in order that you may recognize what it is that will remain" (FmF, p. 311). Recent research into consciousness speaks of "being transformed to a supra-conscious state" which "the death of the separate ego makes possible." "The separate ego

---

[102] It is a commonly known fact of psychology that in most cases the kinds of actions that a patient carries out to overcome a problem are the very ones that maintain his or her symptoms.

must die, if one wishes to reach any form whatever of Being One" (Wilber, *Chakras*, p. 169).

This letting-go, this "dying before you die," as Muhammad (Peace be upon him) calls it, is a painful process that the student cannot put him- or herself through. Only an intimate relation to the teacher, one characterized by deep love and unconditional trust, creates the basis on which such a drastic process can proceed. Led on by this spiritual pact, two people start to share an intimacy that is aptly described by the Persian mystics as "*ham-dam*," literally "being of the same breath."[103]

To guide the student safely through this extremely critical time, the teacher must possess extraordinary qualities of character:

> The capacity to be cold, dispassionate, clinical in certain situations, and not to allow any subjective emotion to cloud their judgment, and to be able, if necessary, to maintain a cold or even callous face to the people they are teaching.[104]

My Teacher spoke of this requirement as "ruthlessness," to be distinguished from "cruelty" principally by the underlying intention.

The love and readiness to sacrifice for the student that is at the root of everything makes such an outward disposition seem paradoxical:

> Indeed, the hardest, most ungraspable direction of the master has its roots in his love for his pupil. . . . And the deeper the existential bond, the more the teacher will have no qualms about the way he deals with his pupil, including giving him or her signs and instructions that on the natural plane would have to remain incomprehensible: signs of his untiring readiness, his inventiveness and his courage. The validation for all this is the presence of the other dimension.[105]

---

[103] E. Vitray-Meyerovitch, *Rumi and Sufism*, p. 141.

[104] Omar Ali-Shah, *Sufism for Today*, p. 60.

[105] K. Graf Dürckheim, *Der Ruf nach dem Meister* (The Call to the Master), p. 62.

Without unconditional trust, a further requirement would be impossible: that of unconditional obedience. This sounds more authoritarian than it is. Both teacher and student freely follow the same overriding law, which the student, however, cannot yet recognize without help.

> The initiatory path also means obedience to the master, who as an embodiment of LIFE is the only and unconditional authority for him or her. To submit to this authority is an expression of the freedom that proceeds from the unhampered bonding to transcendence and grows along with it day by day (Dürckheim, p. 93).

Nor is the assumption made that teachers make no mistakes. They are human and therefore not infallible. Schimmel quotes Al Ghazali in this connection:

> Let him know that the gain he will derive from his master's error in case he should err will be greater than the gain he derives from his own correct opinion in case he should be right[106]

The master-student relationship described by Vitray-Meyerovitch as "spiritual osmosis" is of so great a depth and broadness of reach that even Hz. Mevlâna, one of the most respected Sufi masters of all time, repeatedly expressed his amazement of it:

> For example, Jesus has said: "I am amazed at the way a living thing can eat another living thing. . . ." The true [esoteric] meaning of these words is that the shaikh devours his disciple bones and all. I am amazed at such an uncommon work! (FmF, p. 306).

The living relationship with the master constitutes the external base conditions necessary for the student to be able to transform his or her way of seeing:

---

[106] Annemarie Schimmel, *Mystische Dimensionen des Islam*, p. 155. My heartfelt thanks to Prof. Annemarie Schimmel. Her deeply committed contribution on all levels helped make this project a reality. Encountering her after my *halvet* experience was an unexpected gift.

We also see that the disciple has given up the contents of his own spirit on account of the master's form. For every pupil who comes to the master must first give up the contents of his own spirit and calls upon the master. . . . Baha'eddin asked: "Doesn't he really give up the contents of his own spirit because of the contents of the master's spirit, not because of the master's form?" He answered, "It is not suitable for that to be so. If that were so, then both would be masters. At this point the disciple has hard work to do." (FmF, p. 167).

The master represents the "First Teacher," the prophet Muhammad (Peace be upon him), to whom all spiritual chains of transmission *(silsile)* in Sufism are traced back. Through the initiatory arrangement with the shaikh, the student is connected as a further link in the chain. The level of sacrifice required by connection with a teacher is very high. The Islamic and Christian traditions express these requirements in much the same terms: "What the shaikh demands of you is the same as what the masters of ancient times have demanded, namely that you give up wife and children, riches and high office" (FmF, p. 175), and: "If anyone comes to me and does not hate his father, mother, wife and children, brothers, sisters, and even his own life, he can't be my disciple" (Luke 14:26).

A contemporary Sufi author expresses it as follows:

> The moral character of dervishhood that emerges as the essence of Islamic Mysticism makes it necessary for those who join to give their lives for it.[107]

It is in the same sense that I understand the words with which Carlos Castaneda describes his experiences on an initiatory Native American path:

> In other words, the belief system I wanted to study swallowed me, and in order for me to proceed with my scrutiny I have to make an extraordinary daily payment, my life as a man in this world.[108]

---

[107] Oruç Güvenç, *The Dervish Path and Mevlana*, p. 110.

The masters acting in place of the Prophet vouchsafe security on what would otherwise be an extremely dangerous path:

> Know that the guide is Muhammad. Until someone comes to Muhammad, he cannot reach Us. . . . God's way is utterly frightful, impassable and covered with snow. He [Muhammad] was the first who risked his life, drove his horse onward, and cleared a path. Whoever goes on this path does so through his guidance and generosity. He discovered the way and put blazes all along the trail and set up wooden signs: 'Don't go this way and don't go that way!' . . . The whole Quran is there to make that clear. *In it are clear signs* (3:97); that means: upon these paths we have put roadsigns (FmF, p. 355, 356).

This relationship is not only considered lifelong, it extends beyond the death of the master. It remains "like the dust under the hooves of the horses." Hz. Mevlâna, who compared his teacher Shams with a celestial rider, said:

> The heavenly rider goes by, and the dust is stirred up under his horse's hooves. Now he is gone. But the dust he sent swirling is around us like a cloud even now. May your gaze be straight and bend neither left nor right. His dust is with us and he in the infinite.[109]

The truth of this, however, concerns the spiritual dimension of the master-student relationship. The intentions on the worldly plane are just the opposite:

> The teacher's role is to render himself superfluous to the learner, by helping him to escape from the toils of lesser ideas and of the shallow mind. Until that moment comes, like a guide to a path which is invisible to the learner, the teacher is followed with absolute trust.[110]

---

[108] C. Castaneda, *The Eagle's Gift*. New York 1982, p. 2. The question of the authenticity of Castaneda's accounts is not relevant in relation to the comparisons undertaken in this book.

[109] Quoted according to D. Kielce, *Sufismus*, p. 103.

[110] I. Shah, *Learning How to Learn*, p. 228.

Accompanying Physiological Phenomena

The physical experiences that had begun for me about six months before the *halvet*, which intensified themselves during the *zhikr* exercises, were not familiar to me either from traditional Sufi literature nor from conversations with friends on the Sufi path. Acquaintances interested in the esoteric made me aware of the "kundalini" literature.[111]

This Sanskrit concept is mostly translated as "latent energy reservoirs," "power at rest," or "psychosomatic energy center."[112] It is assumed that Kundalini is the primal energy underlying consciousness and its holistic transformations. The traditional symbol is a snake rolled up at the base of the spine. When this energy is "awakened," it climbs slowly up the spinal canal. In doing so, it opens up the centers of consciousness potential (chakras) lined up in its path, ending with the highest center in the brain. This marks the beginning of a process of enlightenment. When the energy has finished passing through, it is concentrated at the top of the skull. The process as a whole can be seen as a process of purification or achieving equilibrium (Sannella, in White, p. 283). The Kundalini energy remains active once it has been awakened, whether through personal initiation or otherwise (Davis, in White, 1990, p. 425). To what extent these experiences make themselves felt de-

---

[111] The exercises practiced by a number of dervishes under the name *Lata'if* ("subtle" or "delicate") are sometimes referred to in recent literature as "Sufi kundalini," since they can also lead to kinesthetic and visual perceptions. In my opinion, this analogy is not defensible—as such, the differences being more numerous than the similarities.

[112] Cf. J. White (ed.), *Kundalini Energie* (Kundalini Energy).

pends, however, on what the person in question makes of them (Radha, in White, 1990, p. 52).

In a subjective mode, these perceptions, which Gopi Krishna termed "the symptomatology of awakening," have been depicted in very different ways. The Max Planck Institute has carried out a biochemical study of Kundalini. In the experiential accounts, electric sensations, nervous excitements, inner lights and sudden twitches are spoken of, followed usually by a phase in which the symptoms appear in moderated form and the functioning of the central nervous system is obviously changed (Ferguson, in White, p. 276). Also very typical are feelings of vibrating or jiggling, tingling or itching, that spread across the body in a particular pattern (Sannella, in White, p. 287).

Swellings and hardenings of the lower abdomen are also described in a number of cases: "He sensed an unusual fullness in his lower body and, later, a burning sensation in his body that lasted several hours. To his amazement he ascertained that his waist size had increased six inches, without his having gained weight."[113]

> When a practitioner meditates and his kundalinī is activated in the astral dimension or in the dimension of *ki*-energy,[114] his body or his spinal cord will become inexplicably hard. It will be accompanied by a sensation of disharmony at the base of the spine or in the perineum, signaled by something of a tingling sensation . . . a strange, hot sensation much like an electric vibration.[115]

In the Shinto tradition this palpable physiological change is in fact used as an indicator of the level of spiritual awakening:

> As the meditational experience deepens, the practitioner's soft abdomen will gradually harden as a result of the repeated gathering of *ki*-energy in the area of *tanden*. This is especially true when the *kundalinī* is awakened along with the *svādhṣthāna chakra*. An

---

[113] Case study from L. Sannella, *Kundalini-Erfahrung und die neuen Wissenschaften* (Kundalini Experience and the New Sciences), p. 60.

[114] *Ki* or *chi* is the life principle, corresponding to the Sanskrit concept of *prana* (breath).

[115] Motoyama, *Toward a Superconsciousness*, p. 77.

objective test for gauging the extent of a practitioner's progress in meditation practice is, therefore, to determine how hard or tense his abdomen has become. If he has a soft abdomen and the "blood" rushes to his head, he will be unable to concentrate no matter how long and hard he tries.[116]

The emotional states that go along with the awakening of the Kundalini are depicted as ranging from tormented to ecstatic. The following descriptions are representative:

- A blissful, inexpressible experience, an electric delight, streaming through the whole body (Goyeche, in White, p. 280f)
- A feeling of supernatural peace and supernatural calm (Krishna, in White, p. 288)
- Powerful waves of deep ecstasy, spontaneous joy and indescribable peace. The whole body seems flooded with happiness streaming down, with even the countless blood cells dancing (Chaudhuri, in White, p. 59)
- Seen subjectively, it was as if an electric charge of nervous energy raced up my left leg, passed my genitals and then dispersed in my lower back. It was a terrible experience. I knew intuitively that I had unleashed this current through my intense prayer, but I had no idea how to stop it (McCleave, in White, p. 372)
- The phase of adapting to the higher power, [with its] inner conflicts and unbalanced spiritual states, is often very hurtful and painful. That is one of the reasons why reaching a higher consciousness has been compared with a rebirth (Krishna, in White, pp. 224, 226).

White (p. 138) points out, however, that the awakening of the Kundalini does not *in itself* constitute a traumatic or magnificently theatrical event. Rather, the spectacular inner experiences that are so frequently reported are themselves vanishing, transitory events. They count as peaks but not plateaus of human consciousness. In someone whose "enlightenment quotient" is high from birth, such phenomena might well be completely passed over. The unfolding of a higher consciousness proceeds instead "without fireworks."

---

[116] Ibid, p. 43.

The phase in which the organism functions at an accelerated rate under the pressure of the newly released energy can last months or years. In successful cases a transformation of consciousness sets in (Krishna, in White, p. 220). While Krishna postulates that an enlightened consciousness is never possible without biological transformation, Pandit proceeds on the opposite assumption, namely that first a transformation of consciousness takes place which is then responsible for a subsequent alteration in the organism (Pandit, in White, p. 415).[117]

If the Kundalini power is deliberately awakened in the framework of a spiritual training, then certain exercises are prescribed varying with the different traditions: mantra meditations, intensive prayer, or *kriyas*.

The following description of *kriyas* could just as well be a description of Islamic ritual prayer or *zhikr* meditation:[118] According to Khalsa et al. (White, pp. 237, 238), a *kriya* represents a sequence of physical and mental activities that work upon body, reason and spirit all at once. This sequence of activities can consist of all meditation exercises, all physical exercises, or both together, but the combination must fully arouse all the systems that have any importance for a given consciousness transformation. In the case of the *kriyas*, the precise admixture is codified with extreme subtlety and the interplay of the various energy systems is consciously steered.

> There are *kriyas* for every realm of human potential, each with its own effect. The ancient creators of the *kriyas* did not have "just one" mystic state in mind: one must take care not to assume that there is only one state called "meditation."

Some who experience this awakening without spiritual instruction are "sent into shock, believing that mental illness, a nervous disorder or evil spirits are involved" (Desai, in White, p. 61). Be-

---

[117] On this question, see also, "The Authenticity of Mystic Experience," p. 171ff.

[118] Cf. "Methods of Sufi Schooling," p. 141ff.

sides competent guidance and the practice of self-discipline, mental control and purification (Bailey, in White, p. 413), various other measures are recommended to further this process as securely as possible: proper nourishment, regular sleep, rest, loving and harmonious relations with other people (Hopman, in White, p. 318). Sannella urges that the processes be allowed to happen and not be held under control. If the meditator finds that the experience is too violent, Sannella's advice is to stop the meditation exercises and engage in vigorous physical activity (Sannella, in White, p. 288). One can't help noticing that most of the above-mentioned cushioning measures are diametrically opposed to the requirements of an Islamic *halvet*. That could explain why the Kundalini-like processes that I experienced proceeded with considerable intensity.

Krishna, who actively campaigns for a scientific investigation of the Kundalini phenomenon, makes the assumption that given the underlying unity of spiritual experience, the sensations that go along with the awakening of the Kundalini would also have to present themselves to a greater or lesser degree of intensity, in the case of "mystics, Sufis and Taoists." My personal experience of Kundalini-like symptoms which appeared as an accompanying phenomenon in the course of traditional Sufi practices without my being familiar then with the sources here quoted might confirm this assumption.

The literature in general is full of warnings against awakening the Kundalini energy prematurely and without the protective framework of the discipline of spiritual instruction:

> *Don't* meditate with the purpose of awakening Kundalini, because you will probably hurt yourself in the process. It is in fact possible to force it ahead of time, but also extremely dangerous. Strive instead to love more and understand more. Strive to purify your character and train your mind through selfless service, challenging studies and spiritual training. Do this, and Kundalini will awake gently, by itself, and without the unhealthful consequences that one meets with ever more frequently" (White, p. 410).

Scientific Approaches

Recently there have been various attempts to find explanations in the natural sciences for the Kundalini symptomatology. Laboratory investigations of the Kundalini phenomenon are being carried out in various parts of the world. Glueck of the Hartford Institute of Living in Hartford, Connecticut presumes, for example, that the constant repetition of the same sound that occurs in mantra meditation can produce a resonance effect in a person's limbic system. Supposedly, this process finally leads to the appearance of sensations of an electric nature that spread through the head and can become rhythmic and sometimes almost convulsive or orgasmic (quoted according to Ferguson, in White, p. 277).

Bentove (White, p. 291ff) postulated that in the aorta of a person in a deep meditative state, a standing wave is formed that is reflected in a rhythmic micro-movement of the body. The outflow of blood from the heart sets the bodily mass of a sitting, meditative person in motion and causes it to vibrate at its natural frequency. As it moves up and down, the skull sets the brain in motion. In the process, sound-waves are produced and eventually electrical waves also, which propagate themselves inside the skull. This wandering stimulus is responsible for the physical effects of the "awakened Kundalini." On the last part of its journey it passes through a region where a pleasure center is located (pleasure centers are the *gyrus cinguli*, the lateral hypothalamus, regions of the hippocampus, and the amygdala). When the pleasure center is stimulated, the meditating person experiences a state of ecstasy. It can take years of systematic meditation to reach this state; on the other hand, in some individuals it can arise spontaneously. Bentov's observations have shown that these mechanisms can be unleashed experimentally in the laboratory by certain mechanical vibrations, electromagnetic waves or sounds.

Peck, a physicist occupied with the electrical conductivity of ionized media, bases his observation of the Kundalini phenomenon on the theory that the electrical conductivity of the nervous system is altered by certain stimuli and that the alteration makes the nervous system more productive, more sensitive and easier to control (White, p. 278).

In my opinion, recent discoveries in endocrinology are also related to the Kundalini phenomenon. The pituitary hormones, endorphin and encephalin, which occur naturally in the body, are opiates, that is, substances that display effects like those of morphine or heroin. The controlling functions of these hormones include the modulation of stress, pain, moods, sexuality and the basic processes of learning and remembering (cf. Davis, in White).

Rossi[119] goes on the assumption that these hormones can be affected by psychological modulation and hypnotherapeutic intervention, since many of their multiple functions are transmitted directly or indirectly through the limbic-hypothalamic-pituitary system. In my opinion, what goes for hypnotically induced trances can also be assumed for trance states resulting from the practices of various spiritual traditions (not that spiritual-ecstatic states and states induced by hypnosis are to be equated). Here, perhaps is a physiological correlation[120] with the euphoric "states of bliss" that go with the awakening of the Kundalini.

Laboratory experiments on the "neurophysiology of religious trances"[121] carried out at the University of Munich seem to bear this out. Among other findings, the test subjects demonstrated an increase in beta-endorphin, which continued after the session and "is responsible for the intense euphoria after the ecstasy." Furthermore, the EEGs of the "religious trance" did not show the alpha

---

[119] E. Rossi, *Die Psychobiologie der Seele-Körper-Heilung* (Psychobiology of Mind-Body Healing), p. 173.

[120] In the Western literature, formulations like "underlying physiological processes" are customary. However, "underlying" implies a causality that is not scientifically proven and is unacceptable from the spiritual view of the existential oneness of body and soul (*waḥdat al wujūd*). In my opinion, one would do better to assume a correlation—that is, that both variables, for example, depend on a third, rather than being the causes of each other.

[121] F. Goodman, *Ekstase, Besessenheit, Dämonen—Die geheimnisvolle Seite der Religion* (Ecstasy, Possession, Demons—the Secretive Side of Religion), p. 39.

waves so often related to altered states of consciousness, but predominantly theta waves instead.

An oft-mentioned dimension of Kundalini awakening are the extreme mood swings that the affected persons are exposed to. That too can be set in the context of recent insights from endocrinology and biophysiological hypnotic research:

> The evidence of the central role played by the limbic-hypothalamic system and by endorphin and encephalin in a majority of psychological processes and moodswings is by now quite imposing. For example, the demonstration of the existence of numerous neuropeptide receptors in the brain permits us to conclude that structures related to the limbic system (for example, the amygdala and the *gyrus cinguli*) are regions in which, in all probability, moods are biochemically altered (Rossi, *Psychobiologie*, p. 244).

The histological and anatomical basis of the observed physiological changes seems to be just as unclear as ever. The most frequent assumptions involve a change in the central nervous system (cf. Glueck, Bentov, and Peck in White). Other factors, however, could come into question as well—including the autonomic nervous system,[122] the body's electromagnetic field which, as measured in the connective tissue, forms the physiological basis for the meridians[123] or the neuropeptide system[124] (cf. Rossi).

These new methods of neuropeptide research have made it necessary to expand the boundaries of the limbic system to include the modulation of sensory information. Pert (as quoted by Rossi, p. 244) expresses that as follows:

> The rear horn of the spinal cord of mammals . . . is furnished with practically all neuropeptide receptors. Although it has not been previously looked on as part of the limbic system, the neuropeptide

---

[122] K. Ring, *The Omega Project*.

[123] H. Motoyama and R. Brown, *Chakra Physiologie* (Chakra Psychology).

[124] Working with a completely new understanding of mind-body communication, neurobiological research has grouped the autonomic nervous system, the endocrine system and the immune system together under the concept of the "neuropeptide system."

receptors here, as well as at other sensory waystations, can filter incoming sensory information. . . .

In this quest for the origins of the evolution of the neuropeptide system, Roth *et al.* have offered evidence

> that it is older than the central nervous system, the vegetative nervous system and the endocrine system; it is the communication method used by one-celled life forms, plants and lower animal forms. Since nature tends to preserve her systems, it becomes clear that the neuropeptides are a deeper and more universal system of exchanging information between mind and body than the central nervous system is (quoted according to Rossi, p. 262).

The Physiology of Hallucinations

The location of the neuropeptide receptors at the most important waystations in the central nervous system, according to Rossi (*Psychobiologie*, p. 245), strongly suggests the inference that they play an important role in the psychobiological mechanisms of hypnotically induced illusions and hallucinations:

> The neuropeptides, therefore, are a previously unknown form of information exchange between mind and body that is quite possibly the basis of many hypnotherapeutic and psychosocial reactions. . . . From a higher point of view, the neuropeptide system is possibly also the basis of the folk-medicine, shamanic and spiritual forms of healing that have become fashionable in our time under the heading of "holistic medicine" (p. 262).

It is also possible that the neuropeptide system is also the carrier of the bodily changes that go along with consciousness expansion instead of the central nervous system, which many authors presume to be the seat of biological transformation.

The illusions and hallucinations of the hypnotic trance, in my opinion, could have a correlation—on another level, to be sure—in the visions occurring in trances induced by spiritual practices, that is, they might be related to the same physiological processes. However, such considerations are purely speculative. Interdisciplinary investigations in such traditionally widely-separated areas as neurology, molecular genetics, biology, psychology, religion, energetic medicine and cultural anthropology are requisite before any more concrete statements can be made.

Methods of Sufi Schooling

This ritual prayer is not ordained for the purpose of making you stand, bow and throw yourselves down all day long; rather, the purpose is that the spiritual state made visible in the prayer should be with you always. . . .

Hz. Mevlâna (FmF, p. 284)

Various dervish orders have developed differing methods of instruction in the course of time. At the root of them are the common denominators of ritual prayer and *zhikrs*,[125] mantra-like invocations. Because of their central importance for the Sufi path in general and for a *halvet* in particular, a more detailed description of these practices follows.

Ritual Prayer

The ritual prayer is one of the so-called "five pillars of Islam," that is, one of the five duties incumbent on every Moslem.[126] It is con-

___

[125] In the languages of the Islamic world there are different expressions for "praying." Turkish, for example, distinguishes between *namāz kilmak*: ritual prayer, *du'ā etmek*: prayer of petition, *zhikr*: invocational prayer of mindfulness, and *sema*: danced prayer, the mystic round.

[126] In the Sufi orders in the West this matter is viewed differently in some cases. Sheikh Moinuddin al Chishtiyya writes in this connection: "Unfortunately, there are some pseudo-Sufis in the West who foolishly suppose that the *salat* [Arabic for "ritual prayer"] isn't necessary. They say—it is very strange—that ritual actions like the *salat* are mere rituals, which the true spiritual seeker doesn't need. These far-afield people mention Ibn 'Arabi (r.a.) [May Allah be pleased with him], Mevlâna Rumi (r.a.) Imam al-Ghasali (r.a.) and Mansur al-Hallaj (r.a.), as examples of 'truly liberated and free-

sidered the "first and last step," union with all humanity and God. For the Sufi, however, it is not an end in itself, only the basis to which other practices of "getting closer" are added, till finally the dervish's whole being is "drenched" in mindfulness of God:

> If someone carries out his prayers with his whole heart, when he treads the path of God, at first he will observe the five prescribed prayers for a while; then later he will add more and more others, on up to infinity (FmF, p. 172).

The idea is not to circumvent the outer form of Islam, but, on the contrary, to deepen it.

> Led astray by certain poetic expressions of later Persian poets, or else under the influence of wandering dervishes who were anything but true to the law, Europeans have often considered the Sufis to be representatives of a movement that has freed itself completely from the legal prescriptions of Islam and is no longer concerned with belief or unbelief. Thus the word Sufi, in the West, has often become a synonym for 'freethinker.' That, however, is not at all correct (Schimmel, p. 158).

According to one tradition, when one is at prayer, Allah "lifts the veils, opens the gates of the invisible *(kashf)*, so that His servant is standing in front of Him. The prayer creates a secret connection between the one praying and the One prayed to" and serves as a "threshold at the entrance to God's reality" *(al-haqiqat),* the goal of the Sufi path. The result of these efforts is described by Hz. Mevlâna (FmF, p. 302) in relation to the Quran in such a way that the practice of *zhikr*s is already implied:

> In every state the core of his heart is occupied with God, and the outer occupation does not get in the way of the perfected person's inner occupation. As God the Exalted says: *"Men not kept by commerce or trade from the remembrance of God"* (24:37).

---

thinking Sufis.' The truth is that the great men just named were the most ardent and upright followers of the *salat*." A. Moinuddin, *Die Heilkunst der Sufis* (Healing Arts of the Sufis), p. 150.

The question as to what is so important about this ritual can be answered on several levels. From the Western viewpoint it is sometimes described, not very respectfully, as "spiritual gymnastics"[127] on the basis of the outward succession of standing, bowing, prostration, and kneeling. And in fact that is one of its functions. The movements are even, flowing and easy: muscles, joints, and spine are exercised five times a day; inner organs are stimulated; the brain is richly supplied with blood through the repeated bowings; and much more. Practicing Muslims usually remain limber and connected with the earth on into a mature old age. This succession of bodily states forms the outer framework in which the inner dimensions can unfold.

The prayer has its beginning in the preceding ritual washing (*wudu, ghusl*). Here also two levels (at least) are distinguishable: Washing with water leads to outer cleanliness. If no water is available, the "washing" can also be performed with sand (*tayammum*)—so the procedure deliberately goes beyond hygienic measures and reminds a person to be "washed" in the sense of "purified" when standing before the Creator. Next there is a conscious turning toward Mecca (*qibla*) and a "declaration of intention" *(niyet),* which once more brings the purpose of the ritual into consciousness and without which the prayer would not be valid. (From the psychological point of view, such preparatory measures belong in the category of "self-obligating aspects" which enhance inner involvement and focus attention.)

---

[127] The discrepancy between Eastern and Western points of view in this regard is made very plain by Asad: "And in fact people of other religions, who are accustomed to a careful separation of the 'spiritual' and the 'physical,' have a lot of trouble understanding that in the unskimmed milk of Islam these two components, despite differences in their respective natures, go along with each other and are expressed together in perfect harmony. In other words, Islamic prayer is composed of spiritual concentration and physical movements, because human life itself has the same composition and because we must approach God using the totality of the capabilities He has lent us." M. Asad, *Vom Geist des Islam* (About the Spirit of Islam), p. 22.

The ritual prayer symbolizes the unity of body, mind, and soul and signals an inseparable co-working of all these levels. It is as all-embracing as Islam is in its understanding of itself. Even the various bodily positions recall the basic assumption of Islam, the existential oneness of all beings *(tauḥid)*. The prostration *(sajde)*, with the forehead touching the ground, emphasizes the head or cognition and thus symbolizes the domain of human existence. In this position the heart is positioned higher than the brain. Blood flows "from heart to head" and thus recalls the basic premise of Sufism, the harmonizing of heart and intellect. This position is assigned the Arabic letter "mim":

The bow at the waist symbolizes animal life and is expressed with the letter "dal":

The upright standing position *(qiyam)*, the position of being "rooted in the earth," symbolizes vegetative life in close connection with the mineral kingdom.[128] This is expressed by the first letter of the Arabic alphabet, "alif":

(These three letters *alif, dal* and *mim* compose the word "Adam," the name of the first created human being and first prophet of Islam.) The course of the prayer runs through all these stages of being, a reminder that creation is One, that humanity and the earth are One.[129]

The times of prayer are correlated with cyclical cosmic circumstances and bring humanity into accord with the larger natural rhythms of the universe: with the motion of planets, and with seasonal and geographic circumstances.

---

[128] In some traditions the symbolisms of *saijde* and *qiyam* are interchanged.

[129] In the Islamic view, humanity is not supposed to "subjugate" the earth at all. On the contrary, each person has been given a "noble stewardship," that is, he or she possesses nothing but manages the consignment of creation entrusted to him or her.

The text recited in the ritual prayer begins with the declaration *"Allahu akbar"* (God is most great). It ends with a greeting of peace and blessings for the Prophet (Peace be upon him), a greeting for "ourselves and you" (that is, for Muslims and non-Muslims), and finally with a special greeting to the two "recording angels" who "stand behind the praying person's shoulders."

Ibn ʿArabi (FaH, p. 176) offered the following illumination of this ritual obligation:

> Muhammad, you see, has said, in a well-known *ḥadīth*, "And in prayer was placed the gladness of my eyes." For prayer is a very real form of vision, for the reason that it is a secret dialogue between God and His servant, as it also says in the Quran (2:147): *"Therefore keep Me in mind, that I may keep you in mind."* This, then is a ritual transaction, divided in half between God and His servant; one half belongs to God and the other to His servant, as the authentic tradition speaks of God as having said: "The prayer is divided in half between Me and My servant; one half belongs to Me and the other to My servant. What belongs to My servant is what he asks for. . . ." Consider then the imposing rank that prayer holds and how high up it lifts the one who prays!

When a person is totally involved, when he or she is really putting "body and soul" into it, deep states of immersion arise. (A well-known Sufi tale tells of a man who underwent a necessary but much-feared amputation of a limb during the ritual prayer without noticing it at all.) This total inner involvement, which is achieved in the course of time if at all, leads to the direct subjectively perceptible effect that makes it possible for the worshiper to replicate for him- or herself everything that is said theoretically about this "pillar of Islam":

> But whoever in prayer is unable to reach the level of real-live vision has not yet reached its highest goal, and the gladness of his eyes is not in it (Ibn ʿArabi , FaH, p. 176).

Or, in the words of Hz. Mevlâna:

> The [Prophet's] words, "Two sections of prayer are better than the world and everything in it," are not for everyone. It is correct only

for the person for whom it would be more important than the world and everything in it if two sections of prayer got away from him (FmF, p. 74).

Zhikr

Anyone who has ever experienced such a rhythmic *zhikr* with its accelerating tempo and the shortening of the words till only a kind of intense sighing remains knows that even an outside observer can easily be carried away by the power of the experience.[130]

The practice of *zhikrs* can be understood as the "heart" of Sufism: "heart," because it is the central exercise for reaching the goal on the path, the goal of intuitively perceiving the oneness of all being, and "heart," in the sense of Sufi terminology, as being the "organ of recognition" of God's reality. Furthermore, it is absolutely the core exercise of a traditional *halvet.* This fact is expressed in the title of a commentary by Abdul Karim Jili (fourteenth century) on Ibn ʿArabi 's treatment of the *halvet*: "The Unveiling of the Secrets that are Revealed to Those Persons who are Given to the Practice of the *Zhikr.*"

It is also in this light that Sufis understand the Quran verse 29:45: *"Convey unto others what of this divine writ has been revealed unto thee, and be constant in prayer [salat]; for, behold, prayer restrains man from loathsome deeds and from all that runs counter to reason; and remembrance of God [zhikr] is indeed the greatest good. And God knows all that you do."*

These practices, also characterized in a statement by the Prophet (Peace be upon him) as "keys to the gates of realization," go directly back to the Quran: *"Remember God with unceasing remembrance."* (Quran 33:41) The exhortation to approach the Creator through *zhikrs*, that is, "remembering" and "being mindful," runs like a scarlet thread through the holy scriptures of Islam. This word is used in the vocabulary of the Quran when the revelation of

---

[130] Schimmel, p. 250.

higher forms of adoration is concerned.[131] It is also so used, among other instances, in the Quran verse, "*So remember Me, and I will remember you*" (2:152), which, for the Sufis along with the verse, "*He loves them and they love Him*" (5:54), expresses with particular clarity their ardent and intimate relation to Allah, the "Beloved," the "Friend." Both verses express the idea that the original invocation comes from the Creator, not from humanity:

> *Zhikr* is a light whose origin is in the divine and whose purity draws the Sufi heart onward to the Beloved. [132]

Kalabadhi (d. ca. 996) traces the *zhikr* right back to the "primal contract":

> Humanity heard its first *zhikr* when God addressed it with the words: *alastu birabbikum* (Am I not your Lord?). This *zhikr* was locked in their hearts, just as the fact itself was locked in their intellect. As they heard the Sufi *zhikr*, the secret things were shown forth from their hearts again (quoted according to Schimmel, p. 244).

The outward execution of this specifically Sufi form of invocation varies from one *tariqat* (Sufi order) to another but is of central importance in all of them. *Zhikr* can be carried out alone or in groups; aloud or internally (*zhikr* of the heart); while sitting, standing or turning around. Always it is a combination of sound (external or internal), concentration, breathing, and movement. As in the ritual prayer, a person surrenders his or her totality to this holy proceeding. And just as in the case of the ritual prayer, the effect unfolds only gradually. An ancient precept says: "At first you pretend to do the *zhikr*, then you do the *zhikr*, finally, the *zhikr* does you." In the process, the "heart is awakened" or—according to a saying by the Prophet (Peace be upon him) "polished[133]"—which is

---

[131] For example, in Suras 2:152, 3:41, 4:103, 7:205, 13:28, 18:24, 18:28, 20:14, 23:39, 28:13, 29:45, 33:35, 33:41, 37:75, 53:29, 62:10, 73:8, 76:25.

[132] Ruzbihan, d. 1209 in Shiraz.

[133] "There are ways and means of polishing everything. *Zhikrs* are what removes the rust from the heart."

followed by the "happy state in which all booklearning is no longer useful" (Moinuddin).

What is recited consists of holy formulas—for example, the first part of the profession of faith, "*La ilāha il Āllāh*"—or selected "Most Beautiful Names" of Allah. The head (in the standing position, this goes for the whole body) moves rhythmically from right to left, then later back and forth. The combination of sound and movement gives rise to specific breathing patterns, which in some *tariqats* are consciously intensified. For example, the emphasis can be placed on the exhalation. This can lead to hyperventilation, which may be accompanied by convulsive twitching and partial catalepsy. These phenomena are neither sought after nor avoided. If they appear, they are interpreted in some *tariqats* as special signs of grace.

According to Schimmel:

> ... in performing a *zhikr* based on one of the names of God, the wisdom of the mystic leader must be shown to a particular degree, because it is his responsibility to instruct and carefully watch over the pupil, lest the pupil be exposed to serious mental and psychic dangers. The rules for use of these names of God have been worked out by the Sufis in painstaking detail. The name *Al-Fa'iq*, "the Overwhelming One," [for example,] should never be used by a beginner, but only by a high-ranking gnostic. The wrong use of a name of God can have serious consequences for the person affected or those close to him or her, which can even be displayed in the form of physical symptoms, as I know from the personal experience of friends (p. 252).[134]

---

[134] Cf. "Observations on the Thesis of Morphic Resonance," p. 117ff, and "The Physiological Dimension," p. 149ff.

The Physiological Dimension

The question arises as to what physiological processes are stimulated by Sufi practices and to what extent these practices can have transforming effects on consciousness.

It is only very recently that Western scientists have come to investigate the neurophysiological effects of movement, breathing rhythm and sound patterns. Brain research proceeds on the assumption, which it shares with the Sufi tradition[135] and the *kriya* teachings of the Far East, that certain movement sequences go along with specific states of consciousness.

> Now since structures in the brain where feeling and thinking take place are very close to the motor regions of the cerebral cortex, and since stimuli and impulses in the brain tend to spread out and spill over into neighboring networks (a process called diffusion), a drastic change in the motor region will have parallel effects on thinking and feeling. . . . Posture, improved circulation and breathing have an effect on the brain that is not to be underestimated.[136]

In the course of ethnopsychological research it has been possible to demonstrate that certain bodily positions call forth specific altered states of consciousness (Goodman, p. 93). These consciousness-influencing conditions are valid in relation to ritual prayer and *zhikrs* in general and for the circumstances of a *halvet* to an intensified degree. There could be a physiological explanation here for the spiritual development or consciousness expansion that in the Islamic view is stimulated by these exercises.

---

[135] On the subject of the physical-mental-psychic effects of the various positions, see Moinuddin, *Heilkunst*, pp. 138-143.

[136] J. Holler, *Das neue Gehirn* (The New Brain), pp. 160, 27.

Neurophysiological Effects of Bodily Movements

Adults predominantly assume a sitting or standing position. Children, by contrast, run and jump and turn cartwheels and somersaults. . . . That has an influence on the inner ear and thereby on our brains. . . . Violent corporeal movements, unnatural head positions and so on lead to a stimulation of the vestibular apparatus, which sets off increased neural activity in the brain (Holler, pp. 177, 182).

Vestibular stimulation, which presents itself even in the course of the relatively gentle sequence of movements of the ritual prayer, takes place to a much stronger degree in the case of the *zhikr.*

Anthropological investigations show that the so-called "kinetic trance" resulting from these bodily movements is an important component of all indigenous traditions that practice forms of ecstatic prayer:

"Kinetic trance" designates a trance state brought on by vigorous physical movements, mostly rotations, and an unnatural position of the head that leads to a stimulation of the vestibular apparatus. . . . The motor stimulation of the kinetic trance amounts to the practice of a form of nonverbal psychotherapy. In contrast to sensory deprivation, which causes the body to forget, so to speak, this technique has just the opposite effect: overstimulation of the equilibrium and the brain is aimed at producing an out-of-body experience. This can lead to sensory illusions of falling, floating and spinning[137] (Holler, p. 182, 183).

More recent investigations of the workings of the sense of equilibrium have yielded some further interesting indications of the possible psycho-spiritual effects of these Sufi practices:

---

[137] I assume that the subjective feeling of "sinking into" things that I experienced following the *halvet* is also connected with this process. It could be a kind of "deprivation phenomenon," a reaction to the sudden cessation of the intense vestibular stimulation of the previous several weeks.

150

The vestibular apparatus is closely connected to the switching system of the other senses in the brain, particularly the faculties of sight and hearing and the various senses of touch. . . . The signals from the various sensory organs are integrated, classified and examined [in the middle brain] and, if necessary, passed on to the cortex. And in the middle brain we happen upon one of the most remarkable phenomena of the entire apparatus of thought: most of the signals coming from whatever sense organs are integrated here with signals from the vestibular apparatus before being passed on to the regions of consciousness in the cortex. In the event that the vestibular apparatus is too inactive, too active, or out of sync, that can have wide-ranging and enervating effects. . . . This delicate and differentiated sense organ, as the latest investigations show, allows us not only to stand straight but also to think straight, that is, clearly and reasonably.[138]

What from the viewpoint of brain research must be considered an "enervating effect," since it causes "clear and reasonable thinking" to break down, could absolutely be the physiological mechanism that, from the viewpoint of the most varied spiritual traditions, furthers the "awakening of the psycho-spiritual senses" in the kinetic trance and makes possible the perception of other realities for the first time.

It is interesting to examine in this light the external form of the ritual prayer, that is, the interplay of speech forms and movements. The Arabic wording of the prayer is largely fixed, as is the sequence of movements, and its essential form is never altered. The possibilities for individual variations in the Quran verses recited exist only for those bodily positions in which the head is in the upright position, the usual one for human beings. Interestingly enough, the length of time spent in the altered body positions, the ones that directly affect neural brain activity and thereby all bodily functions is prescribed precisely, in exact "doses," if you will, by the length of time required for the exactly worded prayer formu-

---

[138] G. Leonard, *Der Pulsschlag des Universums* (The Pulse of the Universe), pp. 64, 67.

las.[139] Very obviously we are not dealing here with a free, individual dialog with the Creator—there is a form of prayer for that, the "*dua*"—but with a highly complex, purposely structured rite.

The Electro-Physiological Dimension

The times of prayer, it has already been mentioned, are correlated with cyclical cosmic circumstances and bring a person into harmony with the larger rhythms of the universe. The "*Lata'if* teaching" ("the subtlties," i.e, the subtle centers of perception) of the Naqshbandi tradition describes the energetic-physiological workings of this principle of rhythmic resonance.

The energy of the *latifas*, that is, the "delicate centers" of the body, seen from this viewpoint, corresponds to the energy field of the earth as it changes cyclically in the course of each day.[140] This energy field[141] is influenced by the position of the sun and divided into five cycles. These cycles correspond to the five prayer times of the ritual prayer. By means of certain exercises (particularly ritual prayer and *zhikrs*) the *latifas* are called into play and strengthened in line with this teaching. The energy points or fields peculiar to the body that are thus activated begin to correspond to a heightened

---

[139] The preservation of the Arabic language, however, serves for much more than just structuring the time. In the spiritual sense, the text of the Quran being recited is only considered valid in the original language. All translations are understood to be merely "approximations." This practice not only protects the contents from falsification but also prevents any departures from the specific acoustic brain stimulation provided by the original sound patterns since the earliest days. (The thesis of "morphic resonance," starting from a different viewpoint, likewise emphases the importance of the original sound patterns; see p. 117ff.).

[140] Every long-distance flier knows the disturbances that arise when the biorhythms of one's own body are out of sync with those of the geographical time zone—in a word, jetlag.

[141] For a brief description from the scientific point of view of the influence of the plasma field of the sun on the earth's magnetic field and its effects on the evolution of the human nervous system, see L. Sannella, *Kundalini-Erfahrung und die neuen Wissenschaften* (Kundalini Experience and the New Sciences), p. 136 ff.

degree with the global energy field with which their respective cycles are in accord. The state striven for in Sufism, that of the "*Insān al-Kāmil*," the fully developed person, can be understood in this light as a complete mental and physical setting-free, in which the person's body pulses with life-energy, freely and without hindrance.[142]

Researchers from the most varied disciplines consider the electromagnetic field to be the main connection between human consciousness and the outside world. Abraham writes:

> It does seem very attractive to think of the electromagnetic field as some kind of favored intermediary among all the physical fields.
>
> Perhaps the mental field will end up with a mathematical model that is field theoretic, multidimensional, and coupled only to the electromagnetic field, which is coupled to all other physical fields.
>
> We have in our individual consciousness a particular affinity with the electromagnetic field: electromagnetic perception, reception, and so on as epitomized by vision. The easiest thing to affect by the phenomena of mind over matter should be the electromagnetic field.[143]

(One might speculate as to whether the effects of the *zhikrs* that I experienced as my "air body" might have been a subjective perception of alterations in the electromagnetic field of my body.)

Brain research goes on the assumption that the brain can be purposely altered not only through optical, acoustical, and electromagnetic stimulation but also through deprivation of stimuli.[144] Some suggestion of the effects of extreme stimulus reduction come from long-term investigations undertaken in Antarctic regions and in isolation cells. It was demonstrated that the conditions of sen-

---

[142] Cf. A. Dornbrach, "Die Lata'if-Lehre," (The Teaching of *Lat'if)* in *Al-Sufi*, vol. 1, no. 2, 1991.

[143] R. Abraham, T. McKenna, and R. Sheldrake, *Trialogues at the Edge of the West*, pp. 82-85.

[144] Cf. Holler, p. 26.

sory and perceptual deprivation led to a significant increase in alpha activity, hypnotizability and tolerance for pain.[145]

Conclusion

Both of the consciousness-altering techniques depicted above as being poles apart, namely sensory deprivation (absolute isolation) and vestibular overstimulation (*zhikr, namāz*), apply to the conditions of a *halvet* at the same time. The combination of these with the further requirements (heavy fasting, extensive motionlessness, daylight deprivation, and indoctrination with selected Islamic reading materials) causes the *halvet* conditions in their totality to be an extraordinarily powerful method of physico-psycho-spiritual transformation.

Thus the warning against the unsupervised employment of these methods becomes more than understandable.[146] Even just the practice of the *zhikr* in itself, according to tradition, should never be undertaken without the supervision of a shaikh:

> When isolated individuals keep carrying out exercises recklessly over and over on their own, then the least harm that can occur is serious spiritual confusion, but the gravest is death, which has indeed happened before. The Sufis, by contrast, have organized their pupils into *tariqats* so that those who are exercising can be closely watched (Moinuddin, p. 190).

In conclusion it should be mentioned that these Sufi practices are not at all limited to producing drastic consciousness-altering effects, but have additional positive influences on general well-being: The altered consciousness states (or trance) induced five times daily allow the ultradian rhythms that have been disturbed by behavior-induced stress to get back to normal, thereby regularizing

---

[145] A. Barabasz, "EEG Alpha, Skin Conductance and Hypnotizability in Antarctica," quoted according to Larbig et al. in Revenstorf, *Klinische Hypnose*, p. 103.

[146] See the words of Ibn 'Arabi quoted earlier under "Methods of Sufi Schooling—Ritual Prayer," p. 142.

the functions of the autonomic and endocrine systems. These processes work prophylactically against psychosomatic illnesses and according to Rossi could be the basis for shamanic and other spiritual forms of healing (personal communication, 1991).[147]

---

[147] I thank Dr. Ernest Rossi for his personal interest in the psycho-physiological processes brought on by the *halvet* and his repeated readiness to join in some shared reflection, which has had a notable influence on these commentaries on the subject of "Accompanying Physiological Phenomena."

Methods of Sufi Schooling: Do They Make You Well or Make You Sick?

The initiates seem willing to push their bodies to the physiological limits in order to awaken the mind. What the modern world regards as dangerous threats to health, even to life itself, are viewed by the shaman as routes to knowledge.

Achterberg[148]

Western psychosomatic research shows that the functioning of the immune system is weakened by acute and chronic stress,[149] The organism becomes more sickness-prone. The physiological and psychological methods employed by the spiritual teachers of the most varied indigenous traditions would have to be classified, from the Western point of view, as an absolute classic example of "stress" of the most massive kind.[150]

In fact, the cultures engaged in these basic practices acknowledge that the measures leading to consciousness expansion are extremely onerous. Expressions like "dying," "being cooked,"

---

[148] J. Achterberg, *Imagery in Healing, Shamanism and Modern Medicine*, p. 36.

[149] H. Selye, *Stress without Distress*.

[150] Stress is defined as any event in which outer or inner demands (or both) require the adaptability of an individual, a social system, or an organism —or surpass its ability to adapt. Cf. Lazarus et al., "Stress-related Transactions between Person and Environment," in Pervin and Lewis, *Perspectives in Interactional Psychology*.

"washing your heart with blood and tears," or "burning up" show this plainly.

It might be asked how it is that a way of proceeding that according to one kind of judgment "makes a person sick" can be understood according to another kind of judgment as "leading to recovery."[151] In my opinion the difference (that is, as to whether the result will be physical health or sickness, psychosis or expanded consciousness) lies in being embedded in a clearly delineated (spiritual) system of teaching. In the various extremely difficult transition phases on the "way," during which the student is psychologically and physically very vulnerable, this embedding provides the necessary protective structure.

It is also possible that the manifold harm suffered by current seekers on widely differing "New Age" paths (cf. White) can be traced to the fact that on most of these paths, the virtues traditionally considered indispensable (like obedience, discipline, self-control, trust, hope, patience) are scarcely valued at all. The acquisition of these virtues, which often takes many years in the spiritual instruction of indigenous cultures, is so to speak "the student's own[152] contribution" to reducing the risks associated with the transformative processes.

However, the extreme burdens placed upon the student in the course of his training lead to more than just psychological alterations. The literature of Far Eastern traditions continually points out that an expansion of consciousness is necessarily accompanied by

---

[151] From the Sufi point of view all sickness is based on the illusion of being separated, that is, upon "forgetting" the actual existential oneness of creation. The "healing"—which also means becoming truly human—is performed by means of the "re-ligio," that is, "reconnection" brought about by "remembering again" the connectedness of all being. The shaikh is the "soul doctor" who shows the way and thus helps a person to achieve healing (in the sense of "being whole" and "holiness").

[152] In the expanded mode of observation proper to the Sufi understanding of "La ilāha il Āllāh," there isn't anybody's "own" anything any more.

a fundamental biological transformation in the broadest sense.[153] But in the classic Sufi literature too there are isolated references that can be interpreted as descriptions of processes of physiological alteration.

> The Kubrawiyya [Kubra, thirteenth century] chose as their *zhikr* the profession of faïth, which when one practices it under the severe conditions of an initiatory confinement [*halvet*] , is said to influence not just the breath but also the blood, suffusing the pupil's whole being (Schimmel, p. 363).

Interestingly, Rossi, working from a neuroendocrinological viewpoint, makes a deduction that accords well with the above-mentioned assumptions of Eastern spiritual traditions. The mind influences not just feelings and blood pressure, but our very genes and molecules:

> Under the effects of psychological stress the limbic-hypothalamic system in the brain transforms the nerve impulses of the mind's messages into neurohormonal "messenger molecules" of the body. These in their turn are in a position to cause the hormone system to produce steroid hormones, which penetrate the nucleus of various cells in the body, influencing the formation of genes. These genes, for their part, directly cause the cell to produce the various molecules that regulate metabolism, growth, level of activity, sexuality and resistance reactions in sickness and in health. Thus there is an actual connection between the soul and the genes. The mind ends up influencing the production and formation of the molecules of life (*Psychologie*, p. 12).

In my opinion this could be a description of the processes through which the "stress" to which the student is subjected by the teacher leads to the physiological changes that evidently go along with an expansion of consciousness. To that extent, this would be a scientific depiction of the same process characterized by Naray-anananda in the terminology of his spiritual tradition as the "awak-

---

[153] Cf. for example, Krishna, in White, p. 146; Pandit, in White, p. 147; Ring, *Omega Project*, p. 201

ening of the Kundalini Shakti."[154] The "deep sadness" which is understood to be the triggering factor here would then correspond to the psychological "stress" in Rossi's model.

Both spiritual and scientific viewpoints, then, come to the conclusion that the extreme psychological stress of traditional schooling ("Dying before you die") leads not only to psychological changes but to concrete physiological changes as well. Although a psychosomatic mode of observation supposes the interplay of mind and body, the results of empirical research in this area—and also the corresponding assumptions of traditional Eastern schoolings—stand in stark contradiction to current Western theories still based on a Cartesian dualistic view of the total organism:

> The most irritating feature of my investigations was finding out that none of these specialists [in psychoneuroimmunology, neuroendocrinology, molecular genetics and neurobiology] who seemed to know something was willing to share this knowledge with anyone outside his own narrow specialty. As I put together the data from these different specialties and the conclusions they led to, I was led to some surprising thoughts and theories that were quite obviously based on solid research results. Nonetheless, no one was willing to accept them. (Rossi, *Psychobiologie*, p. 12).

Although from a Western viewpoint it is not surprising that the massive stress to which a student is intentionally subjected on a traditional path has psychological side-effects, the question still arises as to the underlying mechanisms as well as the question whether, in bringing about the necessary renovation of a person's psychological-physiological organization, such drastic overloads are really a requirement at all.

The self-transcendence that is the aim of spiritual schooling requires the student to make "quantum leaps" in his or her world picture, that is to say, mental processes. Not just the old spiritual literature, but also the more recent history of Western science indi-

---

[154] Narayanananda, in White. Cf. "The Functionality of Mourning and Loss," p. 162f.

cates how great the resistance is to such requirements of fundamental change:

> At this point, anyone who wanted to have any part in the life of sci-
> ence (at first only in the realm of physics) had to make the effort to
> understand the new ways of seeing. And anyone who wanted to
> understand them and make use of them had to alter the structure of
> his or her thinking and ask other questions and use different meta-
> phors than before. To be sure, anyone doing scientific work is
> ready to fill his or her thinking with new *contents* at any time, but
> it's quite a different matter when new phenomena call for changes
> in the *structure* of thinking. At such a juncture even very eminent
> scientists have the greatest difficulties and react to this requirement
> by mounting a massive and sometimes embittered resistance. "For
> the demand to alter the structure of thinking can make a person feel
> as if the ground is being snatched out from under their feet." The
> change in thought structure required in this case has been rejected
> by scientist after scientist as simply inconceivable. Nonetheless, it is
> a prerequisite for understanding modern physics.[155]

The most persuasive models of the mechanism underlying any
such radical mental re-organization are in my opinion those that
have been fashioned from considerations of system theory and
from the cognitive-theoretical standpoint of constructivism:

> How such a re-organization can be effected is something we know
> a little about from isolated instances in physics, chemistry or biol-
> ogy. For [the psychological reorganization] these can only be con-
> sidered metaphors. What they appear to have in common is that on
> the one hand there is an impetus of being put in flux (for example,
> an abrupt change in environment) . . . from which on the other
> hand a new order is organized.[156]

Prigogine shows how systems evolve:

---

[155] W. Gerl, "Hypnose als Therapie" (Hypnotism as Therapy), in D. Revenstorf
(ed.), *Klinische Hypnose* (Clinical Hypnotism), p. 179.

[156] D. Revenstorf, "Zur Theorie der Hypnose," (Toward a Theory of Hypnosis)
in Revensdorf, *Klinische Hypnose*, p. 96).

... namely in quantum leaps, that is, in a discontinuous and self-transcendent way. The energy that the systems need for the purpose is drawn from outside; but the conditions sufficient for such a qualitative transformation come from fluctuations within their structure. By this process of evolutionary feedback, the systems achieve their new organization (quoted according to Gerl, p. 178).

That means that physical systems have a strong tendency to reorganize *on a higher level* when they are forcibly displaced from their original stability.

In his "model of mental processes," Neisser goes on the assumption that perceptions, imaginations, memories, and thoughts are constructed inside already acquired background templates; these templates are the basis for assimilation and accommodation and form each person's respective current "world view." Certain biophysical and psychosocial events—like psychoactive drugs, developmental advances, or incisive social changes—can bring about more or less pronounced changes in these templates" (according to Peter, in Revenstorf, p. 53).

The "common denominator," the basis on which all cognitive-theory models proceed, lies in the extreme demands made, or pressure placed, on the system. On this point the assumptions of modern Western science agree with those of traditional teachers:

The master is life with its attendant death, dangerous, incomprehensible and severe. A person strives for peace, security and harmony; the master picks up what was just put down, knocks over what seemed to be firmly standing, dissolves what was connected, yanks away the ground a person stands on. . . . The master knocks over the whole well-ordered construction. Yet scarcely is it annihilated and its previous structure destroyed, so that the chaos seems complete and the student lies shattered on the floor, before he or she begins to sense that something new is forming, a new order is putting itself together, a new shape is emerging. And then the student sees the love in the master's severity and sees the purpose in the night the master plunged him or her into: for a new and unsuspected light is rising (Dürckheim, p. 46).

161

The Functionality of Mourning and Loss

An interesting way of seeing the functionality and also the consequences of intense experiences of mourning and loss is expounded by Narayanananda (as quoted by White, pp. 326, 327):

> Even when one is in deep mourning, Kundalini Shakti is awakening [that is, the physiological process of consciousness expansion is beginning] and climbing upwards. In deep mourning the mind stays firmly on one thing, namely the beloved. This constant thinking about one thing and this constant fixation on one object automatically concentrates the mind. This summoning of the mind [activates] the Kundalini-Shakti. For every [form of] deep, concentrated thinking has its unconscious effect on the Kundalini-Shakti. . . . Consequently the Kundalini-Shakti tries to rise. But in deep mourning the Shakti doesn't make it all the way up, because the person has not yet attained purity of body, of the *nadis* [psycho-spiritual energy "channels"] and of mind.

According to this theory, deep mourning, so to speak, "automatically" makes sure that the practices of concentration, considered indispensable to the development of a higher consciousness in the eyes of seemingly all spiritual traditions, are actually carried out. Perhaps this is a further purpose of what is seen in Sufism as the inexorable, extremely painful experience of "dying before you die." In any event, this exposition strikes me as being also a valid description of the tormented, intense, and yet necessary process that I referred to as my "obsession."

The Call to the Path and Its Consequences

It is only on the path of night that one will encounter the dawn.

Kahlil Gibran[157]

The quest to become conscious has grown into a widespread movement in the last few decades, particularly in the industrial nations of the West. This movement is so ubiquitous, so thoroughly "networked" without regard to national boundaries, that Ferguson[158] can speak of a "gentle conspiracy."

In the Sufi view the call to consciousness is always there. It is considered the inner echo of God's primordial question: *"Am I not your Sustainer?"* (Quran 7:172), which seals the bond of the Creator with His creatures for all eternity.

If on the day of the first covenant a drop was sprinkled on him, that drop will draw him to the sea and free him from all confusion and misery. So come! (FmF, p. 158).

To perceive the reverberation of this first cry is seen as a grace:

But grace comes first. When it is given to someone to awake from error and negligence, that is God's grace and purely a gift. If it isn't, why didn't it happen to his friends standing there beside him? Grace comes first, then effort (FmF, p. 121).

"Why didn't it happen to his other friends there?" Transpersonal psychology has not been much concerned with "why," but has rather extensively dealt with the consequences, particularly the consequences for "the other friends there":

The isolation of those who have begun the transformative process is intensified by this inability to explain how they feel and why they are continuing. . . . Once this journey has begun in earnest, there is

---

[157] Khalil Gibran, *Worte wie die Morgenröte* (Words Like the Dawn).
[158] M. Ferguson, *Die sanfte Verschwörung* (The Aquarian Conspiracy).

nothing that can make a person turn back. . . . The personal trans-formation has a greater influence on personal relations than on any other area of life: relations deteriorate or improve, but they seldom stay the same. [When only one partner hears the call,] the other one will quite possibly be angry and feel left in the lurch, feeling threat-ened and utterly unable to see why that partner can't just go back to being the way he or she was before. "If you loved me. . . ." (Ferguson, *Die sanfteVerschwörung*, pp. 39, 102, 450).

The journey begins in earnest "when the holy approval of a seeker appears in the heart of the master. . . . The person so hon-ored will be pulled by an irresistible attraction from his entire exis-tence and knowledge. In this situation, under the wise supervision of the sage, the person's existence is emptied like a cup."[159]

This call to the path, as well as its consequences is illumined metaphorically by Hz. Mevlâna:

> There must needs be an elephant, in order that, when he sleeps supinely, he may dream of the land of Hindustán.
> The ass does not dream of Hindustán at all: the ass has never journeyed from Hindustán to a foreign country.
> There is need of the elephant-like and very robust spirit, that in sleep it may be able to go speedily to Hindustán.
> Because of desire the elephant remembers Hindustán; then by night that remembrance of his takes form.
> The worship commanded in the text, *Remember ye Allah*, is not a devotional work that is within the reach of every rascal; the command Return thou is not a fetter on the foot of every repro-bate.
> But still do not despair, be an elephant; and if thou art not an elephant, be in quest of transformation. . . .
> Of this sort was Ibráhím son of Adham, who beheld in sleep, without veil, the unfolding of the spiritual Hindustán.
> Therefore, of necessity, he burst the worldly chains asunder and dashed his kingdom to pieces and disappeared.
> The sign of beholding Hindustán is that he who beholds it starts up from sleep and becomes mad.

---

[159] Güvenç, *The Dervish Path*, pp. 31, 61.

He will scatter dust upon worldly plans and will burst the links of the chains (that bind him). . . .[160]

That the "grace of being called" is experienced at first as anything but a grace is already attested from the times of the prototypical teacher, Muhammad (Peace be upon him):

We have placed in you a substance, a seeking, a yearning, and We are watching over it and won't let it be lost, but will bring it to its destined place. Say "God" just once and then stand fast, as every affliction rains down upon you! The Prophet said: "Wherever our religion goes, it doesn't come back without uprooting a person and sweeping his house clean and cleansing him." *None touches it but the purified* (Quran 56:79). For this reason you have no peace, but rather pain, because being troubled means being emptied of the initial joys and of the untroubled mood of initial ignorance. . . . You too should also be patient and troubled. "Eating trouble" is an emptying-out. After the emptying, joy appears, a joy that knows no trouble, a rose that has no thorns, a wine that causes no hangovers (FmF, p. 200).

Suffering is never an end in itself but rather a catalyst. For that reason, Sufism emphasizes the joyousness and grace of "being called" without denying the pain:

If you are seek seeking, seek Us with joy for We live in the realm of joy.[161]

However, transpersonal psychology sees the pain not just as a side-effect of transformative processes, but as a prerequisite for them:

Suffering cracks the boundaries of what you thought you could bear. . . . In our woundings we are forced to stop, to shift, to move in new directions, to face what has been hidden to consciousness, to be pruned of our primal growth so that we may bear fruit. . . . In times of suffering, when you feel abandoned, perhaps even annihi-

---

[160]*Mathnawi*, vol. IV, 3068-73, 3078-81, translated by Nicholson, quoted according to Guvenç, p. 79.
[161] Mevlâna, according to Vitray-Meyerovitch, *Rumi and Sufism*, p. 57.

lated, there is occurring—at levels deeper than your pain—the entry of the sacred, the possibility of redemption.[162]

In contrast to many of the "New Age schools,"[163] the ancient traditions and transpersonal psychology indicate the necessity for a massive and continuous personal investment if the development is ever to proceed beyond the initial pain. Transformative realizations cannot be given to a person by anyone else, not do they mostly come about in a "single act of illumination": they have to be acquired. Ibn 'Arabi (FaH, p. 58) expresses this as follows:

This insight is a knowledge that becomes one's own in the course of one's wanderings on the path; for the path is only a path by virtue of being wandered on; this wandering, however, can only be done with the feet.

---

[162] J. Houston, *The Search for the Beloved*, pp. 105, 106.

[163] In the West, particularly the English-speaking West, Sufism is often presented with stark distortions, as if the goal of the ecstatic love experience, the union of "the lover with the Beloved" (that is, with the Creator) were reachable solely on the basis of the appropriate precepts. The massive sacrifices that the path demands of the seeker are rarely spoken of. "Lately all sorts of popularized works have been appearing, particularly in English, that put their main stress on the aspect of the 'dancing servant of God' and the ecstatic experience but give scarcely any sense of the real power and often almost frightening intensity of Mevlâna Rumi." (Schimmel, Bibliography to *Fihi ma Fihi*, p. 376) The selection of Hz. Mevlâna's verses that Western translators make says much more about those translators themselves than about the Sufi path they claim to be depicting.

Spirituality and Sexuality

To be sure, the sex drive is not just there to ensure the production of children; in another respect as well it is a wise arrangement. Because the pleasure that comes when it is satisfied, which if it only lasted longer would be beyond comparison with all others, is also meant to suggest the promised joys of paradise. The earthly pleasure, therefore, is important insofar as it awakens a need for the lasting enjoyment of it in Paradise, thus spurring a person on to the service of God.

Al Ghazzali (d. 1111)[164]

Islam is basically a "pro-sex" religion. However, the connection between spirituality and sexuality is not expressed as explicitly as in other traditions, particularly those of the Far East. In this regard Sufism, however, is much more open than orthodox Islam. The relationship with God (the "Friend" or "Beloved")—in particular, the deepest mystical experience of union with the Creator—is often described allegorically as a love affair. Most of the time, however, such descriptions are understood only as metaphors.

A look through the Kundalini literature shows a clearer picture. The assumption is made that there is a direct but subtle psychophysiological interplay between sexual and spiritual experience, which Krishna (White, p. 196), for example, sees as the actual "missing link" in human evolution. To the Western observer of such ways of seeing, it seems as if sexual energy is transforming itself into higher states of consciousness.

---

[164] Al Ghasali, *Neubelebung der Religionswissenschaften* (Revival of Religious Sciences).

In fact it's just the other way around: higher consciousness is being freed from its chronic confinement into "lower" that is, more bounded and closed-in forms of consciousness or energy. God-consciousness is not sublimated sexuality; sexuality is repressed God-consciousness (Wilber, "Chakras," p. 117).

McCleave, who experienced a Kundalini awakening brought on by intense Christian prayer, assumes that Christian mystics had the same experience:

Perhaps the [Christian] mystics would have been able to express their experiences in greater detail if they had lived in an age in which freedom of speech and research and an honest appreciation of their holiest secrets were all possible. Had all this been the case, they would have admitted that their relationship with God was sometimes decidedly sexual. Concepts like delight, bliss, ecstasy and divine union might have been fleshed out with words like sensual, erotic and orgasmic. The hearts and senses of the mystics were not clamped shut. The mystic making his way to the sacred wedding doubtless realized that the wedding in question was in some part sexual. Something happened to him during his periods of meditation, prayers and other submission-filled efforts to love God and be loved by God. This something, so it appears, was the awakening of the Kundalini. . . . Why, apart from the limited technical vocabulary, were the mystics so limited in their description of the physical aspects of enlightenment? The answer is guilt. The sexual guilt that lies hidden in a person with a "normal" sex life would be sure to prevent that person from accepting or granting recognition to anyone claiming to have a sexual relationship with God. A mystic knew that only another mystic could ever understand him (McCleave, in White, p. 370, 381).

The shifts in perceptual emphasis that occur in the process of a Kundalini awakening are frequently represented in the literature on the basis of a hierarchical model:

When for example, spirit and energy are expressed through the second chakra, one may be overpowered by sensual pleasure, whereas through another chakra, the fourth, a person is filled with love and sympathy and is interested in having concern for others (Rama, in White, p. 26).

However, if the experience catches a person unawares or is accompanied by burdensome feelings of guilt, the sensual pleasure can be experienced as sensual torment.

> As I was deep in meditation on the guru, my mind filled with lustful thoughts. . . . A powerful, lewd desire tormented me. . . . I couldn't think about anything but sex. . . . My whole body felt the arousing lust. The pain in my organ is hard to describe. . . . My mind was continually beset with violent attacks of self-hatred every time I thought about my sexual arousal again and couldn't meditate any further. . . . I couldn't sleep, the self-hatred kept me up late. . . . At this point I would like to add that all these emotional states were really traceable to the sublime workings of a siddha's grace. But because I was ignorant, I fell into confusion instead of experiencing joy (Muktananda, in White, pp. 145-147).

Even from the scientific point of view, various approaches to investigating the connection between spirituality and erotic experience are increasingly being explored.

Arya points out physiological connections with the nasal breathing cycle[165]:

> According to the classic Yoga literature, both during orgasm and in the deepest meditative state of *samadhi,* both nostrils are open. The ecstasy of this kind of meditation is a consequence of the upward-directed implosion . . . of Kundalini . . . which makes celibacy easier and more pleasurable than sex (quoted according to Rossi, p. 166).

Further indications of a possible physiological basis for the erotic experience in trances induced by spiritual practices are drawn from investigations of altered states of consciousness during sleep. By now there is a more and more extensive research literature on the subject of the mind-body relationship between the

---

[165] Psychobiological investigations of clinical hypnosis show a correlation of the nasal cycle with brain-hemispheric activity. Werntz, for instance, demonstrated experimentally that the ultradian rhythms of hemispheric dominance are related contralaterally with similar changes in the nasal breathing cycle (quoted according to Rossi, *Psychobiologie,* p. 164).

limbic-hypothalamic system, the process of dreaming, and sexual activity.

> Under certain circumstances the brain's ACTH-endorphin system appears to be able to cause a shutting-off or shunting-off of the higher centers of the brain, so that the organism operates under the control of the evolutionarily older mid-brain centers. . . . This shutting-off appears to happen during episodes of acute stress, and the shunting-off appears to happen during REM sleep (that is, in the dreaming phase). REM sleep is characterized by sexual arousal (Stewart, quoted by Rossi, p. 254).

The trance states of clinical hypnosis are used to gain access to and to modulate the same complex of stress, dreams, and sexual functioning. Particularly interesting in this connection is one of Erickson's most spectacular cases of psychosexual rehabilitation. In the course of hypnotherapy a woman who had been a paraplegic for more than ten years because of injuries to her spinal cord learned to relocate her orgasmic reactions to her breasts, neck, and lips.[166] This case is often cited to show what psycho-neuro-physiological changes are possible with the help of hypnotic trances. It is conceivable that Erickson in this case might have activated physiological mechanisms similar to those that are at the root of the non-genital-centered orgasmic perceptions of a trance induced by spiritual practices.

Systematic interdisciplinary investigations of these physio-psycho-spiritual phenomena are urgently needed to bring these various interesting but isolated results together into integrated theories or models.

---

[166] M. Erickson and E. Rossi, *Hypnotherapy*, 1979.

The Authenticity of Mystical Experiences

I n the early stages of biofeedback research, one of the assumptions made was that the states reached through biofeedback simulated those reached by mystics:

"As the technology for measuring and training brain waves becomes more sophisticated, unpracticed meditators will have the opportunity to duplicate the psychological states of Zen and Yoga." This is a misconception.[167]

Krishna, who devoted himself to scientific research into the "symptomatology of spiritual awakening" his whole life long, characterizes this assumption as "a grave mistake":

There is such a deep difference between the mystics known to history and the specimens produced by these methods that it does not need any special effort to distinguish between the two.[168]

Here is a perfect example taken from a personal account:

In the course of seven years I succeeded in subjecting the fully autonomous [Kundalini] vibrations to the control of my conscious self. . . . This long process has had many positive consequences for me. Now I am able to experience total bodily pleasure. . . . It takes me scarcely a moment to free myself from stress, conquer physical pain and renew my stores of energy when they are depleted.[169]

In this description it is obviously not any kind of self-transcendence in the spiritual sense that we hear speaking, only at most a self-actualization in the sense of humanistic psychology.

---

[167] Stoya, quoted in G. Krishna, *Kundalini for the New Age*, p. 59.

[168] G. Krishna, *Kundalini for the New Age*, p. 99.

[169] Quoted according to Sannella, *Kundalini-Erfahrung* (Kundalini Experience), p. 82

All sorts of different spiritual traditions warn against this false evaluation. For example, an instruction from the Shinto tradition says:

> It is important that the individual who enters the astral dimension and experiences those phenomena that are consistent with this state does not exaggerate his accomplishment since the astral dimension is not his destination, but simply an early stopover on his long journey to satori.[170]

In Sufism the same warning is expressed in the well-known metaphor of the rose: the thorny stem symbolizes the difficulties of the way, the blossom symbolizes transitory states that are achievable and subjectively speaking are extremely satisfying. There is a great temptation to be "blinded by the beauty of the blossom" and halt at this level. The actual goal, however, is the essence of the rose: its fragrance, which symbolizes the transcendent dimension of reality. In his treatment of the *halvet, Risalat al-anwar fima yumnah sahib al-khalwa minal asrar,* Ibn 'Arabi instructs the seeker to know this danger and be ready to meet it, advising:

> . . . that in the solitude of the *halvet* you should not seek to gain anything from Him but His own self, nor fix your *himma,* the willpower of your heart, on anything else but Him. If everything in the universe is spread out before you ["the rose blossom"], accept it graciously, but don't stop there. Be stubborn in your search, for He is testing you. If you settle for what is offered you, He will elude you. But if you gain Him Himself [the essence, the fragrance of the rose], nothing will elude you. Once you know that, know as well that God tests you by the things He offers you.[171]

The above quoted personal account (as transmitted by Sannella) is a classic example of a seeker who to use the Sufi terminology has been stranded by the "beauty of the rose."

---

[170] Motoyama, *Superconsciousness,* p. 69.

[171] Ibn 'Arabi, *Reise zum Herrn der Macht* (Journey to the Lord of Power), p. 44.

Even Western scientists who have investigated this phenomenon have come to conclusions that depict "manufactured mystics" and "instant enlightenment" as an illusion. Sannella, for example, who has investigated the Kundalini syndrome from a Western scientific point of view, makes a differentiation in this light between the physiological aspects of Kundalini and the total process of spiritual (Kundalini) awakening:

> There are some fairly "normal" people who run through the whole physio-Kundalini cycle in just a few months [all characteristic signs of the physio-Kundalini complex are contained in the clinical descriptions], whereas the literature of Yoga calls for a considerably longer time, generally several years, for the completion of the Kundalini process, even in the case of the most advanced initiates. This strongly suggests that full-fledged Kundalini awakening is a significantly more comprehensive process of which the physio-Kundalini cycle is only a part. It is also possible that the physio-Kundalini is a separate and independent process that is activated in the larger context of a total Kundalini awakening. It would be premature to formulate any conclusive hypotheses on this question (Sannella, *Kundalini-Erfahrung*, p. 100ff).

Rama (in White, p. 30) points out the rarity of genuine experiences:

> These holy, systematic, and extremely advanced teachings [Kundalini], which bring the practitioner to the highest transcendent state of consciousness, have been reduced to a caricature in the West consisting of nothing but breathing exercises and the groundless claims of numerous teachers who claim to be able to arouse the energy in many of their pupils by touch or presence alone. What in fact is aroused in the pupil all too often is the person's latent hysterical tendencies, causing him or her to experience all kinds of imaginary things. The false interpretation of the ancient and venerable teachings leads, not to a true awakening, but to self-deception . . . . Most of the accounts of a Kundalimi awakening that we come upon in the West are purely the utterances of a high-flying imagination.

Perhaps Eastern and Western observations can be made to fit together as follows: a transformative transition into consciousness is impossible without a corresponding physiobiological transformation, but such a physiobiological transformation does not in itself suffice to bring about spiritual awakening.

The question of the authenticity of mystical experiences is not new. It is brought up even in the classic scriptures of spiritual traditions and runs like a scarlet thread through the writings of Shah, who among contemporary Sufi authors is probably the one best known in the West. He repeatedly points out how people tend to confuse enthusiasm and emotionality with mystical experience. Again and again he emphasizes the need for a teacher, the only person capable of distinguishing pseudo-experiences from real ones with any certainty.

However, Ibn 'Arabi, in his treatment of the *halvet*, does describe numerous factors that could help the student to distinguish pseudo-experiences from authentic ones during periods (such as a *halvet*) when he is left to his own judgment:

> For God's sake do not seek the solitude [of a *halvet*] till you know what condition you are in and can judge how adequate your strength is to withstanding your purely thought-based conceptions. If you are ruled by your imagination, then you dare not seek solitude unless at the recommendation of a shaikh who possesses discernment and knows what he is doing. . . . For God's sake, for God's sake, shield yourself from the deceptions of the ego while in this state, for the ego is the great destroyer. . . . Be on guard lest you be visited by erroneous flights of imagination that disturb your exercise. . . . Now I will explain how one can tell the difference between real and imaginary supra-sensory perception. It works like this: If you see a person or some material process, and the perception is still there even when you close your eyes, it's only your imagination. But if for that instant it disappears, then your consciousness is really connected with the place that you have seen in your perceptions. . . . If your experience of these other worlds is that all creatures within them are occupied with the same *zhikr* as you, then your perception is not real but imaginary. In such a case it is your own state that you conceive of as being reflected back to

you in all things. But if your perception of these worlds is that every species there is occupied with a *zhikr* of its own, then that's a case of a genuine perception (*Reise zum Herrn*, p. 41, 42, 47, 51).

Like Ibn ʿArabi, the contemporary scientist and Shinto priest H. Motoyama is also concerned with distinguishing between "real and imaginary supra-sensory perception":

> There is a fundamental difference, however, between a philosophical position that begins in, and is verified by personal experience, and one that is pure, albeit logical speculation. . . . I intend to identify a sufficient number of the differences between what is thought and what is actually experienced to give the reader a clear understanding of the ways in which these philosophical approaches differ. . . . This partial union, and the remarkable experiences that accompany it in the early stages of meditation are not the effects of an hallucination, nor is the state like a hypnotic trance in which the unconscious surfaces. The experiences that a person believes that he has while in a hypnotic trance are not actual, but are mental impressions that are drawn from those past experiences and stored up in his unconscious and that surface into his consciousness. The hypnotic state is merely an opportunity for the unconscious to discharge these past experiences, and regardless of how convincing and detailed the individual's description of the events, their source is the unconscious mind and therefore they can consist of nothing except what he already knows. Because the unconscious mind is the reservoir of memory, it cannot surrender to consciousness anything that is unknown . . . . With hypnotic phenomena, no such correspondence exists between what is seen in the hypnotic trance and what takes place in the real world. Here lies the essential difference between the hypnotic state and the state arrived at through meditation. Hypnotic phenomena are subjective in nature since both their physical and their psychological manifestations are tied to the operations of the unconscious mind. On the other hand, phenomena that occur in meditation, even at its most elementary stage, actually take place in the astral dimension that transcends the psychophysical connection.[172] In meditation the practitioner is transformed and

---

[172] See also the concept of the "imaginal" realm in Henry Corbin, *Mundus imaginalis*, p. 203.

his being is expanded, while in an hypnotic trance the individual remains essentially unchanged and he must rely upon the knowledge of prior experience stored in the unconscious. Consequently, unless the individual is able to recognize that he has moved beyond what he already knows, he has not yet elevated himself above the hypnotic state and emerged from his own shell.[173]

Self-deception in spiritual practices is most often attributed to an inappropriate inner attitude on the part of the seeker.[174] This includes those who in Hz. Mevlâna's sense of the words "set foot on the path in frivolity or salaciousness" or, according to Shah, are looking for sensation, novelty, emotional or intellectual stimulation, social status, security, an exotic pastime, or the like. What with such inappropriate reasons for looking, they are very likely in the Sufi view to stumble on "pseudo-paths." The experiences they have along the way will mirror the motivation that brought them there. The inner attitude of such would-be students, as Shah calls them, makes it all too possible for them to fall prey to exploiters ("false teachers") who promise them automatic progress without painstaking personal effort or a long preparatory stage.

This phenomenon also appears in transcultural comparisons with other spiritual traditions:

That the teaching and practice of Kundalini-Shakti should be so badly abused is no surprise. Whenever and in whatever form the awakening of powers is offered, the self-aggrandizers go streaming off to whoever promises quick and easy attainment of these powers. It is finally by their own hunger for power that they are deceived. All they attain is the illusion of power, never power itself. I remember once asking my master why there were so many false teachers. He answered: "They are a protective device for the genuine pupils. By siphoning off the people who want something for

---

[173] Motoyama, *Superconsciousness*, pp. 52, 56-58.

[174] These "deceptions," however, may have reasons extending beyond the seeker's responsibility: so it is, for example, with the "tests" mentioned when Ibn 'Arabi says: "Be stubborn in your search, He's testing you."

nothing, they unburden the genuine teachers, who can then work with a smaller group of more serious adherents."[175]

According to Shah, initiation ceremonies are one of the most effective means of enticing would-be students with only the vaguest conceptions of what an authentic school might be:

All over the world you will find people willing and anxious to initiate others into spiritual schools. But, as the procedure is still preserved among the Sufis, initiation—the pledge of fealty to a teacher, only takes place "several years after his admission to the Order of Dervishes." This is because, until the student knows enough, and until he has learnt something, he cannot truly commit himself to the deep studies. To get him to engage himself to follow a path while he is still not capable of it is a real mark of ignorance or imposture. [176]

But more is at stake than just protecting potential students from pseudo-paths. Old traditions also have an interest for their own sake in shielding their inherited knowledge from "unworthy objects" or other kinds of misuse. One method of keeping out unsuitable students is the above-mentioned long probationary period that generally precedes an initiation. Another very effective method known to Sufism is to keep "superficiality" at a distance with an "appearance of superficiality," since "one can only protect against a thing by means of the thing itself. Correspondingly, the decree of Muhammad commands praying as follows: 'In Thee I take my refuge from Thee!'" (Ibn ʿArabi, FaH, p. 116).

The following teaching story, from the oral tradition, throws this time-tested technique into relief:

A group of students had a shaikh whom they held in high honor. Only one thing about him repeatedly gave rise to shame and embarrassing situations. In public his behavior was utterly unacceptable. He gave people offense, displayed the most boorish table manners, and in short, his behavior was just impossible. And his

---

[175] Rama, in White, p. 30.
[176] I. Shah, *Learning How to Learn*, p. 272.

disciples were deeply ashamed. One day one of them summoned up his courage and asked the master about that. He got no answer. All this went on for many, many years. Finally it came the time when the shaikh made ready to leave that place and move away. As he took leave of his disciples, he said to one of them: "Now it is time to answer you. Have you never noticed how all the other masters in our city are always besieged by swarms of potential students? And that in their circles there is scarcely time to do the work itself, what with the constant effort to convince the least qualified of these self-appointed pupils that they are unqualified?" Yes, the students had indeed noticed that. "And have you ever stopped to wonder how it is that we have been spared these kinds of disturbances? If a teacher doesn't correspond, from a superficial point of view, with what common people think of as a shaikh, that right there is enough to keep people of superficial judgement away from his door."

The *Halvet* in Transcultural Comparison

For the moon, for the sun, is their setting harmful?
To you it looks like a sunset; in fact, it is a dawn.[177]

Hz. Mevlâna

The dervish exercise of the *halvet*[178] is traced directly back to Muhammad (Peace be upon him), who used to retire to a cave in the Hira Mountains to meditate. Sufis of all centuries have undergone—some of them repeatedly—this forty- or one-thousand-and-one-day exercise. The arrival of the great Sufi saint of the thirteenth century, Hajji Bektaş Veli, in the "Land of Rumi" (Anatolia), for example, is described as follows:

Coming from the land of Kurdistan, Bektaş reached Najef. He visited the Shah[179] and spent some time with him. Then he completed a forty-day *halvet* and left that place for Mecca. He stayed three years. After that he went to Medina and completed another *halvet* of forty days. Then he went to Jerusalem, where he once again underwent a forty-day *halvet*. Following that, he went to Aleppo, where he spent forty days in the Great Mosque. Leaving Aleppo, he went to visit the tomb of David, where he completed a forty-day *halvet*. . . . Then, leaving that region behind, he set out for Rum. Ar-

---

[177] Mystic Odes 91, quoted according to Vitray-Meyerovitch, p. 55.
[178] Etymologically the expression "*halvet*," that is, *al-khalva*, is derived from *khala*: "the Void" (in which the world existed before its creation).
[179] Hz. 'Ali, who is buried in Najef (observation of Annemarie Schimmel).

riving in Elbistan, he underwent a forty-day *halvet* before proceeding to Kayseri (Vilayetname, fourteenth century).[180]

Structure and Methodology

Investigations in the field of cultural anthropology show that the Islamic *halvet* corresponds in its structure and methodology to a "universal schema of initiation into the mystic dimension of being."[181] The ritual withdrawal into solitude, once or several times, symbolizes the central elements of spiritual training: suffering, death, and rebirth. Eliade's investigations into indigenous cultures all over the world show that these first ecstatic experiences almost always contain one or more of the following initiatory themes:

- Dissolution of the corporeal, or being dismembered, or being de-fleshed to a skeleton as a sign of victory over, and thus redemption from, the profane human condition (Eliade, p. 63).
- Ascent into heaven and descent into the underworld as a universal cosmological concept which symbolizes the possibility of communication with other levels (Eliade, p. 264). In the most varied cultures, the initiate who "ascends into heaven" meets a "heavenly companion" of the opposite sex. According to Eliade (p. 79) these encounters, "like every ecstatic experience," are naturally accompanied by erotic experience. However, the close relationship between mystic and fleshly love is too well known for this "change of levels" to be misunderstood.
- Communication with spirits or with the souls of departed teachers, during which all sorts of various instructions of a spiritual and shamanic nature are transmitted. If these instructions (such as visions or dreams) are not followed, that has grave consequences: sickness or death (Eliade, pp. 102, 109).
- The use of caves or labyrinths as places of initiation. This usage goes all the way back to Paleolithic religions (Eliade, pp. 51, 84). Even today such places are of prominent importance in the rituals

---

[180] Vilayetname, *Le Livre des amis de Dieu* (The Book of the Friends of God), p. 37.

[181] Cf. M. Eliade, *Shamanism: Archaic Techniques of Ecstasy* and A. van Gennep, *Les Rites de passage* (The Rites of Passage).

of archaic peoples, being as they are concrete symbols of transition to "other worlds." Often a spot is sought with graves nearby. Contact with departed souls symbolizes the requisite "death" of the self, the "dying before you die."

Another factor common to all archaic cultures investigated is that the initiation rituals are extremely exhausting, at the very least, with most of them being downright painful physically, psychologically or in both respects. According to Eliade (p. 65), the purpose is to make the initiate "forget" his or her past life. On the consecrated paths of Native Americans, this concept is referred to as "altering one's personal history" and is counted as one of the first steps on the path laid out by the teacher.[182]

The successful mastering of a grave physical and/or psychological crisis, whether one is purposely induced by a teacher—or whether an accident, sickness, or tragedy is utilized for the purpose—is considered a prerequisite in many traditions for the vocation of a healer (Eliade, p. 27). This transformation is often confirmed by having a new name bestowed or being taught a secret language. All over the world, "learning the language of the animals," particularly that of the birds, means that one has attained knowledge of the secrets of nature, that is, of the deeper matrix of being (Eliade, p. 98).

Not just the structure but also the methods of achieving consciousness that are employed in an Islamic *halvet* have analogs in other archaic traditions. Concerning this subject, Achterberg has carried out investigations among North American Indians. It is very noticeable that the techniques they describe and those employed in a *halvet* are, in the broadest sense, identical:

> The shamans used a variety of culturally sanctioned means of deprivation to find their way into the ASC [altered states of consciousness]. Their methods have the potential to cause significant physical and mental shifts by inducing electrolyte imbalances, hypoglycemia, dehydration, sleeplessness, and loss of sensory input.

---

[182] See also "The Functionality of Mourning and Loss," p. 162ff.

181

To sum it up briefly here, the changes are occasioned by fasting from food, water, or salt and sleep deprivation, temperature extremes, hyper- or hypoventilation, sustained physical activity, and psychoactive substances. Thus, pressing a body to its physiological limits and inducing metabolic shifts are traditional ways to free the constraints on the imagination.

Through many complex and varied processes, then, the filters that normally prevent direct mental access to the physical body can be lifted. Most of the ways have in common a means of either removing, or significantly altering, or even competing with, the demands the external environment makes on the brain. The variance in the biochemical outcomes of the different methods described above suggests that the routes to the imagination are many, and the *kind* of biological shift that occurs is relatively less important than whether one occurs at all.[183]

Although there is an increasing amount of research into the physiological workings of all different sorts of deprivation conditions, there is scarcely any mention in the literature of the effects of sexual abstinence. That is particularly amazing in the case of what is evidently a cross-culturally practiced method of achieving consciousness. Winkelman posits an interesting hypothesis:

Normally the autonomic nervous system is in a state of balance; heightened activity in one partial region is equalized by a reaction on the part of some other partial region. However, under intense stimulation of the sympathetic nervous systems, the interaction breaks down, resulting in a collapse into parasympathetic dominance. The parasympathetic pattern of collapse can lead to heightened suggestibility, loss of memory and erasure of previous conditioning. These are auspicious circumstances for the deconditioning from previous patterns, assumptions and modes of behavior that constitutes a prerequisite for an expansion of consciousness. Although this state is characterized by discharge patterns in the evolutionary early parts of the brain, it is not primitive, intellectually or cognitively. In fact it seems to constitute a state of optimal capacity for orientation, learning and alertness. From the viewpoint of Far Eastern tradition, this psycho-physiological state, interestingly, is

---

[183] J. Achterberg, *Imagery in Healing*, Boston, 1981, pp. 36, 136-37.

considered the basis of a more objective perception of reality. Sexual activity leading to ejaculation or orgasm results in a general collapse of the skeletal musculature which is characterized by extreme parasympathetic dominance. Accordingly, sexual limitations could serve, first, to insure that sufficient tension builds up in the sympathetic system, and, second, to prevent the collapse so full of significance in spiritual schooling from occurring anywhere outside the ritual phase designated for it.[184]

Altered States of Consciousness and Emotional Occurrences

The contents of altered states of consciousness seem to correspond to a basic universal schema just as much as the accompanying emotional states do. For example, according to Motoyama (*Superconsciousness*, p. 60), in the course of meditation there is at first a spontaneous re-experiencing of emotionally charged events from one's past before reaching the next stage, which is characterized by peace and tranquillity. This also corresponds to the way a *halvet* takes its course.[185]

---

[184] M. Winkleman, *Shamans, Priest and Witches: A Cross-Cultural Study of Magio-Religious Practitioners*, pp. 94 ff.

[185] The parallels in the *halvet* experience to the typical emotional states on the instructional path of the Shinto tradition are extremely conspicuous in the following example, to the point of his using practically the identical words I used in my own depiction: Motoyama, *Superconsciousness*, p. 87)—"When the practitioner is able to transcend the astral world and achieve oneness in the *karana* dimension, he will experience a kind of sublimity that goes beyond simple emotion. After *accomplishing a difficult* task or attaining a hard sought goal, most people have a sense of accomplishment in which there is pleasure but very little emotion *per se*. On the other hand, when a parent greets a child after a long absence from home, the feeling of joy that the parent experiences is primarily emotional. The feeling of joy that coincides with a returning loved one is analogous to "feeling good" in the astral dimension, while the sense of accomplishment that is experienced after completing a difficult task is analogous to "feeling good" in the *karana* dimension." Day Thirty-Six of the *halvet*—"Despite physical weakness I feel unspeakably well.... Also *a feeling of some important task well done*. Redemption. Relief."

The gradual expansion of consciousness, the "journey of the soul," is described from one culture to the next as occurring in stages. The symbolism employed for this succession of levels varies, but the essential and obviously universal content does not.[186] In the Yoga tradition, for example, one also speaks in this context of the chakras:

> Furthermore, they determine the quality of consciousness. As soon as universal consciousness is manifested in the form of a chakra, a special frame of context results through which the individual experiences the world. . . . The varying concentrations of energy from person to person and time to time share responsibility for individuals' different experiences of the world and for their differing experiences at different times (Rama, in White, p. 25).

In Sufi terminology, one speaks of a mutually intertwined sequence of "states" *(ahwal)* and "stages" *(maqamat)* or of "veils" that are gradually lifted. Other concepts used include "valleys," or "oceans" that must be crossed. The number of levels generally stands at seven, but can go as high as forty-five (Al-Qushairi, d. 1074) or even one hundred (Ansari, d. 1089).

---

[186] It is particularly revealing that the above mentioned levels of experience from the Yoga tradition also presented themselves in the same sequence in the Islamic *halvet*. The two lowest chakras—according to Rama, in White—represent the simplest form of expressing energy and are considered to be the states of consciousness most closely bound up with the physical world and the material plane of existence. Corresponding experiences likewise happened to me predominantly toward the beginning of the *halvet* (sixth and seventh day). The next two chakras embody love and sympathy on the *active* plane, that is, accompanied by a deep wish to give of oneself for other people. This dimension of experience predominanted toward the middle of the *halvet* (twenty-fourth and thirty-second day). Chakras five and six embody a turning to the world of "pure forms," as expressed through creativity, intuition and wisdom (thirty-sixth day). Finally the chakras determine the experience of "pure consciousness." The corresponding experience of self-transcendence—not at all expressible in words —occurred, as would be expected according to this schema, only towards the end of the halvet (thirty-ninth and fortieth day).

Ahwal—the plural of *hal*,[187] that is, "states"—can neither be called forth nor kept at bay by the will. They count as gifts of God and can be compared with the "peak experiences" of humanistic psychology,[188] though they are not to be equated with them. These indescribable transcendent "states of bliss," whether ecstatic or characterized by inner peace of a previously unknown extent, are often the harbingers of the *maqamat* (stages) to come. The levels, in contrast to the stages, are reached through a person's own disciplined "hard work" and are also then permanent, that is, one can't fall back to a lower level.

Although theoretically *ahwal* and *maqamat* are clearly bounded areas of experience, in practice there is a complementary relation between them:

A *hal* must be seen as a mystical experience according to its whole being and in line with its dual character as a gift and as a fleeting phase: a flash of light that lights up a person's heart for a while and then vanishes again. It can just as well come upon a beginner as upon the most perfected Sufi; it can happen at any given spot along the way. This flash can light up the section of the heart hidden by the veils; it can spur a person on to reach the next permanent stage. . . . The permanent character of the *maqamat* strongly suggests that they are linked one to another in a hierarchical order. As Hujwiri (d. 1071) already said, one can't go on from one stage to the

---

[187] Such an unexpected experience of a *hal* can be the event that puts someone on the path. Nonetheless, surprising though it seems, these overwhelming states very often have no further effect. An explanation for this lies precisely in the indescribability and extraordinary nature of such experiences. For the person affected, it is just as impossible to make their experience understandable to someone who has not had any such experience as it would be to describe a drug experience to someone who has never had one. What's more, Western rational thinking offers no structure of explanation—except that of a psychotic episode—into which such an experience could be integrated. When a person so affected has no plausible model of explanation at hand, he or she will make a few—usually rather frustrating—attempts to share the experience and then, as a rule, give up. As time goes on and he or she looks back, everything may look very improbable and eventually fade and be forgotten.

[188] A. Maslow, *Further Reaches of Human Nature*.

next till the earlier one has been fully assimilated,[189] till it has been fully made one's own and till all the obligations that go with it have been fulfilled. In fact every *maqam,* even when transcended, stays in the full possession of the seeker, who in addition is radically changed by each of these experiences. . . . Every *maqam* that a person encounters must finally spill over into flesh and blood, altering the person radically (Kielce, *Sufismus,* pp. 65, 66).

Altered states of consciousness, in the ancient traditions, are not pursued as an end in themselves, but as auxiliary tools in the process of spiritual development.

Sensory and Extra-Sensory Perception

The descriptions of sensory and extrasensory perceptions, typically occurring during the rites of initiation, are another area in which similarities are found among the most varied indigenous cultures.

For example, subjective experiences of light, heat, fire and burning in the course of attaining consciousness are so widespread that Eliade has spoken of these light perceptions ("illuminations") as an integral component of the spiritual experience "of archaic humanity back to the most distant ages" (*Ecstasy,* p. 62). A dialog carried on by a medieval Sufi (d. 1300) with his teacher concerning the student's experience of light points out both of the well-known aspects of mystical experience simultaneously: the fleetingness, combined with the through-and-through transformative effect:

> Nasafi said, "Oh Shaykh, anyone who has reached this Sea of Light will be drowned in it and after that never see himself again. All he will see is the Sea of Light."
> The Shaykh said, "This vision is not permanent."
> Nasafi asked, "Oh Shaykh, what is it that is permanent then? Is it vision or beholding the vision?"

---

[189] This corresponds to the contemporary mode of observation of developmental psychological processes. Cf. Piaget's concept of the mutually conditioned process of assimilation and accommodation in cognitive development (J. Piaget, "Piaget's theory," in Mussen, ed., *Carmichael's Manual of Child Psychology*).

The Shaykh answered, "The vision is not permanent but beholding it is."

The Quranic *"Light upon light"* (24:35) is described by Eliade in terms of the shamanic traditions as "a mysterious light which the shaman suddenly feels in his body, inside his head, within the brain, an inexplicable searchlight, a luminous fire" (*Ecstasy*, p. 60). Achterberg quotes an Inuit healer: "Every real shaman has to feel an illumination in his body, in the inside of his head or in his brain, something that gleams like fire. . ." (*Imagery*, p. 34). On the basis of her investigations she comes to the conclusion that the voluntarily produced rise in body temperature ("fire, burning"), which is also objectively measurable, is *not* to be attributed to a redistribution of blood volume from the central body to the periphery:

> The yogins and shamans have apparently found a means to continue an indefinite heat exchange, which means they have the ability to regenerate those chemicals involved, for a long time. We can only conclude that a powerful ability to self-regulate the thermal response is apparent, and note additionally that those who involve themselves in such affairs regard the internal heat as a pathway to knowledge.[190]

References to experiences of vibration and trembling, which can take on convulsive proportions, are also not confined to Far Eastern (Kundalini) and Sufi (FmF, p. 364) literature. Achterberg describes this phenomenon as a spiritual diagnostic technique of the Navajo healers:

> Trembling, or motion-in-the-hand, is induced during the appropriate ritual. The tremblings eventually lead to great body shudders, and the diviner enters into another state of consciousness. These are power states, and in them, the symbols for healing are visualized by the trembler.[191]

In this connection there have been some interesting cross-culturally carried-out investigations according to which there exists

---

[190] J. Achterberg, *Imagery in Healing*, p. 35.
[191] Ibid., p. 49.

a close connection between the so-called "temporal lobe syndrome" (epilepsy-like attacks, spasm-like jerks, muscle twitches, and so on) and psycho-spiritually altered states of consciousness (Winkelman, p. 11). In many of the cultures investigated, this syndrome is deliberately induced, for example, through temperature extremes. These epilepsy-like episodes lead to long-term or permanent changes in the central nervous system, changes that make the affected individuals more susceptible to further attacks of the same kind, thus also making altered states of consciousness more accessible (p. 98). There is no room for pathological interpretations, since the individuals so trained—for example, native healers —are generally the healthiest members of their community from a psychological point of view (p. 97). Furthermore, investigations show that the "temporal lobe syndrome" is accompanied by certain positively valued personality changes: deeper emotional experience, increased interest in philosophical and religious questions, hyposexuality, automatic writing and a strong empathy for the community (p. 98). Evidently these methods lead to the lasting psycho-social and physiological alterations that go along with spiritual transformation.

Another widespread phenomenon of spiritual paths of instruction in all different sorts of traditions is the subjective experience of exiting one's physical body. According to Achterberg (p. 28) this experience is caused by the cross-cultural techniques of sensory deprivation or overloading, or both, by repeated monotonous stimulation. Shamans make use of this "mystic flight," that is, "sending out of the body," to relocate in "lost souls" (Eliade, *Ecstasy*, p. 288). Priests of the Far Eastern religions also act on all different sorts of "planes of being" (Motoyama, personal communication, 1992), even while they physically remain on this material level all the while. Interestingly enough, EEG tests show that the physiological parameters that go along with "out-of-body experiences" represent a physiological anomaly[192] because they

---

[192] Motoyama describes this physiological anomaly" in Shinto terms:

cannot be classified either as one of the various stages of sleep, nor as "stage one" (sleepy), nor as a waking state (Tart/Achterberg, *Imagery*, p. 27).

Western scientific investigations, however, are only equipped in a very limited way to investigate the anomalies associated with spiritual experience. For one thing, the only out-of-body experiences (OOB) accessible to Western research laboratories are characterized by a certain uncontrollability[193] whereas corresponding shamanic states of consciousness are summoned up at will. Furthermore, it has been possible to show that reactions to sensory deprivation are culture-specific (Suedfield, quoted according to Achterberg, *Imagery*). However, since most Western investigations of these kinds of consciousness alterations are not targeted towards

---

When a practioner enters a state of meditation or *samādhi*, his *kundalini* is awakened at the astral dimension, and he experiences a phenomenon called "astral projection" in which he actually rises out of his physical body. Once he has left his material body behind, his being expands and permeates his immediate area, sometimes stretching out and embracing the mountains and the valleys, and occasionally integrating itself with all creation. Although he ascends higher and higher, when he looks back at himself his body remains physically unchanged. But can this kind of meditative experience be dismissed as simple hallucination? Furthermore, if it is not a delusory experience, has the practitioner's being actually expanded in a certain dimension?

Astral projection does not involve a change in the practitioner's physical state. In other words, a levitation of the physical body occurs even though the *kundalini* has animated the individual's astral body and it has departed the physical being and risen into the astral dimension. (*Superconsciousness*, pp 53, 91)

Highwater traces the difficulties that Western scientists have in dealing with "physiological anomalies" back to their limiting definition of reality: "[In the West] it is still exceedingly difficult to speak of any kind of extraordinary event, appearance, or action without apologizing for it by calling it a dream or a hallucination." (J. Highwater, *Primal Mind, Vision and Reality in Indian America*, New York, 1982, p. 79

[193] S. LaBerge, *Lucid Dreaming*.

researching transcendent experiences and do not take place within any spiritual context, the results admit of only very limited generalization (Achterberg, p. 28).

Near-Death Experiences

There is another, quite different direction of Western scientific empirical research that nonetheless exhibits manifold parallels to the *halvet* experience: research into the near death experience (NDE), experiences "at the edge of death."[194] Many of the clinically dead who were reanimated describe—to a large extent, independently of cultural considerations—encounters with light or creatures of light and the running of a "life film," following experiences of "being magnetically drawn" or sliding through tunnel-like structures. These experiences are depicted as being "more real than everyday reality" and generally have a transforming effect on all the rest of that person's life. In a comprehensive study, the *Omega Project*, Ring[195] investigated near-death survivors from two perspectives: on the one hand, their anamnestic data, to isolate those factors that predispose people to experiences of this kind; on the other hand, the long-term consequences of the experience of clinical death. Here is a brief summary of this fascinating study:

- Structurally, the experiences correspond to the above described "universal schema of initiation into the mystic dimension of being" or that of the "shaman's journey" of "separation, transformation, reintegration" or "suffering, death, rebirth (p. 92).
- Most near-death survivors have withstood traumas of the most severe kind at some point in their childhood; they are the "unwitting beneficiaries of a kind of compensatory gift in return for the wounds they have incurred in growing up" (p. 146). (This observation could be an analog to the tribulations that traditional teachers expose their students to.)

---

[194] Cf. R. Moody, *Life after Life*, K. Ring, *Heading toward Omega*, and *The Omega Project*.

[195] My thanks to Prof. Ken Ring for the exchange of experiences concerning our respective areas of research that we shared on a number of occasions.

- Near-death survivors report a number of psycho-physiological changes that take place as residual phenomena of the experience. These include persistent physiological changes, neurological and brain state-specific changes, and unusual psychoenergetic, psychological and parapsychological experiences. These changes generally peak within five years after the experience and are permanent from then on (p. 156, 168). The assertion of Eastern spiritual traditions that consciousness expansion is accompanied by a biophysiological transformation is thus supported by the results of Western empirical research.

Many of the depictions of near-death experiences correspond, in my opinion, to Gopi Krishna's "symptomatology of awakening," that is, the Kundalini phenomenon. Ring makes the same deduction:

My candidate for the driving force behind the psychophysical transformations would be kundalini. In this supposition, of course, I am hardly alone, for the most common assumption about the nature of Kundalini is that to quote perhaps the leading authority on Kundalini in modern times, Gopi Krishna, it is "the evolutionary energy in man." That is, according to Kundalini theorists, it is the latent energy that, once released, transforms the nervous system and promotes the psychospiritual evolution of humanity (p. 169).

Ring himself assumes that the NDE "permanently alters the biological system of the individual, probably (in my opinion) by acting upon the autonomic nervous system" (p. 170).

The results of his empirical investigation lead Ring to wide-ranging conclusions:

Our data suggest that this transformation is in fact *psychophysical*, that NDEers . . . through their experiences undergo certain changes that affect their physiological functioning, nervous system, brain and mental processes so as to permit a higher level of human nature to manifest. . . . I advance the hypothesis that NDEs are a kind of experimental catalyst for human evolution, that potentially, at least, these experiences that we now know have occurred to many millions of persons across the globe are serving the purpose of jump-starting the human race to a higher level of spiritual awareness and psychophysical functioning." (pp. 11, 169)

Interestingly, Ring's evolutionary hypothesis is also advanced by contemporary Sufi authors: "The more people reach this love[196] [that is, the form of being that follows the transforming 'dying before you die'] the more evolution will occur and the more tolerance will grow." (Güvenç, *The Dervish Path*, p. 36) Ring calls the "new person" who is the result of these transformative processes the "omega prototype," drawing on Teilhard de Chardin and B. Greyson, or John White's "Homo noeticus." The Sufi concept of the "*Insān al-Kāmil*" is not hard to recognize here.

Ring refers to this development— and here we come full circle—as the "shamanization of modern humanity" :

> To make it clear and put it into context for you, consider for a moment the general course of humanity's evolution. What began as physical evolution has obviously and especially with the advent of the neolithic revolution became primarily a cultural evolution. But as cultural evolution has shaped our planet's destiny for the past ten thousand years, has also been evident a third form of evolution—the evolution of *consciousness* itself. And we have no reason to think that this evolution has ceased, but rather the opposite: It may be that it constitutes the very frontier of humanity's evolution today. If this is so, I would argue that the findings from the Omega Project suggest that we could be in the beginning stages of a major shift in *levels of consciousness* that will eventually lead to humanity's being able to live in *two* worlds at once—the physical and the

---

[196] In Sufism, "love"—like "heart"—is a clearly defined technical term having nothing in common with the notions of "romantic" love or indeed sentimental "gushing" that are current in the West. Güvenç, for example, describes "love" as follows:

According to Islamic mystics, "love" is the *hal* in which one knows the reality directly. . . . In such a state, a person knows what is true and essential and is directed towards every particle of the universal. If love is manifested in the heart [organ of recognition], it directs one toward conscious living, makes life meaningful, and contains a deep knowledge in the real sense. Past feelings, old viewpoints, and understandings formed by things directed towards the person disappear completely. . . . It opens the heart to new forms and brings a great power of intuition for new manifestations. . . . The (material) world loses is influence. Yet—life continues—in another dimension.

imaginal. This is of course precisely what the shaman in traditional cultures is trained to do (pp. 239-240).

"Imaginal" is not to be confused with "imaginary." Ring uses this expression in the sense of Henry Corbin, who writes thus of mystical experiences:

> . . . it must be understood that the world into which these [visionaries] probed is perfectly *real.* Its reality is more irrefutable and more coherent than that of the empirical world where *reality* is perceived by the senses. Upon returning, the beholders of the world are perfectly aware of having been "elsewhere" ; they are not mere schizophrenics. This world is hidden behind the very act of sense perception and has to be sought underneath its apparent objective certainty. For this reason we definitely cannot qualify it as being *imaginary* in the current sense of the word, i.e., unreal or nonexistent. [The imaginal] world . . . is ontologically as real as the world of senses and that of the intellect. . . . We must be careful not to confuse it with the imagination identified by so-called modern man with "fantasy." [197]

Ring assumes that the "imaginal" element in Corbin's sense is a function of the altered state of consciousness. He characterizes it as a "kind of organ of perception" which the alchemists called *imaginatio vera.* (It is not hard to recognize in this the Sufi concept of *qalb,* that is, "heart as organ of perception.") The perception [of the imaginal realm]:

> . . . is dependent neither on sensory perception nor on normal waking cognition (including fantasy). Because it lies hidden from common view, it can usually be apprehended only in what we now call certain *altered states of consciousness* that have the effect of undermining ordinary perception and conceptual thinking. When these are sufficiently disturbed, the imaginal realm, like the starry night sky that can be discerned only when sunlight is absent, stands revealed (*The Omega Project,* p. 220).

The manifold parallels between the residual phenomena of a *halvet* and those of a near-death experience are mirrored in the

---

[197] Henry Corbin, "Mundus imaginalis," in Ring p. 220.

verbal expression itself: what is a near-death experience if not, in the truest sense, a case of "dying before you die"?

Purpose and Goal

> If you really want to learn, don't be surprised if somebody comes along to teach you (Sufi proverb).

The spiritual trainings of all different sorts of traditions do not proceed at all on the basis of the self-centered goal of individual enlightenment, but have the explicit purpose of being able to serve the community better afterwards. Whereas Western humanistic conceptions of psychological health aim at self-actualization, from the perspective of ancient traditions the aim is rather self-transcendence, which is understood to be what real health is. Achterberg's description of Native American viewpoints is typical:

> For the shamanic cultures, the purpose [of life] is spiritual development. Health is being in harmony with the world view. Health is an intuitive perception of the universe and all its inhabitants as being of one fabric. Health is maintaining communication with animals and plants and minerals and stars. It is knowing death and life and seeing no difference (*Imagery*, p. 19).

The isolation practiced both in Native American traditions and in Sufism (vision quest and *halvet*, respectively), in contrast to traditions in which hermithood or asceticism is seen as desirable in itself, is understood in the context of realization and of service to a greater reality and is therefore only temporary, with concrete time limits. In Sufism this is traced straight back to the "prototypical teacher," Muhammad (Peace be upon him). During his famous "heavenly journey," he came within *"two bowlengths away, or even nearer"* of Allah (Quran 53:9). Nonetheless, after that he was willing to return to the limitations of the material plane, to break away from "gazing straight at divine being" —in order to give a renewed service to humanity, infused with this new knowledge.

Like those in all centuries who have completed *halvets*, Muhammad (Peace be upon him) also feared being distanced from true reality by his unavoidable occupation with worldly things. Hz. Mevlâna describes this conflict as follows:

> For a while He kept Mustafa [that is, Muhammad (Peace be upon him)] completely occupied with himself. Then He commanded him: "Call the people, give them counsel and reform them!" Mustafa began to cry and complain: "Ah Lord, what sin have I committed? Why are You chasing me away from Your presence? I don't want any people!" God the Sublime said to him: "*Cease your anguish, Muhammad! I will not occupy you with people alone. In the midst of this occupation you will be with Me. When you are busy with people, [you will not be even a hair's breath further from Me than you are now]. Whatever business you may be occupied with you will be fully united with Me*" (FmF, p. 136).

Another fear common to those who have completed a *halvet* was also according to Hz. Mevlâna shared by Muhammad (Peace be upon him), namely, that the later fulfillment of wishes made while in "the raw state" might thereby signal a relapse into an earlier state of attachment: before his initiation, while he was still tied to the material dimension, the Prophet (Peace be upon him) once wished, according to Hz. Mevlâna:

> If I only had such eloquence and quickness of speech! When the invisible world was revealed to him and he felt the divine intoxication, he lost all interest and all yearning for the wish he'd made. God the Sublime spoke: "I have given you the eloquence and quickness of speech you wished for." The Prophet answered: "Lord, what good are they to me? I have no interest in them, and I don't want them." God the Sublime spoke: "Do not worry. This will come to pass, and your redemption will still stand, and you will suffer no damage"(FmF, p. 246).

As Ibn 'Arabi sees it, the renewed voluntary return to the "world of multiplicity" after "achieving Oneness" is the sign of the *Insān al-Kāmil*, the spiritually fully completed person:

For the *Insān al-Kāmil*, however, this return to the material dimension is regarded as progress." He quotes Hz. 'Ali on this subject:

> To dwell in separation without having achieved the state of union is to have many gods [*shirk*] . . . . But when the state of union and the state of separation have become one and the same, that is also Oneness [*tauḥīd*].

Conclusion

The world-wide parallels in the area of spiritual training—of which only a few have been discussed here—are so obvious that they have led to wide-ranging speculations about early contacts among various populations. This hypothesis, however, does not appear very plausible, because it is hard to see how these very practices should have been handed down unchanged for at least twenty thousand years while other aspects of the various social systems have undergone such drastic change.

Winkelman (p. 52) instead presumes that altered states of consciousness have a psycho-physiological basis that makes humankind predisposed to magico-religious experiences, which then are formed by the interaction of the biological structure of the human mind with certain social-ecological circumstances, taking shape according to much the same schema the whole world over.

Achterberg puts forward a very pragmatic thesis: the explanation lies in the simple fact that these methods worked. A process of trial and error led to the development in widely separated cultures of the same effective techniques. That would also imply that these methods function independently of any world view, that is, that they are culture-independent apart from certain outward forms. In producing the effect, belief in it is no more or less required than belief in gravity is required to make objects fall to the ground:

> The ancient way is powerful, and taps so deeply into the human mind, that one's usual cultural belief systems and assumptions about reality are essentially irrelevant (Harner, quoted in Achterberg, p. 16).

Universal truths should show themselves in all traditions and in every age. (Islam says that prophets with the same message have been sent to all peoples in every age.) Seen in that light, the numerous parallels mentioned earlier among such different cultures as those within Sufism, the Native American shamanic tradition, the Far Eastern religions and many others is not to be wondered at—regardless of which hypothesis you adduce as an explanation.

The extraordinary transforming power of a *halvet* obviously has to do with its being directly rooted in a cross-cultural, cross-temporal teaching system that is not based on speculation but on the actually lived-out experience of all humanity. The effects on all levels are so extensive that during this period of isolation one is, in the truest sense of the word, "catapulted" beyond one's current manifest state of being. It takes a long time after that, perhaps years of the most intense efforts, to make the reality glimpsed there something that one also lives "in this world." "The real *halvet* begins after the *halvet*," goes the Sufi saying. Because concrete *life,* the actual "embodiment" of this "exact knowledge," is what matters. Perhaps that is finally the touchstone that can show the difference between a real transformation and illusion and self-deception.

The Land of Truth

Once upon a time there was a man who thought that normal life, such as most people know it, couldn't possibly be all there is. He went looking for the true teacher of the age. He read many books and joined many communities, and he heard the words and saw the deeds of one master after another. He followed the commands and carried out the exercises that appealed to him the most. Often one of his experiences would put him in an exalted mood, then the next time he would be all confused again; and he had no idea what stage he was in or where or when his search might end. One day this man had fallen to thinking about his life when he suddenly found himself near the house of a certain wise man held in high esteem. In the garden of the house he met Khidr, the secret messenger who shows the way to the truth.

Khidr took him along to a place where he saw people deeply mired in suffering and torment. He asked who they were: "We are those who did not follow the true teachings, who were not honest about our obligations, who followed self-appointed teachers," they answered. Then the man was taken by Khidr to a place where everyone looked well and full of joy. He asked who they were: "We are those who did not follow the true signs of the path," they said. "But if you didn't pay attention to the signs, how can you be so happy?" asked the wanderer. "Because we chose happiness over truth," the people answered, "just as those who chose the self-appointed thereby also chose misery."

"But isn't happiness a person's ideal?" the man asked further.

"The goal of a person is the truth. Truth is more than happiness. A person of the truth can put on any desired mood or get along fine without any at all," they responded. "We acted as if truth was happiness and happiness truth, and people believed us. That's why you too have imagined till now that happiness was the same as truth. But happiness makes you just as much a prisoner as pain."

All at once the man found himself back in the garden, with Khidr at his side.

"I will grant you a wish," said Khidr.

"Then I would like to know why I have failed in my search and how I can be successful," said the man.

"You have just been wasting your life," said Khidr, "because you have been a liar. Your lie consisted in striving for personal satisfaction when you could have striven for the truth."

"And yet I have reached the point where I have found you," said the man, "and that is something that scarcely happens to anybody."

"You have encountered me," Khidr explained, "because for one moment you possessed enough uprightness to set your sights on truth for its own sake. This one moment of uprightness gave me reason to answer your call."

Then the man was overcome with yearning and the desire to find the truth even if he should lose himself in the process.

Khidr, however, made ready to depart, and the man started running after him.

"You don't want to follow me," said Khidr: "I'm going back to the normal world, the world of lies, where I have to stay in order to do my work." And as the man looked round, he saw that he was no longer in the garden of knowledge, but in the land of truth.[198]

---

[198] Version of Idries Shah in *Denker des Ostens* (Thinkers of the East), pp. 58-60.

Appendix: *Halvet* Questionnaire

H*alvet* experiences are extremely subjective and thus are always unique and essentially incomparable. Nonetheless, what follows are brief accounts, standardized in questionnaire form, from other people who have completed *halvets*.[199] This will perhaps help the reader to gain an impression of the workings of this traditional dervish exercise that extends beyond the description of a single case study. All the accounts are by Middle Europeans of various nationalities (Muslim and non-Muslim) who–in contrast to me–had not come in contact with the Islamic cultural domain before entering the Sufi tradition.

Age: thirty   **Sex: male**   **Date: March 5, 1992**

1. *What were the dates of your* halvet?

January, 6, 1992–February, 15, 1992

2. *What were your reasons for going into the* halvet?

Yearning for clarity and peace. The wish to purify myself and forge deeper into life.

3. *Please describe what seems most important to you about your experiences.*

That, as Yunus[200] writes in his poems, it takes mastery to find truth in the world of values, to let eternal truth and love do their work through them. When I exhaust all my possibilities, God gives me more and helps me in mastering the obstacles on my way to Him. That everything and everyone I see, I myself am, and many facets are very strange to me and touch off great amazement and all kinds of other emotions.

---

[199] My wholehearted thanks to the *halvet* veterans who were willing to share this most personal of experiences.

[200] Yunus Emre, Turkish mystic, d. ca. 1321.

4. *What concrete changes have there been in you or your life since the* halvet?

I made a momentous decision: deciding to come to Vienna and take a completely different job. Concretely taking responsibility for my son, who lives in Vienna. After the *halvet* it became possible at the same time to reach great peace with my close relations and clarity towards them. So this decision has been like a miracle for me, the way that this one decision has caused so many diverse aspects to be set free and to be touched and led toward further growth. That a return to the roots is a necessity of my life, as well as the admitting of errors that goes along with it.

5. *Would you go into a* halvet *again? Why or why not?*

YES! Because it is a holy, whole, cleansing, weighty, and beautiful time with God. It offers the possibility of giving the ego directions to God, to educate it if God wills, and teach it to surmount obstacles and to sense in weakness God's eternal presence and help. It looks to me like a possibility for humanity to bring the causes of mistakes, difficulties and confusions from the outside to the inside, thus freeing and cleansing the connection to *all* human beings! And thereby also to encounter a whole spectrum of problems–from environmental responsibility and war to personal relations and inner development–in the light of God.

6. *Would you recommend a* halvet *to others or warn them against it? For what reasons?*

Advise them to do it, see question 5. All those years of psychotherapy compared to a connection with the Infinite in forty days!

7. *Did you experience physiological changes during or following the* halvet? *If so, what sort?*

Extreme bradycardia.[201] Pulse often about thirty-five (but I have an athlete's body); after about two weeks the hair loss I have had for about the past five years ceased. Sometimes extreme heat, then cold, then cool, pleasant, rippling sensations on my skin and down my back. Extreme constipation in the middle of the *halvet* with related tiredness and confusion (retroinfection from the intestines?).

---

[201] Slowed heartbeat.

Towards the end that wasn't a problem any more, even when there was still difficulty. Even dealing with problems had become something else. Back pains, lower spine, upper spine, strong inner division perceptible! Lost thirty-five pounds. Afterwards very hungry for spices and milled grains (polenta, wheat grits) and *iskembe sorbasii*[202]!

8. *Is there something else about your experience that is important to you but not covered in the previous questions?*

Age: forty-three   Sex: female   Date: September 10, 1992

1. *What were the dates of your* halvet?
June–July 1992
2. *What were your reasons for going into the* halvet?
To get to know myself and to deepen my being.

To test the limits of my personality/ego using a new method not previously known.

To develop myself on the Sufi path, to advance in my spiritual unfolding.

3. *Please describe what seems most important to you about your experiences.*

I think there were *several most important* experiences:

The "unusual" states arising during the *zhikr.*

The surmounting of physical barriers.

The "imparted" information–in images and lucid sequences *in dreams.*

Other things of which I can give no description because words fail me.

4. *What concrete changes have there been in you or your life since the* halvet?

Physiological and emotional changes.

Cognitive changes in relation to perceptions of the world and everyday occurrences.

---

[202] Turkish cuttlefish soup.

A new kind of deeper emotional experience.

5. *Would you go into a* halvet *again? Why or why not?*

Yes, without the slightest doubt. For me it is a wonderful psychological method by which I was "deepened" on conscious and unconscious levels and am now more mature. It is an integrating experience that furthers ONENESS (with oneself, with nature, and with God). Furthermore, though it hasn't been long, in fact I feel the desire to repeat the *halvet.*

6. *Would you recommend a* halvet *to others or warn them against it? For what reasons?*

Yes, but only for individuals with no grave psychological problems and no chronic physical disabilities such as diabetes, ulcers, circulatory problems, etc. I think a *halvet* is worth recommending, though it is important that the person in question would really like to have such an experience, deeply desires it.

7. *Did you experience physiological changes during or following the halvet? If so, what sort?*

Yes, during and after. Some were stunningly unexpected. (I'm not sure if this question calls for a description or explanation?) [203]

8. *Is there something else about your experience that is important to you but not covered in the previous questions?*

For me it was a unique and unforgettable experience of the discovery of myself. Let me add a few general observations that seem to me worthy of mention:

---

[203] Additional comments (February 7, 1993): On some days, very strong hunger feelings (I was starving!) which, however, then passed. My bowel stopped up on many days during the halvet and also following. At the same time, heavy gas buildup (eructation and flatulence). Increased urination during the first few days, sometimes with a strong odor. Cold feet for hours at a time and the need to use Shiatsu (a kind of massage) to stimulate circulation and keep my body temperature normal (97-98.6 degrees F). The interval between my periods was reduced from twenty-eight days to twenty days. In the forty days of the *halvet* I menstruated twice, though without any further complications whatever.

I assume that the increasing slowing-down of the rhythms of activity that occurred during the *halvet* (including intestinal and elimination processes, sleeping and waking states, and daily activities) was responsible for leading to a much clearer consciousness: a consciousness of the psycho-physiological imbalance we normally live with and the resulting disharmony of body, mind, and soul.

I personally am convinced that this slowing-down of rhythms—including the above-mentioned physiological dimension of these processes—helps to maintain psycho-physiological balance just as much as the meditative and contemplative states and the various parapsychological experiences that may occur during a *halvet*.

Age: forty-one **Sex: female** **Date: April 1992**

1. *What were the dates of your* halvet?
1) September 1990
2) June 1991

2. *What were your reasons for going into the* halvet?
I realized that I had sunk into a rut that I needed to get out of once and for all. Despite my anxieties about a *halvet*, I was ready to really put my trust in myself and God. Wanted to find the reason for my life, to realize my mission. . . .

3. *Please describe what seems most important to you about your experiences.*
Experiencing divine love and mercy. Watching my life pass before me and realizing what had previously been hidden from me. Seeing the outline of my life and the necessity and possibility of accepting it. To be able to see the matrix of my life, as well as the necessity and possibility of accepting it; to see my entire life as a preparation—starting from the structure my family had, as well as my role as a child—up to today. Working through the realization of all my faulty conduct to reach a deep forgiveness of the faults of others. Feeling a deep peace in just being, a oneness with the earth, people, and God. Looking within me and finding my limita-

tions and impermanence and at the same time finding everything. Understanding the paradox of life and letting it be. Achieving a new form of openness and closeness with all family members and partners. Not being lonely during the forty days and putting my whole life in service of humanity in gratitude for this experience. Heaven and hell are both here at once.

4. *What concrete changes have there been in you or your life since the* halvet?

I'm much closer to people, more generous, kinder, more forgiving. Much closer relations with my mother and daughter, resumption of close contact with my brother, clearing-up of relations with my father. Building up a new and deep friendship with my ex-husband; breaking-up my household for my daughter's benefit, awakening to a mother's role; learning to be alone, to deal with pain and grow in the process. Complete restructuring of my understanding of myself. Recognition of utterly neglected parts of me, which have now been given some room to live. The meaning of a partnership in the individual and spiritual sense is coming into focus, and the desire is awakening for a fulfilled woman's life that is not played out exclusively or even principally on the job. Starting to integrate music into my life. I can now accept the rules of this world without wishing to break or undermine them.

5. *Would you go into a* halvet *again? Why or why not?*

I did a second *halvet* in June 1991. Because it seemed to me that the task of sorting through my past that I had set myself once back outside was now pretty well carried out, and a burst of energy directed toward the future seemed important. I would do a *halvet* again if the tasks remaining from the first two seemed to be completed or if external necessities should permit.

6. *Would you recommend a* halvet *to others or warn them against it? For what reasons?*

Yes: if you're at a turning-point in your life, if you're confused, if you're ready to look at yourself in the mirror. For me there is no possible way that mind and heart could encounter each other more deeply, where a direction emerges so clearly, one that can really be followed. But when you're back outside, the other part of the job begins. Namely to put into action, amid the maelstrom of life, what was realized in the protected space of the *halvet*. Otherwise it remains just a wonderful memory.

7. *Did you experience physiological changes during or following the halvet? If so, what sort?*

What was different was my sensations. For a while afterwards I could physically feel the effect produced in my own body by negative thoughts and words that I let slip out of negligence and fatigue. Mild stomach over-acidity. Difficulty withstanding the urge to overeat. Total uprightness of the spinal column. Decreased sensitivity to light, noise, crude people. The ability, so to speak, to draw deeper within myself (in the bodily sense) and to be secure there or to protect myself through concentration.

8. *Is there something else about your experience that is important to you but not covered in the previous questions?*

The second *halvet* was completely different from the first. What became clear to me in an external context during the first *halvet* became clear to me in an internal context during the second. Many realizations that I knew from hearsay suddenly became comprehensible and were concrete. During the first *halvet* I came to understand why I am a Muslim; during the second, why I am a Sufi. The first *halvet* clarified my relations with my mother. The second *halvet* clarified my relations with my father. In the first *halvet* things were indicated in dreams. In the second *halvet*, tasks that are of significance to my life took concrete form. Found a connection to my being in the sense of purity and individuality and the energy source that springs from it. The concept of guilt melted away. The possibility of tolerant acceptance opened up. My previous relationship to my ex-husband dissolved completely, and I was able to encounter him and his wife in openness and love–something that had been previously impossible for me. Am finding a relationship with my future husband that matches the "glimpsed" qualities and is opening up whole new realms for me. The tempo of my life has been noticeably slowed since the second *halvet*, from which I conclude that I was just pushing myself before. Experiences on other levels can't be standardized.

Age: twenty-three   Sex: male   Date: August 6, 1992

1. *What were the dates of your* halvet*?*
January 15–February 29, 1992
2. *What were your reasons for going into the* halvet*?*
I felt the need for isolation and sensed that my development and my life had reached a point where without this experience, I would have gone no further.
3. *Please describe what seems most important to you about your experiences.*
Life is lived for a moment, the only truly existing, all-embracing moment, that exists because of love, for love, and by means of love. From a poem by Niyazi Misri[204] "If you cannot see the face of God in everything, you have failed."
4. *What concrete changes have there been in you or your life since the* halvet*?*
My way of seeing things.
5. *Would you go into a* halvet *again? Why or why not?*
If I have the need and the possibility, *yes.*
6. *Would you recommend a halvet to others or warn them against it? For what reasons?*
If asked about a *halvet,* I could only recommend it.
7. *Did you experience physiological changes during or following the halvet? If so, what sort?*
Disappearance of my addictive behavior (up till five minutes before my *halvet* started I was a heavy smoker: now I don't smoke any more). I had a lung inflammation during my *halvet.* My hair loss stopped; afterwards it started again but in a much weaker form than before the *halvet.* My body makes much better use of nourishment than before (unfortunately, that means I gain weight very easily, which wasn't so before).

---

[204] Turkish mystic of the Khalvatiyya order, d. 1697.

8. *Is there something else about your experience that is important to you but not covered in the previous questions?*

The real result and real experience can't be conveyed in words, presumably it wouldn't even be right for me to try. They say that during a *halvet* a person's heart is gradually made to open. I think I sensed that physically. In a *halvet*, I believe it is possible for a connection to divine knowledge to be established. To be sure, a forty-day *halvet* is no guarantee of anything. The job is to transfer that experience into the other world.

Glossary of Islamic Personages

'Ali ibn Abi Talib,[199] cousin and son-in-law of the Prophet Muhammad, fourth Calif (successor) of the Prophet (ruled 656-661). The Shiites consider him the only true successor of the Prophet and the first Imam (leader in prayer and war) of the *Shia.*

'Aṭṭār, Faridaddin, Persian mystical poet, d. 1220 in Nishapur, in northeastern Iran. He is known chiefly for his allegorical Persian epics. His *mantiq uṭ-ṭair* (Conference of the Birds) describes the journey of the thirty soul-birds who set out to find the God-bird Simurgh; the *Musībatnāma* (translated by Isabelle de Gastines as "Le Livre de l'Ġépreuve") describes the experiences of a mystic during the forty-day confinement. *The Ilāhīnama* (translated by J.A. Boyle, Manchester 1976) depicts conversations of a king with his six sons. The best introduction to his life and work is: H. Ritter, *Das Meer der Seele* (The Ocean of the Soul).

Baha'eddin Walad, Mevlâna Rumi's father, preacher in the province of Balch, Afghanistan; emigrating from there, he was professor of theology in Konya 1229-1231. Best study is Fritz Meier, *Bahā-i Walad.*

Bektash, see Haji

Beyazid Bistami, mystic from northeastern Iran (d. 871), famous for his asceticism and his lofty pronouncements, above all his remark, *subḥāni, mā a 'ẓama schāni* (Praise be to me! How great is my majesty!), which has often been taken together with Hallaj's *anā'l-ḥaqq* as an expression of "deification."

---

[199] The transliteration of Islamic names is not standardized, it varies with the nationality of the author. An Arabic word like *Hallaj* might appear as *Halladsch* (in German transliteration), as *Hallac* (in Turkish transliteration), and so on.

Ghasali (Ghazali, Ghazzali), Abu Hamid al- (d. 1111 in Tus, eastern Iran), the great systematic theologian of "moderate" mysticism, whose principal work, *Iḥyā' 'ulūm ad-dīn* (The Revivification of Religious Sciences), lays out in forty chapters the duties of a Muslim, with the actual "mystical" stages appearing in the last ten chapters. This is because a person prepares for death in forty stages. Ghasali's influence on the lifestyle of moderate mysticism cannot be overestimated. Many parts of the *Iḥyā'* are available in European languages; a good analytical overview is G.-H. Bousquet, *Ih'ya' ouloum ad-din, ou vivification des sciences de la foi* (Vivification of the Sciences of Faith), Paris 1955. The "mystical" parts have been translated by R. Granlich, *Die Lehre von den Stufen der Gottesliebe* (The Doctrine of the Levels of the Divine level, Books 31-36); his work on the names of God, *'al-maqṣad al-asnā...*, has been translated by David B. Barrill and Nazih Daher, *The Ninety-Nine Beautiful Names of God,*

Gurgani, Abu'l-Qasim, teacher of Hujwiri, d. 1076.

Haji Bektash, Turkish folk mystic who came from eastern Iran to settle in Anatolia, where he died in 1338. He is the founder of the Bektashi order, which became known for its influence on the Osmanic elite troops, the Janite Hordes. The order has taken on several Shiite traits: women are admitted, and the folk humor of the Bektashis is known all over Turkey. See J.K. Birge, *The Bektashi Order of Dervishes.*

Hallaj, Al-Husain ibn Mansur al-, mystic from southern Iran, who lived in Iraq and was noted for the severity of his asceticism. His pronouncement *anā'l-ḥaqq,* "I am the Absolute Truth" —that is, "God" —is offered as a reason for his grisly execution in Bagdad in 932, but it was actually political reasons that led to his death. For later Sufis he is the "martyr of divine love," who paid with his life for "revealing the secret" of the union of God and humankind in love. Even today Muslim poets and thinkers refer to him and his role of "lover." The comprehensive biography is that of L. Massignong, *La Passion d'al-Hoseyn ibn Mansour al-*

Hallaj, martyre mystique de l'Islam, in two volumes, Paris 1922; expanded edition, Paris 1974 (English translation by Herbert Mason, *A. Hallaj, Mystic and Martyr of Islam*). Selection from his works: A. Schimmel, *O Leute, rettet mich vor Gott!* (People, rescue me from God!).

Hujwiri, Ali ibn Othman al-Jullabi al-, mystic from eastern Iran, d. 1071 in Lahore, where he is venerated to this day under the name of Data Ganj Bakhsh. Author of the first mystical instructional work in Persian, *Kashf al-mahjub*, translation by R.A. Nicholson.

Ibn 'Arabi, Muhy'ddin, born 1165 in Ceuta, Spain, d. 1240 in Damascus. The great teacher of theosophical Sufism. His *Futūhāt al-makkiyya*, (The Mecca Revelations), contains the mystic's experiences and insights in five hundred sixty chapters; his *Fuṣūṣ al-ḥikam* (The Bezels of Wisdom) treats of mystic prophetology. An excellent biography is that of Claude Addas, Ibn 'Arabi, *La Qûete du soufre rouge* (The Quest for the Red Sulphur); the best analysis is William Chittick, *The Sufi Path of Knowledge*.

Ibn Ata Allah, Egyptian mystic of the Shadhiliyya order, d. 1309 in Alexandria. Author of the *Hikam* (Wisdom Sayings); a comprehensive study: P. Nwyia, *Ibn Ata Allah et la naissance de la confrérie shadilite* (Ibn Ata Allah and the Emergence of the Shadhilite Order). His work on the *zhikr, Miftāḥ al-falaḥ wa miṣbāḥ al-arwāḥ*, is a classic exposition of the names of God and their effects. (An English translation, *The Key to Salvation*, is in preparation by the Islamic Texts Society, Cambridge.)

Ibrahim al-Khawass, d. 904, Arabic mystic, famous for his absolute trust in God.

Jili, Abdul Karim al-, built on the ideas of Ibn 'Arabi and gave a classic description of *Al-Insān al-Kāmil* in his work of that name. He died between 1408 and 1417. See also R.A. Nicholson, *Studies in Islamic Mysticism*,

Kalabadhi, Abu Bakr Muhammad, Muslim jurist from Bukhara, d. 990, authored a work on Sufism, *kitāb at-ta 'arruf,* offering brief, spare descriptions of the levels and waystations of the mystics. (Translated by A.J. Arberry as *The Doctrine of the Sufis*).

Kubra, Najmaddin, mystic of central Asia, d. 1221, buried in Ur-genj. Author of highly interesting works on the Sufi path, with descriptions of visionary experiences of colors and shapes. The groundbreaking work is that of Fritz Meier, *Die fawā'iḥ al-jamāl* On the subject of his teachings about light, see also Henry Corbin, *L'Homme de lumière.*

*Mevlâna (Maulana: "*our master"*) Jalaluddin (Celalettin) Rumi* (1207-1273), spent the greatest part of his life in Konya, Ana-tolia. The greatest singer of mystical love in his lyrical *Dīvān,* comprising thirty-six thousand lines of verse; his didactic poem in couplets, the *Mathnawī,* is prized as the "Quran in the Per-sian tongue." His discourses, *Fīhi ma fīhi* (In It What is In It), take up the central themes of his poetry. His son, Sultan Valad (d. 1312), institutionalized the mystical turning, the *semāʿ,* which is why the order of the Mevlevis, which dates back to Mevlâna, is often called "the order of the whirling dervishes." *The Mathnawi* (ed. and trans. R.A. Nicholson) is available in several editions; recommended commentary: A. Schimmel, *I Am Wind; You Are Fire;* also by A. Schimmel, *The Triumphal Sun.*

Nasafi, Aziz al-, Persian mystic who was occupied above all with the notion of the perfected person (d. ca. 1300). Translation: Sa-belle de Gastines, *Le Livre de l'homme parfait.*

Niyazi Misri, Turkish mystical poet, d. 1697 in Lemnos.

Omar ibn al-Khattab, second successor of Muhammad, famous for his severity and uprightness (ruled 634-644).

Qushairi, Abu'l-Qasim al-, mystic from eastern Iran (d. 1072). His *Risāla* or "missive" is one of the most read works on the subject of "sober" Sufism; a good selection, though limited to the mysti-cal aspects of the *Risāla,* is B.R. von Schlegell, *Principles of Sufism;* on the subject of Qushairi's account of *zhikr* experi-ences, see Fritz Meier, *Al-Qusairis tartib as-sulūk.*

Ruzbihan-i Baqli, mystical writer resident in Shiraz (d. 1209), in-terpreted the ecstatic pronouncements of the Sufis, (*Sharḥ-i shaṭḥiyāt: Les Paradoxes des Soufis;* edited Henry Corbin); in his *ʿAbhar al-ʿAschiqīn (Le Jasmin des fidèles d'amour,* edited by Henry Corbin) he describes the aspects of love in language of the greatest subtlety.

Shams, Shamsuddin of Tabriz, wandering dervish whose arrival in Konya in the fall of 1244 set off a mystic shock in Mevlâna Rumi that turned him from a theologist and jurist into an ecstatic poet. Shams disappeared, probably murdered, in December 1248, and Mevlâna identified with him so totally that many of his poems bear the name of Shamsuddin.

Yesevi, Ahmed, Turkish mystic from Yassi in central Asia, where he died in 1166. First author of a Turkish anthology of *hikam,* verses of wisdom. The order that goes back to him is known for its "sawing *zhikr.*"

Yunus Emre, Anatolian mystic poet, died 1321. His simple mystic verse has influenced Turkish lyric poetry down to the present day. See *The Drop That Became the Sea* in the bibliography.

Zubair, az-, allied himself with the Prophet Muhammad (Peace be on him) as a young man. During the wars of succession he fought in the so-called "Slaughter of the Camels" of 656 on the side of A'isha, the Prophet's widow, and against the party of 'Ali. Famous for his transmission of the *hadīth.*

Glossary of Medical and Psychological Terms

amygdala: part of the limbic system.

***archetypes*[200]**: age-old images or conceptions that have been handed down genetically since earliest times and are common to all people.

archetypical movements: a concept employed in ancient Oriental music therapy to denote sequences of movement that can be traced back through written records and cave drawings to the beginnings of humanity and which are manifestly carried out for holy or healing purposes.

autonomic nervous system: supplies motor fibers to the heart, the stomach, the pancreas, the small and large intestines, the sweat glands, peripheral blood vessels, and other internal organs, tissues and glands. Its main function is to regulate physiological processes involving these internal organs, such as blood pressure and body temperature, and to prepare the body for emergencies by initiating appropriate physiological adjustments.

bradycardia: slow heartbeat (less than sixty per minute).

catalepsy: remaining for some length of time in a certain bodily position, possibly even an uncomfortable one, with heightened muscular tension.

central nervous system: the brain and spinal cord, part of the nervous system.

***collective unconscious, Jung's*: the most influential system of the psyche, of which the individual is fully unconscious. It is the inherited tribal basis of personality structure and contains the influence of the cumulative experiences of all previous generations and even that of the human race's animal past.

cortex: the outer layer of the brain, which principally controls conditional-reflective and analytical functions and influences all

---

[200] Entries marked with an asterisk are taken from the *Lexikon der Psychologie*, the rest are from the *Roche-Lexikon Medizin*.

the organic functions and the deeper centers (including the vegetative centers) of the central nervous system.

dehydration: lack of water in the body.

endocrine: eliminating substances into the bloodstream.

gyrus cinguli: belt-shaped *gyrus* situated between the furrow containing the corpus callosum and the furrow containing the cingulus.

hippocampus: "horn of Ammon," site of the olfactory center of the cerebral cortex, with a central function in the limbic system.

hyperventilation: unnecessarily heightened pulmonary respiration, can lead to muscle cramps.

hypoglycemia: abnormal depression of the blood sugar level.

hypothalamus: the part of the midbrain located under the thalamus. . . . Is effective as central regulatory organ for the vegetative functions such as those of nourishment absorption, water absorption, body temperature, circulation, sexuality, and sleep.

* *ideomotor movements*: a condition, controlled by emotion or affect, that leads to motor reactions unintentionally and without the participation of the will.

kinesthetic: having to do with the sense of movement and position.

kinesthetic hallucination: the experience of a bodily movement that in reality is not happening. Such hallucinations occur after a long boat trip.

* *levitation*: paranormal upward floating of an object or a person, generally in connection with a physical medium.

limbic system: it regulates affective and impulsive behavior and the link between it and the vegetative organic functions, and is probably also of importance for the memory.

lucid dream: dream in which the dreamer becomes sufficiently conscious to steer the events of the dream.

neuroendocrinology: study of the nervous system and the endocrines.

* *parasympathetic system*: part of the autonomic nervous system with trophotropic effects on rest, nourishment and elimination of waste.

215

perineum: the "dam," soft-tissue bridge, about 3 cm. wide, between anus and scrotum.

sensory deprivation: long-term absence of all sensory inputs; its effects on individuals include heightened suggestibility, thought disturbances, weakness of concentration, depressed mood, possibly also hallucinations (as with extreme social isolation).

* *sympathetic system*: part of the autonomic nervous system with ergotropic functions in heightening physical activity.

* *synchronicities, Jung's*: correlation between outward and inward realities that can't be explained causally. According to Jung this correlation has its basis in archetypes.

* *transpersonal psychology*: that branch of psychology which is concerned with the spiritual life of the individual and attempts to include the wisdom of the sacred traditions. It therefore goes beyond the constitutional realm of the body and includes, in particular, soul and mind, as well as higher states of consciousness..

vestibular apparatus: the functioning unit serving the sense of balance. Appropriate stimuli are acceleration and gravity. It causes an excitation of sensory cells.

BIBLIOGRAPHY

Abraham, R, McKenna, T., and Sheldrake, R.. *Trialogues at the Edge of the West*. Sante Fe, 1992.

Achterberg, J. *Imagery in Healing: Shamanism and Modern Medicine*. Boston, 1985.

Algan, R. and Helminski, K., trans. *The Drop that Became the Sea: Lyric Poems of Yunus Emre*. Putney, 1989.

Arabi, ibn al-. *Die Weisheit der Propheten (Fusus al Hikam)*. Graz, 1986.

Arabi, ibn al-. *Risalat al anwar fima yumnah sahib al khalwa minal asrar*. Freiburg, 1984.

Arabi, ibn al-. *El Nucleo del Nucleo*. Malaga, 1986.

Arasteh, R. *Toward Final Personality Integration*. New York, 1975.

Arya, U. "Meditation and the Art of Dying," in E. Rossi, *Die Psychobiologie der Seel-Körper-Heilung*. Essen, 1991.

Asad, M. *The Message of the Qur'an*. Gibraltar, 1984.

Asad, M. *Vom Geist des Islam*. Köln, 1984.

Attar. *The Conference of the Birds*. London, 1961.

Bailey, A. "Die Gefahr des Kundalini Erweckens," in White, ed., *Kundalini Energie*. Munich, 1990.

Barabasz, A. "EEG alpha, Skin Conductance and Hypnotiziability in Antarctica," in D. Revenstorf, ed., *Klinische Hypnose*. Berlin, 1990.

Barabasz, A. "Restricted Environmental Stimulation and the Enhancement of Hypnotziability: Pain, EEG alpha, Skin Conductance and Temperature Response," in D. Revenstorf, ed., *Klinische Hypnose*. Berlin, 1990.

Bentov, I. "Die Mikrobewegung des Körpers als ein Faktor in der Entwicklung des Nervensystems," in White, ed., *Kundalini Energie*. Munich, 1990.

Castaneda, C. *The Eagle's Gift*. New York, 1982.

Chaudhuri, H. "Die Psychophysiologie von Kundalini," in White, ed., *Kundalini Energie*. Munich, 1990.

Corbin, H. *Mundus Imaginalis or the Imaginal and the Imaginary*. Ipswich, 1972.

Davis, J. *Endorphins.* New York, 1984.

Desai, A. "Kundalini Yoga durch Shaktipat," in White, ed., *Kundalini Energie.* Munich, 1990.

Doore, G., ed. *Opfer und Ekstase.* Freiburg, 1989.

Dornbach, A. "Die Lata'if Lehre," in *Al Sufi,* vol. 1, no. 2 (1991).

Dürkheim, Graf. K. *Der Ruf nach dem Meister.* Munich, 1986.

Eliade, M. *Shamanism: Archaic Techniques of Ecstasy.* Princeton, 1972.

Erickson, M. and Rossi, E. *Hypnotherapy.* New York, 1979.

Ferguson, M. *The Aquarian Conspiracy.* Los Angeles, 1980.

Ferguson, M. "Kindling und Kundalini Effekte," in White, ed., *Kundalini Energie.* Munich, 1990.

Floor, E. "Die biologischen Grundlagen von Kundalini," in White, ed., *Kundalini Energie.* Munich, 1990.

Gennep. A. *Les Rites de Passage.* Paris, 1909.

Gerl, W. "Hypnose als Therapie," in D. Revenstorf, ed., *Klinische Hypnose.* Berlin, 1990.

Ghasali, al-. *Neubelebung der Religionswissenschaften,* vol. 2. Halle, 1917

Hilmi, Shebenderzadeh Ahmet. *Erzählung nach dem Roman A'mak-i Hayal.* Berlin, 1985.

Ghasali, al-. *Die Nische der Lichter.* Hamburg. 1987.

Gibran, K. *Der Prophet.* Olten, 1987.

Gibran, K. *Worte wie die Morgenröte.* Freiburg, 1988.

Goodman, F. *Ekstase, Besessenheit, Dömonen: Die geheimnisvolle Seite der Religion.* Gütersloh, 1991.

Goodman, F. "Schamanische Tranceeinstellungen," in G. Doore, ed., *Opfer und Ekstase.* Freiburg, 1989.

Goyeche, J. "Kundalini zur Vorbeugung und Therapie gegen Drogenmissbrauch," in White, ed., *Kundalini Energie.* Munich, 1990.

Güvenç, O. *The Dervish Path and Mevlana.* Vaduz, 1981.

Hart, O. van der. *Rituals in Psychotherapy.* New York, 1983.

Highwater, J. *The Primal Mind: Vision and Reality in Indian America.* New York, 1982.

Holler, J. *Das neue Gehirn.* Südergellersen, 1991.

Hopman, T. " Symbolische Ausdruckweisen der Kundalini durch das Unbewusste," in White, ed., *Kundalini Energie.* Munich, 1990.

Houston, J. *The Search for the Beloved.* Los Angeles, 1987.

Khalsa, S. et al. "Kundalini Energie," in White, ed., *Kundalini Energie.* Munich, 1990.

Kielce, A. *Sufismus.* Munich. 1985.

Krishna, G. "Bedeutung und Implikation einer wissenshaftlichen Untersuchung des Kundalini-Phänomens," in White, ed., *Kundalini Energie.* Munich, 1990.

Krishna, G. *Kundalini for the New Age: Selected Writings of Gopi Krishna.* New York, 1988.

LaBerge, S. *Lucid Dreaming.* New York, 1991.

Larbig, W. and Miltner, W. "Hirnelektrische Grundlagen der Hypnose," in D. Revenstorf, ed., *Klinische Hypnose.* Berlin, 1990.

Lazarus et al. "Stress-related Transactions between Person and Environment," in Pervin and Lewis, *Perspectives in Interactional Psychology.* New York, 1978.

Leonard, G. *Der Pulsschlag des Universums.* Munich, 1992.

Lexicon der Psychologie, Arnold, Eysenck, and Meili, eds., Freiburg, 1991.

Maslow, A. *The Farther Reaches of Human Nature.* New York, 1971.

McCleave, M. "Christliche Mystik und Kundalini," in White, ed., *Kundalini Energie.* Munich, 1990.

Moinuddin, A. *Die Heilkunst der Sufis: Grundsätze und Praktiken.* Freiburg, 1984.

Moody, R. *Life after Life.* New York, 1975.

Motoyama, H. and Brown, R. *Chakra Psychologie.* Freiburg, 1980.

Motoyama, H. *Toward a Superconsiousness: Meditational Theory and Practice.* Berkeley, 1990.

Muktanada. "Sinnliche Erregung," in White, ed., *Kundalini Energie.* Munich, 1990.

Narayananda. "The Primal Power in the Kundalini Shakti," in White, ed., *Kundalini Energie.* Munich, 1990.

Nasafi, A. *Kitab al Insan al Kamil.* Teheran, 1962.

Pandit, M. "Kundalini is nicht die einzige Wahrheit," in White, ed., *Kundalini Energie.* Munich, 1990.

Peck, R. "Eine Forschungsanmerkung über der Kundalini Energie," in White, ed., *Kundalini Energie.* Munich, 1990.

Pert, C. et al. "Neuropeptides and their Receptors: A Psychomatic Network," in E. Rossi, *Die Psychobiologie der Seel-Körper-Heilung*. Essen, 1991.

Peter, B. "Hypnotische Phänomene," in D. Revenstorf, ed., *Klinische Hypnose*. Berlin, 1990.

Piaget, J. "Piaget's Theory," in Mussen, ed., *Carmichael's Manual of Child Psychology*. New York, 1970.

Radha, S. "Kundalini: ein Überblick," in White, ed., *Kundalini Energie*. Munich, 1990.

Rama, S. "Das Erwachen der Kundalini," in White, ed., *Kundalini Energie*. Munich, 1990.

Revensdorf, D. "Zur Theorie der Hypnose," in D. Revenstorf, ed., *Klinische Hypnose*. Berlin, 1990.

Ring, K. *Heading toward Omega: In Search of the Meaning of the Near-Death Experience*. New York, 1985.

Ring, K. *The Omega Project*. New York, 1992.

Roche-Lexikon Medizin. Munich, Vienna, and Baltimore, 1987.

Rossi, E. *Die Psychobiologie der Seel-Körper-Heilung*. Essen, 1991.

Roth et al. "Evolutionary Origins of Neuropeptides, Hormones and Receptors," in E. Rossi, *Die Psychobiologie der Seel-Körper-Heilung*. Essen, 1991.

Rumi, Mevlana Jalaluddin. *Love is a Stranger: Selected Lyric Poetry of Jelaluddin Rumi,* translated by K. Helminski. Putney, 1993.

Rumi, Mevlana Jalaluddin. *The Mathnawi,* translated by R.A. Nicholson, 3 vols. London, 1926.

Rumi, Mevlana Jalaluddin. *Open Secret: Versions of Rumi,* Putney, 1984.

Rumi, Mevlana Jalaluddin. *Von Allem un von Einem (Fihi ma Fihi),* translated by Annemarie Schimmel. Munich 1988.

Sannella, L. *Kundalini Erfahrung und die neuen Wissenschaften*. Essen, 1989.

Sannella, L. "Kundalini, kassisch und klinisch," in White, ed., *Kundalini Energie*. Munich, 1990.

Schimmel, A. *Mystical Dimensions of Islam*. Chapel Hill, 1975.

Schimmel, A. *Mystische Dimensionen des Islam*. Köln, 1985.

Schuon, F. *Den Islam verstehen*. Munich, 1988.

Shafii, M. *Freedom from the Self: Sufism, Meditation and Psychotherapy.* New York, 1985.

Shah, I. *Denker des Ostens.* Reinbek, 1988.

Shah, I. *Das Geheimnis der Derwische.* Freiburg, 1982.

Shah, I. *Learning How to Learn.* San Francisco, 1981.

Shah, I. *Die Sufis.* Munich, 1990.

Shah, O. *Sufism for Today.* Paris, 1991.

Sheldrake, R. *The Rebirth of Nature.* London, 1990.

Seyle, H. *Stress without Distress.* New York, 1974.

Stewart, J. "Brain ACTH-Endorphin Neurons as Regulators of Central Nervous System Activity," in Brunfeld, ed., *Peptides.* Copenhagen, 1980.

Stoyva, J. "o.T.," in G. Krishna, *Kundalini for the New Age: Selected Writings of Gopi Krishna.* New York, 1988.

Sufi, Abd al Kadir. *Der Pfad der Liebe.* Munich, 1986.

Tart, C. "A Psychophysiological Study of Out-of-Body Experiences in Selected Subjects," in J. Achterberg,. *Imagery in Healing: Shamanism and Modern Medicine.* Boston, 1985.

Tennyson, A. "Complete Poetical Works (1898)," in R. Arasteh. *Toward Final Personality Integration.* New York, 1975.

Tucek, G. *Yunus Emre: Seit ich mich selbst vergass. . . .Gedichte und Leider.* Zeining, 1991.

Vilayetname. *Le Livre des Amis de Dieu: Les Saintes des Derviches Bektashis.* Paris, 1984.

Vitray-Meyerovitch, E. *Rumi and Sufism.* Sausalito, California, 1987.

White, J., ed., *Kundalini Energie.* Munich, 1990.

Wilber, K. "Gibt es did Chakras wirklich?" in White, ed., *Kundalini Energie.* Munich, 1990.

Wilber, K. *Halbzeit der Evolution.* Bern, 1987.

Wilber, K. *Wege vum Selbst: östlicher und westliche Anzätze zum Pers önlichen Wachtrum.* Kösel, 1988.

Winkleman, M. *Shamans, Priests and Witches: A Cross-Cultural Study of Magio-Religious Practitioners.* Tuscon, Arizona, 1992.

Acknowledgements

The publisher wishes to thank the following publishers for permission to reprint excerpts from their books:

Asian Humanities Press for permission to quote from *Toward a Superconsciousness* by H. Motoyama.

Bantam Books for permission to quote from *Kundalini in the New Age* by Gopi Krishna.

Bear and Company for permission to quote from *Trialogues at the Edge of the West* by R. Abraham, T. McKenna and R. Sheldrake.

ISHK Book Service for permission to quote from *The Secrets of the Dervishes* and *Learning How to Learn* by Idries Shah..

Murrow Company for permission to quote from *The Omega Project* by K. Ring.

New American Library-Dutton for permission to quote from *The Primal Mind: Vision and Reality in Northern America* by J. Highwater

Pocket Books for permission to quote from *The Eagle's Gift* by Carlos Castenada.

Post Apollo Press for permission to quote from *Rumi and Sufism* by E. Vitray-Meyerovich.

Recommended Reading on Sufism
Most of these books can be ordered from Threshold Books: 802-254-8300

'Ali ibn Abi Talib. *Living and Dying With Grace: Counsels of Hadrat Ali,* translated by Thomas Cleary. Boston, 1995.

Asad, Muhammad. *The Message of the Qur'an,* Gibraltar, 1984.

Bayrak, Tosun. *The Most Beautiful Names,* Putney, Vermont, 1985.

Chittick, William. *The Sufi Path of Love: The Spiritual Teachings of Rumi.* Albany, 1983.

Chittick, William. *The Sufi Path of Knowledge: Ibn al-Arabi's Metaphysics of Imagination,* Albany, 1989.

Eaton, Gai. *Islam and the Destiny of Man.* Albany, 1985.

Emre, Yunus. *The Drop That Became the Sea: Selected Lyric Poetry of Yunus Emre,* translated by Refik Algan and Kabir Helminski. Putney, Vermont, 1989.

Helminski, Kabir. *Living Presence: A Sufi Way of Mindfulness & The Essential Self.* New York, 1992.

Hilmi, Ahmet. *Awakened Dreams,* translated by Refik Algan and Camille Helminski. Putney, Vermont, 1990.

Ibn 'Arabi. *What the Seeker Needs,* translated by Bayrak and Harris. Putney, Vermont, 1992.

Rumi, Mevlâna Jalaluddin. *The Essential Rumi,* translated by Coleman Barks and John Moyne. New York, 1995.

Rumi, Mevlâna Jalaluddin. *Feeling the Shoulder of the Lion: Selected Poetry and Teaching Stories from The Mathnawi,* translated by Coleman Barks, Putney, Vermont, 1991.

Rumi, Mevlâna Jalaluddin. *Love is a Stranger: Selected Lyric Poetry of Jelaluddin Rumi,* translated by Kabir Helminski. Putney, Vermont, 1993.

Rumi, Mevlâna Jalaluddin, *Jewels of Remembrance: A Daybook of Spiritual Guidance,* translated by Camille and Kabir Helminski, Putney, Vermont, 1996.

Rumi, Mevlâna Jalaluddin, *The Mathnawi,* 3 vols., London, 1926.

Rumi, Mevlâna Jalaluddin. *Open Secret: Versions of Rumi,* translated by Coleman Barks, Putney, Vermont, 1984

Rumi, Mevlâna Jalaluddin, *Rumi: Daylight: A Daybook of Spiritual Guidance*, translated by Camille and Kabir Helminski, Putney, Vermont, 1994.

Rumi, Mevlâna Jalaluddin. *Signs of the Unseen: Discourses of Jalaluddin Rumi (Fihi ma Fihi)*, translated by W.M. Thackston, Jr. Putney, Vermont, 1994.

Rumi, Mevlâna Jalaluddin. *This Longing: Poetry, Teaching Stories, and Letters of Rumi*, translated by Coleman Barks and John Moyne, Putney, Vermont, 1988.

Rumi, Mevlâna Jalaluddin. *Unseen Rain: Quatrains of Rumi*, translated by Coleman Barks and John Moyne, Putney, Vermont, 1986.

Schimmel, Annemarie. *I Am Wind, You Are Fire: The Life and Work of Rumi*. Boston, 1992.

Schimmel, Annemarie. *Look This Is Love!: From the Divan of Jalaladdin Rumi*. Boston, 1990.

Schimmel, Annemarie. *Mystical Dimensions of Islam*. Chapel Hill, North Carolina, 1975.